SONG OF MYSELF

SONG *of* MYSELF

ANNE LORNE GILLIES

MAINSTREAM
PUBLISHING

EDINBURGH AND LONDON

For my children —
one day

She thinks, part woman, three parts a child,
That nobody looks . . .
Like a long-legged fly upon the stream
Her mind moves upon silence.
                    W. B. YEATS, Long-legged Fly

I turn the page
To a girl who stands like a questioning iris
By the waterside, at an age
That asks every mirror to tell what her heart's desire is.
The answer she finds in that oracle stream
Only time could affirm or disprove.
                    C. D. LEWIS, The Album

First published in Great Britain 1991 by
MAINSTREAM PUBLISHING COMPANY (EDINBURGH) LTD
7 Albany Street
Edinburgh EH1 3UG

The publisher acknowledges the financial assistance of the Scottish Arts Council in the production of this volume.

A catalogue record for this book is available from the British Library

ISBN 1 85158 368 8 (cased)

Typeset in 10/11½ Imprint by BEECEE Typesetting Services
Printed in Great Britain by Billings & Sons Ltd., Worcester

OVERTURE: OBAN 1985

'Rachel was never in Oban before, was she mummy?'

'I was so. I was in your tummy wasn't I?'

'Huh. That doesn't count.'

'It does so, doesn't it mummy?'

'Please be quiet can't you. Can you not see that poor Granny's upset? How would you like it if you came back to look at your home and it was all spoiled?'

'Can we go to MacTavish's Kitchen for chips on the way back mummy?'

There are times when it's a mistake to take the kids along. This is turning out to be one of them.

It's confusing the issue. They want to ask questions, confirm impr ssions, hear old tales again. They want to talk. Perhaps they even want, somehow, to help.

I want to think. To feel. To smell. To touch. I want to remember things I may never tell them about. Certainly not today anyway. Not until the hurts subside, the memories resume the sunny soft-filter of once-upon-a-time films. Today I am irritable with loss and impotence.

After all it wasn't showmanship that made me leave the car down below the gate. I never set out to make a pilgrimage on foot, a sentimental recreation of the journey I made a thousand times throughout my formative years. But the gate (our gate, our right-of-way to our own past) was padlocked against us. Here, where I picked September brambles, and heard, with the acute sense of childhood, end-of-season bees droning in harmony with a buzz of distant pipers — all now, like the bees, dead or gone away — today I stood shut out. And when we climbed the gate I took with me an anger which sharp-edged the memories.

Yes, this is the gate which Jumper jumped, the cow who would a-wandering go, until my mother sold her, miles up the glen, whereupon she walked all through the night and jumped back in again. This is the gate where we stood and waited for the tiny black dot in the distance to turn into Sine, our collie, who knew by telepathy whenever one of us was

5

coming up the road, walloping along, tail birling, to walk us home. Where I told the drug-eyed man I'd rather be raped than murdered. This is the road where I learned to ride my bike on Christmas morning, walked to my first school dance on a wild rainy night, stood beneath frost-bright stars and savoured my first long kiss. There are the net-curtained houses which I thought so friendly until a letter turned the smiling windows into hostile spy-holes. And here is the land which my father garrisoned with cattle to ward off the compulsory purchase order, young man full of dreams, old man fighting rheumatism to keep his tenuous hold on a little, uneconomic slice of the Highlands: could they not have left him a year or two of peace at the end of it all?

Here is the ditch where, one dark night, my brother and I discovered the ancient boy-scout trying to pitch his tent en route for a jamboree in Mull. Mud etching his wrinkled knees, his kilt drooping and bedraggled; his tiny monkey face smiling squintly in our incredulous torch-light. All the way on a moped from Derbyshire to our ditch. And where my father struggled for hours to save a drowning stirk, waist deep in the slough of despond, until abandoning the unequal struggle.

And here is the house, for so long our delight, our bane, our womb, our worry; now boarded up, its face blank, as if it too is shutting out sharp memories. How many times did I wish for an ordinary house with ordinary sanitation, ordinary electricity, ordinary aspirations? How often did I wish for parents generous with their time, unbowed by burdens? And now, perversely, how I wish for my own children a world where pictures were woven in firelight, where the seasons were not punctuated by self-centred celebrations, but by Nature, gift-laden, uncompromising.

The hay-field where once we fought the capricious Highland weather-gods has long been overgrown with tarmac and concrete buildings. Now where cattle grazed and children sledged, the soft belly of the recumbent hillside has been hacked out and the carcase left unburied; the brave-sounding, blackmailing official plans (local employment, amenity enhancement) conceived in the first flush of Thatcherism, now seem to have died with the hill. Some day someone will make a bomb out of this land — after a tactful period of mourning has elapsed of course. Meanwhile my gentle parents live out their lives amid the keening of city traffic.

I wish I hadn't brought the kids to see this disfigured corpse. They have no images to breathe life into its sad contours. Some day I'll need to paint again my childhood's landscape. Today I can't trust myself to speak.

We haven't been up to Oban much recently. Not since Granny and

Grampa came to live near us in Glasgow. Cutting my link with the Argyll earth. Nowadays we only seem to come up for funerals. There's a depressing thought, eh.

Used to come up every holiday. Like teuchters the world o'er. 'Going home' it was known as — long after you went to University in 1962 and then away down south to train as a singer. Whenever you saw a car with an SB registration you looked to see if you knew the driver, even in the middle of Tottenham Court Road. How daft can you get? And remember the time you were in your kitchen in Oxford listening to the Third Programme when this cailleach came on singing a Gaelic milking song with the sound of milk hitting the pail in the background. I know it sounds like an awful cliché, but the walls really did dissolve and the whole place filled up with the smell of the byre at home: lime-wash and Udsal and wet straw and warm milk. In your nose, on your cheeks, making your eyes smart. You could feel it palpably draining away after the song was done, and you were left wiping your runny nose on a patterned English tea-towel and looking out blankly on a garden full of frost-bitten English vegetables.

'Where are you going your holidays?' folk would ask.

'We're going home — as usual,' you'd reply — even after you'd settled in Glasgow with a husband and one . . . two . . . three children. It was so handy. My son could just run wild, and my father was so much mellower now that he was retired. We always remarked on that, my mother and I. So much more relaxed with the grand-children. It's always the way. And it was nice going down town with the kids. All the Oban folk stopping and saying how like William your wee boy is and the baby's just the image of yourself. Of course they never said anything about you being on the telly. They're very laid back, the people of Oban. They have their own way of paying you compliments. One day my mother took us down in the car to get our messages in Willie Low's. A knock came to her window. Well what do you know. A parking man. In a peaked cap. That's an innovation, isn't it, Mother? For Oban, I mean? Well yes, I suppose so. There's just the one. We have a traffic light too, now, you know.

'Oh Mrs Gillies, Mrs Gillies,' the parking man said sorrowfully, 'I'm terribly sorry but you can't park here.'

'Yes, I know' my mother replied. 'I was just stopping to let Anne out.'

'Och here Anne, it's yourself. I never saw you sitting there. Aye aye — and the children too. Well well it's nice to see yous all. Are yous up for long? Och well, Mrs Gillies, just you leave the back door of the car open while you're in the shop — make it look as if there's something going on and they'll never take you.'

I've been asked to write an autobiography. There's going to be all hell let loose when I tell folk that. Of course you turned them down Anne? I hope? Oh for heaven's sake.

It is a well-known fact that people who put themselves forward are tempting providence — especially women. Rule Number One: 'Is dona thig maighdeann gun bhith beusach': 'it ill becomes a maiden not to be modest'. Oral Gaelic sources suggest a history of burying female poets face downwards. Women sang at their work, crooned beside cradles, keened beside graves and spurred their heroes on from the side-lines of the battle. To praise, lament, satirise and rehearse the past was man's work. You could easily forget that, typing away down there in Glasgow. And — not being a native-born Obanach, let alone a native-born Gael — that would just confirm everybody's worst fears, wouldn't it? (Rule Number Two: never do anything for fear of what folk will think of you.)

My family's natural reticence has been, if anything, amplified by their need to accommodate — and to be accommodated by — the surrogate culture: chameleons, taking colour from the surrounding terrain. To them my musical vocation — clearly inherited from the distaff side — has already proved all too dependent on the fuel of notoriety to be thoroughly acceptable. And now this. Anyone else would just take the money and write about the bens and glens of home. Anodyne, picturesque and modestly saleable both sides the Atlantic. But not me. They know me and my unruly member. They have my best interests at heart. Oh yes. Remember what that girl said about the poor English teacher when we were in Second Year in Oban High School:

'Oh Anne have you heard the latest. You'll never believe it. Isn't it terrible. It's all round the town that Mr Smith has published a book of poems and he's called his mother an elephant!'

'Mum-my! You said we could stop and have chips in MacTavish's Kitchen. You promised.'

'Och for goodness' sake. Granny's tired. And so'm I. I want to get away down the road. It's a long drive. The sooner we get going the sooner we'll get home to daddy. Why don't you eat the rest of the sandwiches and then have a nice wee sleep? We can get chips in Glasgow.'

'Granny doesn't mind do you, Granny?'

'Well it's really up to mummy. She's in the driving seat.'

'Och for goodness' sake. Now I'll have to go all the way back round the one-way system and MacTavish's'll be crowded and it'll be dark by the time we reach Loch Lomond. I hate driving round there in the dark with the state of that road. Well, thanks very much, kids.'

'Hurraaaaay. Can we get ice-cream too?'

After they moved to Glasgow my mother came back up every week on the train to teach cello in the school. She couldn't bear to think of her pupils having to stop dead like that when they were getting on so well. Six hours in a train at her age, all through the winter, with her bad chest. She couldn't keep that up for very long of course. Just till her pupils got a wee bit further on — or left the school.

She really missed Oban, my mother, even with us just along the road, even after she got into the Glasgow Chamber Orchestra. That was something she couldn't have done in Oban. There were never that many musicians in Oban all at once. Not classical musicians, I mean. Enough for a piano trio, in our kitchen on a Friday evening. Enough to accompany Gilbert and Sullivan in the Argyllshire Gathering Hall, or The Messiah *in the Cathedral. But nothing like enough for symphonies and concerti like they play in the Chamber Orchestra. That's given my mother something to look forward to every week. But she still misses the smell of the sea.*

I don't think I really took on board how upset they were at the time. I was so busy trying to find them somewhere to live close by us, where they'd feel reasonably at home. A garden — that was the most important part. Much more important, really, than the house itself. After all that space around them. The hills. The sea. The blessed peewits. My father's pretty much of a hermit at heart. He can be contented enough anywhere as long as he's not too aware of his bourgeois neighbours. He looks exactly the same now, sitting in his living room in Glasgow surrounded by books and newspaper cuttings, as he did in our kitchen at home. Except fatter. Less exercise. Doing your garden in Pollokshields isn't at all the same as walking miles up a Highland hill to collect your cows.

But I'd been more worried about him falling over a precipice, or taking a heart attack halfway over a dyke. An old guy in his seventies crashing about the hillside in all weathers. To be perfectly honest, I thought it was all quite a blessing in disguise when the Council came up with their crazy scheme to knock down the dùn and use the earth to fill in the bog to make playing-fields for the youth of Oban. It forced my father to come to a decision, though he must have had a quiet laugh to himself when the Council's JCB fell right down into a bottomless pit as soon as they started work. Well you had to admit it sounded a bit like a Judgment; we've always suspected that dùn was an ancient burial mound of some kind, even if it was pointing in the wrong direction; and anyway, nobody got hurt. As long as my parents didn't have to stay around to see the desecration taking place in front of their eyes it was probably all for the best.

It wasn't until I was up in Oban recently, on the way to sing at the Mull Festival, that it really came home to me what it had been like for them.

I was sitting on the pier waiting for the ferry when I saw Al Birrell in his overall and wellies. I've known Al since I was five. I was in love with him when I was seven. After he grew up he sometimes gave my father a hand with the cattle — taking them up to the bull and the like.

'Hi Anne' he said, leaning in his laconic Oban way on the door of Rhona's Volvo Estate. (Rhona plays the harp and stays right opposite my parents in Pollokshields.) 'How're you doing? Where're you off to?'

I told him, and then he started asking after my parents. He told me about the day he and my father took the beasts to the Mart, to sell them when my parents were moving to Glasgow. There were tears in Al Birrell's eyes, standing there in his wellies on the Railway Pier. I hadn't really thought about my father walking home on his own after selling all his beasts.

'There's a lot of folk in Oban think it was terrible what happened to your folks,' Al said. 'After all they did for the town. And the waste of the land. Just lying there. And the hill like that. It's terrible right enough.'

'Och well, Al, it's nice to know we're missed. Even if we weren't natives of the place. Even if my parents had only lived there for thirty-odd years.'

'Are they sleeping?'
'They seem to be.'
'Isn't it typical. They always fight all the way home and then fall asleep just when we reach the outskirts of Glasgow.'
'You were just the same when you were their age.'
'What nonsense. I was a paragon. Anyway. Are you all right, Ma? Not too upset?'
'Och no. Not really. Though I must admit it was much worse than I expected. What a mess. What a mess. I was glad your father wasn't there to see it. It'll be bad enough describing it to him.'

I'm not going back up there. Too depressing.

Though of course I still think of Oban as home. And I seem to be stuck with my Oban name. Lorne: as in 'Oban and . . .' Adopted when I joined Equity — to differentiate me from the other Anne Gillies. Anne Gillies, Skye, that is. Of course she's been dead for years now, but I've become really attached to my Lorne, even if I do have to put up with people calling me 'thon singer, whatdyoucaller, aye thon Lorna Anne Guinness'.

On the other hand I like Stirling too. Whenever I'm singing there I take a great pride in reminding people that that was where I was born. The headmaster at Cambusbarron School came round to my dressing-room the other day with a photocopy of the school register for 1949. I was only there for one term, but there was my name: 'Anne Gillies, 21:10:44 — Townhead, North Third, by Stirling, father Iain, quarry manager.' It's really beautiful where we lived — quite a few miles outside the town in almost total isolation. We often go back to look at it and listen to the peewits and the burn. It hasn't changed a bit.

'Thank you very much,' I said to the headmaster. 'You really know how to make a girl feel her age.'

'Och aye, it was long before my time,' he laughed. How chivalrous can you get?

Not that we intended to stay in Townhead, even if the landlord had let us. No Gaelic in Stirling. Not since the Reformation.

'Wake up kids, we're nearly home.'

Glasgow. Their home. Just about the last place on earth I ever thought I'd end up in. But as it turns out it's not that different from Oban. It has the same 'Hullo-cheerie-bye' as you enter and leave shops, the same 'are you OK hen' if you drop your messages on the pavement. But without the same claustrophobia.

And — irony of ironies — the girls are being taught in Gaelic in their local primary school — the very thing we wanted, but didn't get, all those years ago in Oban. In 1985, in the middle of the city! How times change. Not that Gaelic-medium education was handed to us on a plate. The Regional Council took some persuading. I used to read the kids bedtime stories. Now I go to meetings instead. Well, this is the last chance for the culture. We have to do more than just be parents. We have to fight. I wonder if they'll thank me for it when they're forty, or harbour resentments about me sacrificing my time with them on the altar of my own principles. Scotland? Gaelic? Where are they now? And was it all worth it, Mummy? My crusade my children's cross. My father's crusade . . . My grand-father's crusade . . . That's what it's all about really, eh? Bad cess to my Covenanting ancestors.

'No you can not get more chips. Say good-night to Granny now. Good-night, Ma. Keep your pecker up. And don't you be worrying about this book of mine. I can't see myself getting the time to write it anyway.'

ONE

The world stretched away endlessly at first. A landscape of sounds with here a taste, there a smell, a colour, or a fear in the foreground.

The cry of peewits and the murmur of a mileaway burn: comes the scrape of a dry-stane dyke, the suck of wellingtons in mud, slime on the reservoir wall. The din of grass-hoppers, the dialogue of sheep; scent of yarrow, scratch of lichen, drool of cuckoo spit, spring of moss, taste of knees, islands of nettle-rash in a sea of docken juice.

The motorised push-bike, away beyond the gates where the pitted road is floury with summer drouth, brings your mother back to you. From the greys of her old age, from the haze of her faraway work, she rides sun-haloed towards you, with her strong knobbly tobacco-smelling hands, her crisp striped blouse, and her secrets: her smiles, her smells, the long hair coiled away behind the soft neck where you hide your face, drowning in her warmth, lulled by the tunes she whistles in and out on every breath. Your secrets, which you recreate when she's not there, burying your face in her brown and orange checked coat as it hangs on the back of the kitchen door, plunging your hands into its gritty pockets, hiding from your fat-bottomed granny with her piercing coal-black eyes.

We were Bad. Paddled under the bridge in February and caught cold to Worry our Mother. Locked ourselves in the larder with its mouldering jars and had to drink salt to be Sick and Sorry. Walked for miles across hills following a sheep path or a bird-call and had to be Given Tea by Kind Ladies and Brought Back Home by our Poor Mother. Got stuck, scared, pecked, stung, grazed, dirty, wet, chased, over-excited, wheezy, frightened, lost, bitten, and caught short.

We were a Constant Worry. Why could we not have been delivered fully-grown and toilet trained? The edgy china pot stood little chance against the subtle pleasure of defaecation on a hillside, caressed by wind and grass, or the sharp hubris of retention with its dreadful nemesis. 'Dirty little girl' says Granny, throwing it in the fire. 'Dirty little girl' hisses the fire.

There were high spots.

The fank-day, when you looked down from a dawn window and found the usual yard transformed with seething wool and your breath caught at the sugar-pink of sunlight through lambs' ears. Afterwards, when Tom had gone home for his tea and the sheep had wagged their tails and recovered their dignity, you wandered between the long grey planks and plucked wool from the skelfs, puffing it away like dandelion clocks.

The scent of lily-of-the-valley and fresh scones when we called on an old lady in a floral apron.

The great snow wiping out the world; the cocoon, igloo, burrow (what was it?) that your father built, the silence inside it roaring, and the perfect, terrifying black thing embedded in its whiteness. No-one saw it but me. Did it move? Don't take your eye off it. Don't tell about it. There's sure to be a Perfectly Logical Explanation for it. Huh.

Evenings ben-the-hoose. A fire-hot face, a wooden music-stand, Bonnie Prince Charlie in gilded royal-blue books, and the night window, too dark to see the tiger's flat face against the glass outside.

The wee green car — your bare thighs sticking to bottle-green leather in the dicky. Queer holidays in my father's office, mountainscape of boxes and paper. Kalamazoo? Huge men who birl me round on the balding velvet chair, its brass studs making patterns on my thighs; my father calling us strange hearty names: Wee Anne. Young William here. Outside, machines rape the rockface behind a screen of dust. Lorries hurry up the road like dung-beetles. Past the ancient lime-kilns to feed upon the fresh hill-wound. The noise is thick and there is white dust on your lips. Behind the quarry the lily pool. Seething frogs. They will not let me see it. It is too terrible. My brother has seen it and there have been frogs crawling in his cot at night.

A day at Aberdour. People all walking in the same direction, drawn like iron-filings to the sea. A hand-knitted swimming costume, green and moth-eaten as seaweed, and you sitting up to the waist in a warm crystal rock-pool; wine-red anemones fluttering and tensing, tickled by wave-ripple; pink pearly shells like the scraps in my book; pastel streamers on a kiss-me-quick hat. I run round and round my mother like the merry-go-round: leave your poor mother be — you're tiring her out. The kiss-me-quick hat is dusty on the wardrobe: I wear it to run down to the gate.

A trip to Ballachulish on a bus that sings in the Gaelic I am going to learn one day. I join in. I'm singing a Gaelic song, Mummy. Shurrup, my brother whines. Glencoe where my father used to stay before he moved to Stirling. After he left London to live in the Highlands. He saved up all his money to come here and then lost it in the slate quarry. Then he had to go and work in the quarry in Stirling to get some more money so that he could have us. Poor Daddy. He liked it better in Glencoe. It hangs in my childhood's memory, dim landscape touched and re-touched by time. Dark mountains looming with Gaelic — Bidean nam Beann, Stob Coire nan Lochan, Buachaille Eite Mhòr — the devil left his finger-prints on their boulders, Cluny MacPherson hid among their sheer slits, the Red Fox spewed his Campbell blood at their feet. The fast-flowing river, bubbling over brown stones, foaming around flat slabs, overhung with sandy turf — awning for royal salmon. Easy to hear the Caoineag on its banks, weeping before the Massacre; easy to see the ghosts under the bridge after a night out in the King's House Hotel. Easy to put pictures on my father's tales: the wake with the coffin stuck half out of the window; the *cailleach* turning back the clock on the mantelpiece 'so that you won't have to run for your train without a good breakfast inside you'. From the window of my father's cottage the Burial Isle — dead kings, dead chiefs and dead ordinary, side by side in eternal clanship.

My grampop on a visit from London. Mummy's daddy. My grampop lives in London but my granny lives with us. He is sitting on my bed playing The Beethoven on his fiddle and singing nursery rhymes in French to take my mind off the battle for breath. Sometimes my granny sings The Beethoven as she goes round the house: 'It's Gordon Tanner it's Gordon Tanner who's going to play The Beet-ho-van'. We write our own songs too. There is a rude one about a frog and one about Uncle Navel and one about Barnacle Bill the Sailor. Barnacle Bill is my toy lamb. Some auntie made it out of hospital lint. That's all you could get at the time you know.

One evening bananas appearing all around the kitchen door, the most yellow, the most wonderful things I have ever seen, exotic enough to make a magician of my father. Did we eat them?

There were fears. Black fears, like night, and Virol, and the taxi that will come and take you away to school; like the burnt grass on the fir-cone hill and the beady eyes of the clocking hen. Orange fears, like the nightmare tunnel that swirled my mother away from me, like the glutinous orange juice with its fishy after-taste, like the back of your eyelids if you dared to look at the sun, like the glowing wattles of the cock, like the eyes of the English hound that howled on *Saturday*

Night Theatre. Grey fears, like the dirty face on the back of my bedroom door, like the wolf that devoured Monsieur Sagan's little goat, like the mists that devoured the poor Highlandmen after Glencoe, like the thick sputum that chokes your chest and makes you claw the air, like things you don't understand.

There were joys. Broken biscuits, sugar-studded, in a turquoise and orange tin; a tomato eaten in careful quarters; finding my mother's lost brooch — what a clever little girl: I got another tomato; brushing the hairs over my father's baldy patch; the *MacFlannels, Down at the Mains*; building a house in the Smiths' loft, large as you can make it — a mansion which goes on haunting my dreams, still not fully-explored; fried potatoes and my father fat in a boiler suit whitewashing a ceiling; a pair of emerald green sandals (greener than grass, greener than the leather seats in the wee green car, greener than the frogs in the lily-pond) bought in Stirling Arcade in a shop with golden necklaces like snakes by the plate-glass doors.

There were things you couldn't have, however much you wanted them. Like the golden necklaces; your mother when she fell asleep in a chair; the balloons that silly dentist promised to give you if you blew up his black rubber mask; ice-cream — you were not deceived by the pink blancmange your mother made in egg-cups; a wooing-goat — a lovely wee wooing-goat. There is so such a thing as a wooing-goat. It's in Mummy's song. Robert Burns wrote it so there. Duncan Gray cam here tae woo ha ha the wooing-goat. I want a wooing-goat, Mummy. Mummy he said I was stupid.

You couldn't make a sound when your father checked his pools or your mother listened to the Sunday concert; the wireless saved its moon-noises for then. You couldn't expect attention when your brother was very ill. You couldn't scratch your eczema or it would only get worse. And now that you were a big girl you couldn't stay at home when the taxi stopped at the white gate. We saw a squirrel on the road to school. The taxi-driver was a nice man.

School was grey. I didn't understand school. I didn't understand why it had to be so fighting, so yelling, so falling over outside. So quiet, so ominously purring inside.

Muffled sounds of voices chanting, the water-fountain scooshing, a door opens and spills out a strange buzzing.

Following other people around I wonder how they understand so much. They know everything. Each other's names, the teacher's name, the games, how to skip and play conkers and plunkies and slide on ice, how to ask out to the toilet, how to scream. They are sliding on ice. I am watching. We are all in trouble it seems: the bell's gone, the bell's gone, when did it go I never heard it, we're for it, the heidie'll murder us. Obediently I follow them in, wheezing to keep up in my tight coat, scared to slip. I don't understand the headmaster:

'Come away ben, infants, come away ben. We nearly started our service without you.' What are infants? Why isn't he cross?

I stay inside my head-house, waiting to understand: the hard dun-coloured plasticine, the slate, the cat on its mat, the getting up, the sitting down, I can see no rhyme or reason in any of it. And why, may I ask, do people laugh when I speak, I swear they do.

Usually I can't think of anything to say — not like them. I don't know anything about all this. I know other things but nobody would be interested. If I do think of something to say I try it over to myself first, my hands shaking, my tummy turning over. If it sounds all right I might say it out. But by that time they're away onto something else. Then I get quicker at it. I have said something. They turn in astonishment. They laugh at the way my words come out instead of listening to what I'm saying.

No-one has ever done that before. They tell everybody else. You should hear Anne Gillies speaking. What a laugh. Every afternoon the big girls surround me, sticking their faces into mine, smelling of sweaty armpits and sour milk. 'Speak,' they command me, laughing in anticipation. 'Go on, say something.' So I speak, and so they laugh, and so I smile and smile until head aches, muscles twitch. My hands shake inside my coat pockets.

I never told on them, but someone must have: the merciful teacher takes to keeping me in every day until the taxi comes, letting me play in a corner of the classroom with a shiny plaster tea-set, blue on the outside, brown on the inside, the realest thing in the whole school. I love it. I might have grown to love the teacher. Miss Flett. Flett. Flett. But she is very high up in the room. Her round face bobs above me like a white balloon. I take the songs she taught us home to my mother, carrying them carefully as eggs.

O will you buy my sybies and will you buy my leeks
And will you buy my bonnie lassie wi the red cheeks.
I willnae buy your sybies I willnae buy your leeks
But I will buy your bonnie lassie wi the red cheeks.

'What are sybies, Mummy?'

'I don't know, darling. We'll ask Daddy when he comes home.'

Water water wall-flower growing up so high
We are all fairies and we must all die.
Except for Johnnie Stewart the youngest of us all
He can dance and he can sing and he can play the violin.

'Will I die, Mummy?'
'Not for a long time, darling. Dainty died because she was very old and tired. She just went to sleep very peacefully.'
'Will you die, Mummy? I don't want you to die.'
'O I'm not going to die yet-a-while. Not till I'm a very cross old lady.'
My mother comes every day at dinner time and takes me to the toilet in the town. One day the big boys told me there was an old man in a hut who sold apples. My mother takes me to the hut on the side of a very smooth green wee field — square with sloping sides. The hut is full of tools and cans.
The old man looks aggrieved.
'Me, selling aipples missus?'
I want to cry with embarrassment, tug at my mother's coat. But the old man takes an apple from his piece, splits it with his big black thumbs and offers me half.
'Oh no — we couldn't,' my mother says.
'Och dinna be daft missus. Here lassie help yersel.'
I don't understand any of it. What are lies? What are swears? Why can't I trust words any more? The explanations lie like a film of oil on the surface of my brain.

Auchencruive. Auchencruive. Auchencruive. A beautiful Gaelic name. My mother went there and learned how to milk a cow. She was away and my Daddy made boiled eggs.
But we have no cows. A cart-wheel lies askew in the cow-shed. A cart-wheel, clocking hens, bales of wire and nettles; a tweed hat belonging to Adams (who he?) hanging on a nail; pram-wheels, tin-trays, rusty staples, kindling. The sheep are not ours. Tom Davy, gentle golden-brown shepherd, like Jesus meek and mild, looks after them. He dips them in our fank.
But it turned out they all belonged to this Adams: the sheep, the fir-cone hill, the fank, the cow-shed, the cart-wheel, the house, Tom Davy. Grampop comes up hastily from England to capture it in

17

watercolour. Paints my big brother in the foreground as an afterthought: small Scottish blob beside the fir-cone hill.

One day a van came to take our things to Oban. To our new house where we would stay forever and learn Gaelic. My father would go in the van with the men, my brother and I would go in a train with my mother and my granny.

At Stirling station I am allowed to choose: a *Rupert Annual* and a bar of pink and white nougat.

'O you mean nugget, dear,' the shop lady says. 'Is it for the wee lassie? Are you going far dearie?'

I sit in the corner of the train looking out the window, nursing my *Annual* and licking the paper off my sweetie: frivolous luxuries underlining the momentous nature of the occasion. I see mountains — high and pointy. Stupid. They're not mountains. They're slag-heaps darling. Ha ha stupid. It grows too dark to see outside.

I am tired of Rupert and Algernon and the join-up dots. Tired of my peely-wally face in the window. Tired of my sweetie. I close my eyes and pretend to sleep. Going away. Going away. Going away, the train says.

Leaving it all behind.

North Third where Daddy went rowing and I made a wee ball with slime. I kept it secret in my hand all day, rolling it and rolling it till it was round and hard. Look Mummy — I've got a sheep's toalie. Dirty little girl. She swept it off my hand and it rolled away in the grass. I was crying. Why didn't you tell me you old silly? Playing tricks on your poor old mummy. We searched and searched but my ball was gone. And then we walked along the grass at the side of the road towards the second burn. There were hundreds of daisies. You could sometimes get slime at the ford. But there was none that day.

Todholes where we never went but I loved its name — over the hills and far away. Across the burn and the crying lambs and the peewits. Will there be peewits in Oban? My mother says she hopes the peewits will come with us. She couldn't live without them, though it will be lovely to be by the sea. Will it be like Aberdour? Tods are foxes, not toads, you know. Toads don't live in holes do they?

The Gillies Hill. We have a hill called after us, granny, did you know that? Jaggy and black against the white sky thick with tall trees. I had new white socks on and by the time we got there they were all black. Bright black. Where were we going that day? Can't remember, but Daddy was with us. I think.

The crossroads where my father had his accident. We were having our tea one night and somebody brought him home with glass all in his face. His hands were shaking and had blood on them.

Cambusbarron and the big grey school and the taxi that I caught my fingers in. They opened the door and my fingers were all mashed like porridge. I howled all the way home. My mother heard me a mile away and ran down to the gate. It wasn't your fault, she told the poor taxi-driver.

The people in the taxi — Ella and Jimmy and Johnnie. You could go to their house sometimes. When you were asked. Birthday parties like. The Smiths' house was huge. Their mother made jellies shaped like rabbits and then we played houses in the loft outside. There were beds with patterned shawls on them and all. At Johnnie's birthday party you had on your mother's silky dress from when she was wee — sort of orangey with pale round spots. Not the one in her photograph with the smocking at the front. That would have been far too posh. The silk was very cold on your arms. There were musical chairs and then they took all the chairs ben to Mrs Stewart's best room. There was a white table-cloth and date sandwiches. You were shivering in Mrs Stewart's best room. We don't use it that often you know Mrs Gillies. No wonder she's cold, poor wee lamb. We'll put her over here beside the electric fire. The electric fire was interesting: I looked at it all the time. Dusty silver with black lines that went orange and crackled when she turned it on. We'll put both bars on. But I didn't get any warmer. Perhaps she's not well. Yes I think that must be it. I shivered and shivered. My mother picked me up off the chair and buttoned my coat up and carried me piggy-back all the way home whistling through her teeth, in and out in and out, like she's doing now only you can't hear it for the train. My head was very sore.

We went into another house at Christmas time and they had mistletoe and a wee baby in a cot. It had done wee round shiny toalies in its coat and was doing something awful with them. I won't think about that. And in another house there was a big black tom cat that came in and out the window. Everything smelt like the cat. The cat stood on the window-sill and did a wee-wee at the pot-plant. Straight out the back like a water pistol, its paws trembling with the effort. We were giggling and poking each other under the oil-cloth. The old lady didn't see it at first. She was making tea at the stove. Then she saw. Ah ye dirty skite. Ye scum. Go on away oot o that ye dirty big skite. We were dying of laughter. Don't smile or they'll ask you what you're thinking about. Penny for your thoughts dear. No fear.

Where's my daddy now? Is he out there? I try to see through the window. You can see the train lights reflected on the ground and you can see cars and lorries sometimes, but you can't see very clearly. There's rain streaming across slanty-ways and dripping off the wee metal bits on the inside. Daddy's out there in that rain. Like at Glencoe. Like the Covenanters. Come hither Ewan Cameron — in the book with tissue paper between the pages. It always makes me feel sad. Don't be daft. That was long long ago. Daddy's not wet. He's in a lorry.

I've been in a tipper at the quarry and it was raining then too and the wipers scooped back and forth back and forth. That was quite long ago too. Before I went to get my teeth out the day we got Woggle Pixie in the Arcade for a reward and then I wet the seat of the wee green car on the way home. Don't worry darling. It was the anaesthetic that did it. It often has that effect. I hope Granny didn't leave Woggle Pixie behind. Not that I play with him now. Not since he lost his wheelbarrow. He won't woggle right any more. None of these new-fangled toys ever works, my father says. Och Iain. It's only a wee token to cheer her up. To make up for the balloon. You do agree what a silly man that dentist was, breaking a promise to a child. But there was a girl living near my father who only had a stick with rags tied on it to play with. She thought it was a dolly and my father's mother said they all had to be careful not to tell her it was only a stick. I wonder what my granny was like.

Will all our stuff get wet? The mahogany wardrobe with the monsters on it? All the Bonnie Prince Charlie books? Oh help. My nugget's stuck to my skirt. Don't let them see.

I pull it off. It's gone all hairy. Did you have a nice wee sleep then dear? We're nearly there.

The rain is still slanty-ways across the darkness when we reach Oban. We get off the train and hurry in under the glass shelter bit. A teasy man takes my ticket. A man with a moustache and a cap takes our stuff on a big buggy and wheels it away across the wet street. We have to hurry to keep up. Smell the sea, smell the sea, my mother says, trying to keep our spirits up. My granny is grim with lizard-skin handluggage, my brother icy silent with suppressed excitement. In the hotel he bounces wheezily on the big fat slimy eiderdown and then presses a button on the wall. I am watching the car lights skite like crabs across the ceiling. A lady with a black dress knocks on the door.

'Yes. Can I help you?'

No, we don't think so. Why?

'Well, you rang didn't you?'

My granny is black affronted. Look at that — making a perfect nuisance of yourselves and upsetting your poor mother when she's got so much to worry about. Don't you know how to behave?

'Och it's all right dear,' the lady says. 'They're only children. Are yous from England? Are yous here for long?'

For ever and ever amen.

P.S. Why's everybody speaking English?

TWO

'Is that them now? Surely this must be them now?'

We are in a little room empty except for a fire in the grate. Except that I am sitting. What on? Looking out of a window with no curtains. I think there are orange walls. Perhaps. The two bedrooms have slanty ceilings with drippy sky-light windows and dry pink flaky paint — damp wooden planks halfway up all the walls: you can run your fingers up the grooves to pass the time. They come away black with mould. The other downstairs room has a green and white china range with big round iron knobs where the squares meet. Esse, it's called. Everything makes a noise — your feet clattering on the bare floors, your voice echoing. It is misty damp outside and getting dark. Soon we won't be able to see a thing. There is no sign of the van yet with all our furniture. And the oil-lamps. Every time we hear a car engine we jump. But the cars are all away over in The Houses. It seems very noisy after Stirling. You can't work out where the sound is coming from. The train roars by. The railway line is behind the house. That's where we came in yesterday. But the train sounds as if it's down by the bay. Funny acoustics, they say. Must be bouncing off the sides of the glen. I hope my daddy is all right. My mother is trying to cook chipolata sausages but there's no heat in this range. Daddy will bring the paraffin stoves. He'll fix the flues. I have still got my nugget.

I have explored outside, but it's too big and wet. Though different big from Stirling — high instead of wide — and different wet from Stirling: moist on your face, drops sticking to your hair like blue pearls. You can smell it. It hangs over the edge of the rock behind the house, drips off the hanging trees, and swirls down into the yard, drops sticking to the high hedge like hair. There are seagulls. No peewits. I don't like the sad noise the seagulls make. They're crying. I don't like going to the lavatory outside. There is a damp black bakelite seat and a queer smell and you get wet on the way there and back. You'll just have to get used to it, my granny says grimly.

Then they come. Daddy! Daddy! It's completely dark and everything is getting wet and spoilt. They couldn't get up the road, the lorry got stuck, but never mind all that now — we're here that's all that matters and you just keep out of the way. Now where on earth are those lamps? The big boy is trying to get round the corner of the wee windy stair: fourteen steps, I've counted them ninety-nine times today already. He is going up backwards, bent all twisty with the wardrobe on his back and his legs scrabbling underneath him and suddenly there is an awful crack. Oh Lord a mirror — seven years bad luck? What was that crack, the man asks. That was my heid, the boy says. Oh, that's all right then, says the man. I tell my mother and my granny. Wasn't it funny. They think it's very funny. I'm very proud of myself for making them laugh. They usually smile tolerantly. 'That was my heid — that's all right then' I say over and over again.

We can eat the sausages now. They taste very good. A different taste from Stirling sausages don't you think? But I bought them in Stirling dear. Oh.

The man and the boy get cups of tea and a sandwich then they must be going. Cheerio cheerio. My father looking very self-conscious and slipping them ten bob each like a conjuror as he shakes hands. We must have gone to bed in our new rooms. I suppose. Christmas? It must have come. I suppose.

We stay in a croft on the edge of Oban. It's called Dalintart Farm, but it's not really a farm at all. Ferguson sold all the good bits to the Burgh Council to build The Houses on, and then he sold what was left to my father. We couldn't have afforded it otherwise. Ferguson's got a big new farm now. You see it from the bus if you go down to Easdale.

You can tell we're not part of the town because the road's pitch black at night and the postie comes late and the Burgh dust-cart doesn't come at all. They were just finishing off the last of The Houses when we moved in, but they didn't bother to bring the electricity across to our house, or the gas or the mains water, even though they were so near, and they didn't put up a proper fence that would keep the boys out of our corn and our cows out of their back gardens, or a proper gate at the end of Dalintart Drive to save me having to go all the way round our road in the dark. Anyone would think the Burgh Council didn't want us to live here at all.

But then we're not quite country either. Not with The Houses right up against our road and the people chucking their old bedsteads across and letting their dogs loose on our cows to chase them down into the bog. The people in The Houses probably think my parents are mad, keeping cows and making hay and things on top of them both working full-time in the hospital. But they have to do it willy-nilly. The Burgh's just waiting for the excuse to say we're not using the land and poof! They'll buy it off us like it or not. Of course you couldn't make it pay the way it is just now, but my father's draining the bog so's he'll have enough arable to really farm, which will make us all feel a lot safer in case he loses his job at the hospital — which could happen at any time the way things are going in the NHS. Of course my father won't be able to use the bog until the Burgh decide to drain their side of the fence — which of course they never do. It's a Hazard, that bog. One day a cow will go down in it and drown.

The people in The Houses think we're rich because we've got our own farm. Oh yes, I say, we're very rich: we've got cupboards full of toys. You should see them. But we cut the corn with scythes and sickles and turn the hay with gap-toothed rakes. The real farmers round about must think we're mad too I suppose. With their tractors and combine harvesters and milking machines. But I love watching my father sowing the corn on a Saturday afternoon, throwing rainbows of seed out of a tray like the ice-cream girls have at the pictures, right hand, left hand, right hand, walking along slowly, cigarette dangling from his bottom lip, squinting up at the blasted seagulls. I think that's him happy. I love watching them making stooks, tying the corn round itself like a school scarf. I do not love everyone getting irritable sitting indoors waiting for the rain to stop and what if it doesn't stop before next week and I have to go back to work and where'll we all be then? I love the land. I hate the land. I can't do anything about any of it.

Indoors is sostenuto in summer. Staccato in winter. Indoors is perverse with people.

There was always Granny. In her brown portrait she is eternally young, in a muslin dress with richly sheened black hair and rounded cheeks, her bowing arm liquid as caramel. In London, in her girlhood, she had been a Prodigy. Welsh fire and English ice. She never went to school, never had to cook or clean, channelled all her malleable contours into mellow music-flow. Her violin was round-bellied and deep-chested, fashioned in Cremona; it sang with a warm alto resonance throughout its range. But the hands that coax and flutter over it in our kitchen are crooked with age, the music, still technically flawless, edged with disappointment.

It was Granny who produced bland loveless meals on a row of flickering Valor stoves. Granny who laid sticks in the cold grate, lit lamps and cleaned sooty funnels with spit and rolled newspaper. Granny who heated irons in the fire and left vengeful black trails on school shirts, threw potato peelings across the door-step and washed dishes in an inch of listless greasy water. Granny who bought Government stock and voted Tory to annoy my father. Granny who tightened her lips against the world and drank black tea long after the war was won.

It was Granny who bought the piano, who introduced me to Mrs Middle C and the fat lazy D who hung below the line. Granny who showed me the joy and longing that lay waiting beneath the cool ivory. Granny who thumped out the *Students' Song-book* one evening and Mendelssohn the next. It was years before we began asking ourselves why Grampop lived so far away.

Granny goes to the pictures once a week dressed in a fur coat and pearls, sits among the pensioners in the front row knitting in the darkness. It was Granny who danced like a girl in the meths-soaked embrace of Alec McMaster, while the cinema queue watched and applauded.

Madam will you walk will you talk
Madam will you walk and talk with me?

'Is this person annoying you, Mrs Cathie?'
'Not in the least, young man.'

No I will not walk, no I will not talk
No I will not walk and talk with you.

Once upon a time Granny had played in the picture-palace, when my mother was a girl. Granny was a trouper all right.

It was years before we found out how Grampop had sold her fiddle when she was expecting her first.

'You won't be needing that any more now, will you dear?'

But Granny had given secret mandolin lessons, keeping one lesson ahead while feeding the babies; had gone without sugar-buns, pawned her jewels and played at the picture-palace until she had saved enough to buy another fiddle. She took the children every year to Llandudno, or Buxton, watching demurely while Grampop conducted his orchestra and flirted with the soloists in his silk opera cloak.

Grampop's picture hangs above the mantelpiece in my mother's bedroom, opposite Uncle Colin. Uncle Colin lives in New Zealand

and sends koala bears at Christmas. Grampop lives in England and comes up on holiday now and again, billeted in the corrugated iron bothy in the yard, night-thunder of cow-scratching haunting his sleep; he picks his disapproving way between the goose-turds to empty his chamber-pot in the hedge, only once standing beside Granny to glower uncomfortably at my brother's new Box Brownie.

By the time I have completed the jig-saw Granny has grown deaf and senile, bent as an old badger in a world beyond music, beyond love. But that is much later.

My mother is several people, all of them perfect.

At the hospital she is starched and fresh as a girl; black elastic waspie-belt above broad hips, fresh-laundered white uniform buttoned over a fraying lace slip; with her gentle voice, her proud badge-of-office, her cellist's fingers that can play scales on spines, ruthless vibrato on pain-spots, she moves among her machines, disappears behind her floral screens. At once sensual and unearthly in the dry ultra-violet light, utterly unaware of the spell with which she binds me and her patients. Her mahogany dressing-table is dusty with their unused gifts — bath-salts and bath-cubes, scented soap, perfume and talcum powder — ironic tributes to a woman who pours icy water from a fly-strewn ewer, a woman sweet-smelling with fresh sweat and udder-cream.

In her bed she is warm and lazy as a cow, opening her arms drowsily to melt you into her dreams.

On the hill she is a monster, lurking, growling, grunting, hidden among gorse and bracken, leaping out to ambush you, terrify you into squealing, laughing flight, pounding down the path behind you like a stampeding elephant on her huge feet. Or a sketchy artist with a pre-war paint box. Or a naturalist, labelling, identifying, filling the world with things you strain to see. Or a teller of tales, of fox-glove fairies and toadstool rings, lady-birds and puddle-ducks.

On her bike she is a bent-backed brown bear. I clutch her rain-soaked fur, hiding my face from the wind, holding my legs out stiffly to avoid her heels, metal digging through knicker-elastic as we bump over potholes. In the friendly shops she is courteous, shy, knowing everyone, knowing no-one. She used to have lots of friends, when she was a girl in London.

Lots of delicious naughty things happened to my mother to make me laugh. A man sent a rescue-party up Stob Coire nan Lochan because he saw her through his telescope weeing on the ground and thought she'd fallen and broken her ankle. Her pants fell off in Soroba Road right in front of a Man and she had to shy them into the siver. Once she fell asleep standing up and came down like a felled pine right on top of an astonished patient. One day she was on the pot when my father brought the rates assessor into the bedroom and she had to stay squatting down behind the bed, talking to him across the eiderdown, pretending to be hunting for spiders. O giggle and gurgle and rude noises round the tea-table and laughing so loudly you didn't hear Daddy coming past the window, and the silence that fell like an axe as the cat streaked off out the door was a queer welcome home for a man after a hard day's work.

My father. A much more complex jig-saw. A man thirled to First Principles, constantly illuminating the outside world with parables, yet impatient of directing a childish hand towards the easy bits of his own jumbled portrait. Scornful of Half-baked Ideas, yet wantonly leaving indigestible adult conclusions lying around where a child can pick them up and swallow them whole. Humane, gentle, yet completely uncompromising. Does he not realise how inadequate his own high standards make others feel? The cunning cat creeps back to the hearth when his back is turned, but I want his notice, long for his approval. Searching past my girlish, peace-loving mother, my disillusioned granny, for a way to my father's heart, the nonplussed child concludes that there is only one thing for it: she will have to try and learn to Think Like a Man.

EXTERIOR: THE ROAD: LONG SHOT. My father striding along, with springy steps that make his shiny head bounce up and down. His arms swing in military style, his raincoat flaps open behind the lovat sports jacket. Tighten to MID-SHOT as he sucks air in through flaring nostrils, throws back his shoulders, inflates his barrel-chest, hawks and spits hugely.
FATHER: Better out than in.
(ANNE, trotting to keep up, wheezes mournfully.)
FATHER: Come along, cough it up and spit it out.
    Tighten to CLOSE-UP: the shining bump on Father's forehead — half a pickled onion under taut skin, well-known sign of Great Wisdom.
FLASH-BACK: EXTERIOR. SOMEWHERE IN LONDON. Granny Gillies's daily help lets Baby Father's pram go shooting down a hill. Baby Father falls out on head at bottom: CLOSE-UP: bump developing on tiny bald forehead.

BABY FATHER (waving rattle): Eureka.

Father's face: spare, domed, clever, kindly, crinkle-skin, stream-lined, worried, unsoftened by hair. Everything Father does is serious-minded, intelligent, extremely Important. Nothing undertaken lightly.

Father's hands: elegant even when calloused, thorn-scratched. Hand-writing painstaking, rounded, precise, emphatic, meticulous, self-conscious, digs into paper. Father always remembers to make carbon copies.

Father can build a wall, clip a hedge, make toy furniture, plant vegetables, plaster ceilings, plumb a sink, slate a roof, dig a damp-proof course, wash dishes, put up shelves, lay a fire, cross-breed cattle, paint a window, mend a rocking-horse, muck out a byre, pay bills, tarmac a road, rotate crops. But not until he is ready. Not until he has drawn a plan, taken measurements, worked out a system, thought it all out. Father stays up late, working things out, making lists, doing sums, drawing neat technical diagrams: the side-elevation of a doll's house, aerial view of a flower-bed, a fool-proof system for winning newspaper competitions, beating the Inland Revenue: 'You will rush things, all you people.'

There is nothing my father cannot do, when he has the time, or the room, or the tools, or the money, or the Relevant Information. 'One day the Sheriff's Officer will come and take all the furniture' my mother says.

But we understand really. We don't mind. We wouldn't change him. We get on meantime, hoping he won't notice our makeshift measures, the brush-strokes, the bits of string and insulating tape, the bent nails, the lumps of putty, globs of glue. My granny plunders sale-rooms, my mother smuggles in cheap rubbish from Woolworth's. My father sighs and shakes his head: 'You're all the same, you people.' 'Can't you get the accountant to sort all this out,' my mother begs. 'Isn't that what we pay him for?'

After months of sparring, the Inland Revenue wearily pays my father a hefty tax rebate. And when the house falls down, the bits my father built will stand triumphant.

My father's speech: considered, erudite, well-informed, leavened but not lightened by flights of sardonic word-play: London, the great stinking wen, corrupted by Anglo-American, pluto-democratic, Wall-street thuggery and fuelled by the selfish greed of unthinking yahoos. Yahoos? Please God don't let me giggle. Millions now living are already dead.

Conversing with my father is like competing in *Top of the Form*. My brother always wins. It feels like.

My father's talk is peppered with names, tossed off nonchalantly. You try in vain to sort them out: living/dead; heroes/friends; famous/obscure; goodies/baddies: Carlyle, Willie James, Attlee, Knox, MacDiarmid, William Power, Aquinas, Compton MacKenzie, Paul Robeson, Willie Blake, Mendel, Art O'Brien, Jung, Rory Erskine of Mar, Dr Johnson, Darwin, O'Casey, Tom MacDonald, Edward Dwelly, Terence MacSweeney, John MacLean, Edward the First, Burns, John Murdoch, John MacCormack, Brian Boru, Walt Whitman, Nietzsche, Iain Lom, D. H. Lawrence, Synge, Ramsay MacDonald, Viscount Stair, Wallace, Francis George Scott, de Valera, Toulouse Lautrec, Big Chief Sitting Bull, Campbell of Islay.

What? You've never heard of Kenneth MacAlpin? You hear that, Mary, she claims she's never heard of Kenneth MacAlpin. No-one ever listens to a word I say in this house.

Every room is full of books. In bookcases made out of gelignite boxes: Gaelic books, Irish books, Welsh books, Fabian Society pamphlets, Penguin Classics, Pelicans. Periodicals, dictionaries, encyclopaedias, atlases.

Histories of Scotland, the Highlands, Ireland, the Celts, the working-classes, the French Revolution, the Jews, the English.

Celtic art, social anthropology, psychology, biography, humanism, religion, poetry, farming, gardening, house-keeping, medicine, musical theory, botany.

Copies of *The Listener* and *The Scotsman* in the byre, the dairy, the bothy and under the beds.

Cuttings and quotes and notes and references heaps in corners.

Hidden away in drawers: your grandfather's papers. Vital clues to solving the jig-saw.

'No, darling, I never knew your grandfather. He died before I married Daddy. But I wish I had known him. He was a very wonderful man. You'll have to ask your father about him.'

But my father gets unaccountably irritated. When he gets time he's going to write a book about his father and set the record straight. Some bits I ought to know — hasn't he told me often enough? Some bits I'm far too young to understand. Why don't I remember it right if he's told me about it already? Why won't he tell me again? It's not fair. If it means all that much to him why doesn't he explain it in a way I can understand? What's the great mystery? I have no bother remembering all the other stories he's told me. About his parrot that said 'where's

Iain?' every day at exactly the time he was due home from school. About how his mother knew a girl who broke off her engagement because her fiancé went into the Gents when they were out on a date. About his Auntie Jeanne who was an elegant Parisienne — she would never bite her finger-nails like that. About the time his red-haired auntie was in a coffee-shop and somebody said, 'Oh you red-headed red-headed red-headed red-headed red-headed old bitch' — that was a parrot too. About the old man who'd been at sea and when he went dotty the daily help used to say, 'The old gaffer be a-hollerin' until at last he covered himself in grease and belayed himself into the bed to wait for the end. About the man from the Bank who got drunk and sat down in the tube station and they had to run all the way down the up escalator to rescue him before his botty got shaved off at the bottom. About the man who gave away his house and his money and all his things and took his family of wee children up on top of Hampstead Heath to wait for the end of the world. Funny wee gossipy stories like that.

But he doesn't gossip about your grandfather. All that was far too important. Too Complex. (Too Painful? adult consciousness whispers, belatedly eroding the edges of my childhood confusion.) You can try to re-construct some of the snippets though. I like to think of him as a schoolboy in London, writing letters to John Murdoch, raising funds for the Highland Land League and charming the birds out of the trees to speak Gaelic to him until he became completely bilingual: a Gaelic scholar, teacher, playwright, propagandist — promoting the concept of self-knowledge, cultural awareness, national identity, as the only route to universal understanding. (What worm is this which asks why his own children were not bilingual? The cobbler's son is aye ill-shod? Hush. Be still.)

My father passed his Common Entrance Exam at fifteen, but they couldn't afford to send him to university so he became a librarian, then a bank clerk. But his real work was at his father's elbow — from the shared ideals of his own boyhood to co-editing the *Scots Independent* newspaper in his young adulthood. Where would he have been now if his parents had not died young — within a few months of each other — and my father left to keep the family together until the youngest of his sisters (my mother's best friend) came of age? That was when he felt free at last to come up and live in Scotland. To Ballachulish . . . Stirling . . . Oban . . . To pursue his ideals? Promote historical awareness? National identity? Assist in economic regeneration? Take part in a cultural renaissance? As a desk-bound servant of HM

Government, answerable to a non-elected Board of local big-fry? Hamstrung by children, the Inland Revenue, the Burgh Council, the weather?

Sometimes I worry about how sad my father seems so much of the time. I hope it's not my fault. I will try to do really well at school to make him proud of me. All you people are far too concerned with personalities anyway, instead of getting on with the issues. Dear father, live forever.

Lastly my big brother. Named after his grandfather. Older than me. Cleverer than me. Stronger than me. Wittier than me. Shyer than me. Gets iller than me. Gets more upset than me. Gets more pocket money than me. Gets to stay up an hour later than me. Can run across narrow bridges and leave me behind. Come back here you wee bugger and help your sister across that bridge. Here don't speak to my big brother like that mister. So that's my family.

What do you mean, I haven't told you anything about my big brother? I've told you everything about him. He's there all the time. Half of 'us'. Us good, us bad, us scared, us fighting, us playing. Surely I don't have to keep saying that all the time? 'My brother and I this' and 'my brother and I that'?

What d'you mean, 'What's he like?' Oh for goodness sake. This is very embarrassing.

My brother has a hen called Blackie. He has trained her to come when he calls. He has a teddy made out of a camel dressing-gown called Teddy Poo who is going to the grave with him. He likes stamp-collecting and fishing and his bike's got four gears and he's got moles on his cheeks. I have no hen because every time I get one they die and I can't get them to do anything anyway. I have a china doll called Rosamunde that I'm not allowed to take outside because it was my mother's and I like skipping and playing peever which of course he doesn't. I hate stamps but I don't like to admit it because Look at all the Things You can Learn from it so I collect the Hungarian ones with the pretty flowers, and I hate fishing because you might catch something and have to kill it but I don't mind sitting looking at my bony legs bending in the water and sometimes he gets wild with me for frightening the fish. And I have no gears on my bike and no moles on my face, only the scar where I scratched my chicken-pock, which is the sort of thing he doesn't do because he has more self-discipline than me. Otherwise we're exactly the same. Us. I'm jealous of him sometimes but other times I feel about twenty years older than him. So what? Why don't you ask him what he thinks of me? We both have pigeon chests and skinny legs and usually we just get on with things together.

I call him Will. The kids at school call him Willie. My parents call him Liam. Everybody else calls him William. I am just Anne. Anne Anne Anne Anne Anne Anne Anne. After my mother's nurse: 'Old Anne'. What a boring name. When I grow up I'm going to change my name to Lesley. Or Bridget. My mother really loved Old Anne. Thank goodness she did, otherwise she might have called me Lily after my granny.

Sometimes we get asked to go to parties. Dear William and Anne please come to my party . . . Horrors. He won't go and I don't want to go but I usually end up going myself and saying he's not well. His asthma again. Posh parties in big houses down the town with bannisters and put your coat in the bedroom dear. Bright lights with big shades and powder-blue eiderdowns. A number pinned on to you as you come in — all the odds this side, all the evens over there no peeping now. Catch the plate before it falls or do a forfeit. All the pretty roses on the carpet. Thank you very much for the lovely party as you put your wellies back on and trudge home carrying his bit of birthday cake in a paper napkin. Not posh ones in halls with professional entertainers (someone's uncle with a mike) in and out go the dusty bluebells oooooh hokey cokey cokey. On the way out a lucky bag with coconut ices you spit out on the road. No wonder he doesn't want to go to parties. I wish I had the nerve not to go either.

Mind you he went to the Philatelic Society Party — that was him dragging me for once. It was really weird. All these old men playing games: pass the parcel and win a set of tweezers, do a forfeit and win a magnifying glass. They invented this game where you had to try and judge how long a minute was. Each team-member has to come out and sit on a chair for a minute. All watches off, please, gentlemen. It would have lasted half an hour if we'd all done it right. They told us afterwards that the only person who sat for exactly sixty seconds was young William Gillies. He told me on the way home that he took his pulse, basing his calculations on an average 70 beats per minute and allowing a little for the excitement of the occasion.

What do you mean he sounds very boring? He is no such thing. Either that or I must be boring myself. He makes me laugh and when I went to get an injection at the dentist he made up a story about the three Biddles who all lived in different parts of the globe — Biddle A who lived in the North, Biddle B who lived in the East and Biddle C who lived in the West. It was very funny and it made me stop crying. Even when we're fighting he makes me giggle — much to my own annoyance. Like the time I said to him, 'Please don't do that, Will, I appeal to you,' and he said, 'Oh no you don't.' Quick as a flash. It took me a minute or two to get the joke. My granny says she's going to knock our two heads together, so then we go away and think up awful things to do to my granny or make up rude songs which I'm certainly not going to tell you about or my brother will never speak to me again. He'll probably never speak to me again as it is. Telling about his Teddy Poo I mean. Excuse me. Is nothing sacred?

My brother takes me places that would be too far for me to go myself and he usually waits for me if I'm getting peched. I help him to collect clovers and elderberries and things for his wine. He makes very good wine.

But our best expeditions are at night in bed. The lamp blown out, the torch confiscated, the books put away. Bump bump creak down the fourteen stairs Daddy with histrionic sigh or Mummy with nightie-by-kitey.

Momentary silence. Then from his bed, 'What was Davy doing?'

'Well Davy had made breakfast of oatmeal and water, and then gone down to the burn to wash out the pot when he looked up and saw the flash of a red coat far away on the horizon. What was Alan doing?'

'Alan had been keeping watch all night, lying on a flat boulder while Davy slept. He had eaten the gruel Davy made and was polishing his *sgian-dubh* with heather-roots when he saw Davy signalling frantically from the burn. Turning, he saw the red-coats advancing. Gripping his dirk between his teeth he began crawling on his belly up the mountain-side. What was Davy doing?'

'Well Davy . . .'

Alan Breac was always strong, always brave. Davy Balfour always got wounded or captured or stranded and had to be rescued by Guess Who. But by golly they had some good times together until 'You two go to sleep up there or I'll come up and give you a good clump.'

THREE

Outdoors is like a member of the family too. A dynamic entity in its own right. Just as familiar, just as unpredictable, exasperating, beloved, resented, fickle; just as seminal an influence as any other member of the family; just as likely to help or frustrate you.

Sometimes it seems that outdoors changes you — making you respond to its nuances, its cloud, its light, its pressure. Sometimes you impose yourself on it, painting its contours with your mood, seeing only what you choose, beauties or blots, selecting parts to use, obstacles to give in to or rebel against. Sometimes your relationship with it is an extension of someone else's plan, determined by their whim, their will; but ultimately outdoors has the upper hand, power over the most powerful, uniting the rest of us in impotence or awe. Abstract with animal, vegetable and mineral connections.

Did you ever wake up on a summer morning with excitement tasting like candy-floss on the back of your tongue and go out and sit in the grass, straight-legged, bare-legged, drinking up the dew? Did you pull out a single floret from a juicy white clover and milk it with your teeth? Dig for ground-nuts, sniff meadow-sweet, smoke acorn pipes, kiss bog-cotton, eat wild strawberries, crack ripe hazelnuts? Have you sat on a high hill with Cruachan at your back and Mull rising straight out of the sea in front of you and heard bagpipe music rising like smoke from chimneys far below?

And have you thinned turnips when the ground is sodden and glittering with beetles? Howked tatties till black fingers, black boulders, black tatties merged into a single freezing misery? Turned hay with your ears thundery and swollen with midges and felt toads squirming in furrows underneath your sandals? Have you fallen bare-legged on sharp stubble or rubbed your eyes to jelly, wheezing for dear life in the seedy heat of a hay-loft? Have you been a child among hell-bent adults while sea-gulls, washed inland, hover like vultures over damp crops? Have you watched the wind flatten corn or your father's cheeks taut and flushed with strain?

The railway line cut the hill in half. A path wound upwards, over

34

rivulets, under the railway bridge, and away: up to the burn, the waterfall, the rowan tree, the cave, the windy summit and the dark forestry beyond — bluebells, coo of ring-doves, soft pine-carpet and sudden sunlight on pale transparent grass. At the railway bridge you stopped, putting your fingers in the holes in the stone: there were magic tunnels. You could find the entrance only if you stood under the bridge when a train went by. You heard the train coming and ran. But you always missed it. Above the tunnel you could play hide and seek in the bracken and not be found for hours: one day my brother ran right over me — his big spongey sandal flat on my face. Or sit in the cave whistling on grass-stems. Or play houses in the hazel-grove.

Below the railway line, terraces of sheep tracks for running down jerkily, one leg straight for balance, and a huge boulder to lie flat and look out for red-coats. Iris leaves to sail and reeds to peel. Moss tuffocks to bounce on in the bog the other side of the strange grassy *dùn* stretched like a sphinx above the hay-field. Wild rose-petals to boil for scent.

Then the house crouching hard against the damp, tree-hung rock-face, like a foetus newly-pushed from the womb, still attached to its mother by the gurgly spring with its corrugated iron lid where all our water comes down from, straight down the tap into the sink in the byre below.

Peeling lime-wash pecked by generations of hens. Two smiling windows, three rusty sky-lights. On one side the dairy, filled with bikes and dilapidated chicken-coops; under a sheet of plaster-board the bath my father is going to put in one day, home from home for spiders. The big red-roofed barn with its huge sliding door that never slid but bumped and juddered and sent down flakes of old blue-green paint where you bounced your ball; there are round holes with red clay pipes in them for ventilation and birds' nests — you can't get the ball in the holes but you keep trying. The hen-run, tumbled round with blackthorn briars and honey-suckle, flanked by hazel, oak and birch trees, a piece of corrugated iron wedged into a loop of rope for a swing, big red troughs full of stagnant black water. On the other side the two byres and the stable, iron latches in worm-eaten doors, birds' nests in rhone pipes, rusty water-butts full of blood-red witches' brew, and a concrete drain-cover ideal for peever.

The hens scratch idly among the groundsel in the yard, bathe luxuriously in the ash-heap, talk to you querulously under the door as you sit tearing toilet-paper patterns in the chilly sentry-box with its cauldron rich and brown as a winter stew. The garden was mystical, entirely surrounded by a high hedge, it lay not dead but sleeping. If you can open the broken gate you can hide like Tom Thumb under the rhubarb leaves, or give yourself the *sgùrr* eating plums and curly kale.

I respected the hens, feared the snaking geese with their vicious beaks, ignored the sheep billeted on our hillside by Jackson the Butcher, avoided the horses billeted on our *dùn* by big girls from down the town. But I loved the cows. Daisy, Dixie, Daffy, Dearg . . . They came and went, were born or bought, joined or left our family, and behaved or misbehaved much as we did ourselves. All girls together.

On the *dùn* where I rolled or sledged, they were my big sisters, condescendingly aware of my presence but busy with the real work of eating, digesting, evacuating. When they escaped to raid the gardens and chew the washing over in The Houses I was their granny, bustling with a horny walking-stick taller than myself, nagging and chiding and whacking their bums along the street, up the ginnel, through the gap in the fence. Bad girls: go home at once. Watching a cow drown, slowly sucked into the bog, huge white-rimmed eyes swivelling to plead for help we could not give: I was a mother then, a frail, helpless, mourning mother.

In the byre they were my aunties. I sat in the shadows, listening to the sough of milk on pail, my mother's low voice conversing, the air thick with dust-specks and female mystery. I learned to read their slime, the restlessness in their rolling eye-whites. Recognised when their heat or their calves were due, saw the great holes swell like gargoyles, laughed to see the ridiculous dignity with which they squeezed their pregnant wames through the narrow door. There was mystery beyond me the day we took Daisy up the hill to the bull: as we watched the heavy heaving bodies, enthralled, the farmer's collie came up quietly behind me, possessing my shoulders with his tall front paws. I laughed, turning my head towards his great black muzzle, but the farmer prised him off me roughly, striking him with intense, incomprehensible emotion. Humans definitely stranger than animals.

There is nothing more beautiful than a calf. In the byre, waiting, wishing you could help, you turn away, suddenly afraid. But unseen sounds are more frightening still: the heaving, the men's voices peaking urgently, the gush of juices. You peep between your fingers and see the steaming grey package, dead as a bunch of firewood, lying on foaming black straw. Oh my God. The calf is dead. You turn away once more — from despair, from the huge veined jelly-fish your father carries on his graip out to the manure heap. And in that moment a ludicrous cawing sound explodes into the air, tearing hysterical laughter from deep in your guts, whipping you round to see a miraculous animal climbing to its silly knees, bedraggled, wobbling, adorable. Muffin the Mule arising from the foam.

Making you love the byre, the hissing storm-lamp, the deep shadows on the wall, your father's hollow eye-sockets and the glow of his trembling cigarette. Making you love the vet; his strong bare freckled arms as you hold the soapy basin up to him; his pale handsome lips drinking whisky. As the calf sucks your finger and you draw its slimy, gaping nose down into the milk-pail you rejoice in possession, in maternal power; making you forget the real mother left alone, empty in the byre, her swollen teats the instruments of our human imperialism. Later the betrayal lies heavy upon you. As she bellows and howls through long nights you stuff your ears and cry into the pillow.

Bit by bit the calf grows boring, tramps on your feet in the stinking darkness of the barn, knocks the torch from your hands with its hard blunt impatient head. The calf grows greedy, finding its feed without your help, finishing it in a few ungrateful sooks, butting your thighs for more; you begin to weary of its budding horns, its budding bullishness.

The day the calf is let out of the barn is a festal day. A Family Occasion. The first warm day. The calf has never seen light before. Hesitates, experiments, sniffs, balks, shies sideways at a thistle, then begins to dance: stopping starting leaping darting tasting bellowing baying blowing flying wheeling kicking quivering snorting flirting frightened curious amused amazed hungry distracted blinking turning flying jerking stretching jumping kicking up its heels then running away and away and away while we laugh and clap and gurgle and wheeze and cough and double and clutch and imitate in excitement and sympathy and love. My joy is the calf. My calf is the joy. My relief infinite, I turn towards summer. A child again. Can I get new sandals Mummy?

This was my reality. Far away from that stupid school with its narrow wooden desks and its radio broadcast *Nature Study* lessons with accompanying illustrated booklet and teacher's notes. Half an hour away in the rain, further if you had crisps to eat, or on soft spring afternoons when you lingered over king-cups in the dry ditch socket, or autumn when you staggered home drunk and gorged with brambles, touched every second rose-hip with your finger-tips and swung on every gate.

Wouldn't life be wonderful if you didn't have to go to school. You'd have thought it might have been better in Oban. In the Highlands.

'What are you gaping at?' the girl snarled.

'I'm not gating,' I whispered to the wind. Sic.

The playground sloped down steeply. I clutched the cold railings that separated girls from boys, looking down at my new fur-lined ankle-boots. To move was to be whipped by ropes, knocked spinning, stung by back-handers, muddied by balls.

I got my ankle-boots in a big shop called Huttons during my first dinner-time at the school. I remember my mother coming into the classroom to collect me. I remember standing looking at the sea opposite Huttons. Spray was lashing up onto the pavement. They let me wear my new boots out the shop and they tied my old shoes up in a brown paper parcel. Then I had to go back to school. The lights were on everywhere because it was winter.

I recall little else of my first year at Rockfield School. Not my teacher's name, if I ever knew it. Not her face, or those of the other children in my class if I ever saw them. The vaguest memory of sums I couldn't begin to do, a green rubber mat you sat on like the cat, hands that shook when you tried to hold a pencil right, and pictures stuck on yellowing cardboard that you took from pockets in the wall if you finished off what you were meant to be doing.

Then gradually images begin to surface, disjointed, arbitrary. Edna Molloy, a dark, vivacious girl in my brother's class. She lived near the school and got birlies-round from Ronnie the Jannie. I wished she would play with me.

Miss MacTaggart, my Primary Two teacher. No face, just a name — it made me think of moss agates like in my mother's bracelet.

Miss Skinner with her huge breasts and posh voice, who came out to bring in the lines wearing a high-necked Chinese silk blouse and embroidered silk slippers with toes that curled up like two Viking long-ships. Her class could recite 'the King asked the Queen and the Queen asked the Dairy-maid'; they could do all the actions with costumes and a real cow's head. (A real cow's head, memory?)

A white-haired man with a plum-coloured waistcoat and a plum-coloured English voice who came to teach music sometimes in the gym. The others called him Old Loin-chops. I hated Old Loin-chops' tatty tatty taffatiffies and the way he taught scales by making fun of people in the class:

Billy Billy Fergus-un
Kissed all the girls and made them run

I hope Old Loin-chops doesn't think of anything to rhyme with Anne Gillies.

Loin-chops wanted to run a concert. He gave every class something different to do. I can't remember what my brother's class got. My class got an English song about daisies pied and violets blue. A concert, Mummy. By some magic a new dress arrived for me to wear, silky and fine, with a pale tracery of daisies. In a cardboard box with tissue paper. Daisies pied on a violet blue dress, to wear at my first concert. We knew all about first concerts in our family.

But teacher says, 'You, Anne Gillies. If you really want to take part you will just have to stand there and open and shut your mouth. You will be so good as to make no sound. You croak like a frog.'

I feel my face hot. I won't tell my granny. She won't know. Please don't tell granny, Mummy.

It was snowy the day of the concert. We were sent home early to get ready. I crunched up the perfect snow behind the Games Ground grandstand: no-one has ever been here before me. I can't wait for the concert. To get my dress on. It was warm in the house and my father was there. That was strange. He had got off work specially because we had a visitor. I didn't know anyone was coming. They were talking and talking about Scotland. It's our school concert tonight. Not now, darling. Leave Daddy in peace to talk.

I don't remember anything about the stupid concert anyway.

Every day I watch the other children, and listen carefully to everything they say, trying not to gape. See the dirty red-haired family that everyone despised: the little one was Offalot and when he came to school the teacher had to take him into the cloakroom to remove his stripey pyjamas from underneath his trousers. There are fat green slugs poking from his nose.

Hear about the tar that falls down from the ceilings in Dunstaffnage: one girl had to have her hair cut off, and Linda's mummy doesn't keep well. I like to look at Linda, dark-haired and pale-skinned like a fairy princess. When she breathes her chest goes up and down like a bird's. I do it too, to be like her. When I remember. When her mother died she went to live with her granny. The others knew what to say when she came back to school: what a lot of words they poured round her. I hope they won't find out if my mother dies. Don't die Mummy.

Watch the girls buzzing, droning around the big dark coarse-faced girl in calipers. Her mottled legs blue and purple with crusts like cheese-rind: she is a tyrant, harrying and scheming. They will do anything for her. I dream of being palely, interestingly ill like the girls in books — a broken leg would be fine — smiling up through my pain at a sea of loving faces. Or consumptive. Dying. Well nearly dying. My brother fell at dinner-time and broke his arm and went to the hospital for a stookie. I fell on the brae and went to the Jannie's room to have wee black stones dug out my knee.

In Primary Three a huge brown wooden cut-out kangaroo hangs on the classroom wall. When my glands are sore I can't bend my head up to look at it. There is also a Mercator's Map. What that? And a new boy with fair hair who lifts one side of his top lip up like a horse snickering. Who he? The teacher is nice. Very quiet. She is the Free Church minister's wife, fluffy hair and a fluffy twin-set. But she gets ill and other teachers come. Not so nice.

The dinner-hall is along the road past the place where Fay's father works. Grains spill out of Fay's daddy's place onto the pavement, and he stands smiling in the wide doorway in his dusty navy-blue boiler suit. The dinner-hall smells of stale lentil soup. I stop going there. I don't like it there. The potatoes get stained with beetroot and one day I dropped my fork and went down under the table to get it and when I got back up they'd taken away my ham. I'd eaten up the horrible lettuce and potatoes and left the ham to the last and then they went and took it away. From now on I would rather walk home, even if it does take all dinner-time. In the toilets in the playground there are brown splashes on the pan and dirty paper in coils everywhere. Girls climb up and look down at you through chicken-wire. The smell is bitter brown.

I am anxious to please, but people are unfathomable: after school I went to play with a girl in her flat in Albany Street. Well she asked me. There were white cloths on the back of the settee and her mother was big with a red face and greasy hair. And then I came home feeling very pleased with myself. But my mother was very upset. Where have you been till this hour? We've been worried sick. We've nearly called the police. She makes me give back the coloured bangle the girl gave me. Neither a lender nor a borrower be. Then the girl is very upset. Throbbing with rage on the yellow floor beside the piano in the gym-hall she utters a terrible incantation:

Give a thing and take it back
God will ask you What Is That.

I await divine retribution, trying to reconcile gentle Jesus meek and mild with the wild light in Mary MacTaggart's eyes.

Without warning two girls suddenly pal up with me. I am perplexed. What have I done to deserve this? They stroke my hair and my cheek, pull at my elbows, link arms each side, fix me with point-blank stares. Then without warning, as if by some secret signal, they decide to fall out with me. I never know when it's going to happen; or why. They come towards me very fast along the corridor with linked arms, smiling at some point just above my head; at the last minute one side-steps and the other walks straight into me, banging my forehead, bouncing me off the corridor tiles.

'Oh here sorry, Anne, I never saw you.'

Sometimes they fall out with each other, pulling me between them like a bone. I smile a lot and try not to upset anyone. It goes on for years.

Towards the end of Primary Three Mrs Dobbins belts me for talking in class.

'What page are we on?' I whispered to the girl who sits beside me.

'You. Yes you. Out here this minute.'

My hand is very sore and there is a scratchy thing in my throat but I will not cry. I hate Mrs Dobbins. She has a big fat nose. I pretend to have it in my hands under the desk — plasticine, squashy. I knead it.

I don't talk in class after that.

They don't teach Gaelic in Rockfield School.

But a teacher comes down from the High School sometimes and we do gym. We have to use the corridor, turning somersaults on the cold concrete floor. Tuck your heads in hips up, up, up, *UP*, head under and straight over. I hear my back crunch like a football rattle. On sunny days outside in our knickers to bend stretch out in up down stretch and change. Come on, sing! He wears a blue bonnet blue bonnet blue bonnet he wears a blue bonnet and a dimple in his chin don't tell me Anne Gillies is the only one who knows the words. On snowy days outside in our knickers to build a snow wall. Gloves looking daft on the ends of skinny white cotton arms, blue-legged, chain-gang shoulders back chests out work work *WORK* that's the way to keep warm keep that snow coming while she runs on the spot, sheep-skinned, fair-isled, beating her wings in their suede mitts and screaming like a wild goose.

Mens sana in corpore sano. As my father would say.

One day I said 'holy mackerel' in the playground. I don't know why. I must have heard it.

'Oooh that's terrible, Anne Gillies,' they all said. 'That's Our Lord.' Eh?

Twice a day we say our Lord's Prayer and once a term we go to the Parish Church in twos along the pavement. The town looks funny at this time of day. Very empty. And it smells fishy. Women are gathered on the pavement outside the Parish Church like at a wedding. Mammy. Mammy! They wave to their mothers, embarrassed but pleased. My mother isn't there. She's at her work. And Fay's mother lives at Dunstaffnage and Linda's mummy's dead.

The church is enormous. And who is playing the organ? I stare up at the silver pipes, but there's nobody there. The minister here is Duncan MacDonald's father — he's all fat and smiley, not like the Free Church one who comes into the school. You can tell from their voices that both of the ministers can speak Gaelic. But they don't. Not to us anyway. Most of the other ones in my class come here to the Sunday School, so they're quite used to the beautiful red velvet cushions and the golden eagle and the light-bulbs that look like ice-cream cones and the way the sun cuts great wedges through the coloured windows. I like the lambs in the windows and Jesus is very handsome with a neat brown beard. I have to look along the row to see what we're meant to do. I hope we don't have to kneel down on the skelfy floor.

I don't think I've ever been down the town on a Sunday. Sundays we eat biscuits in my parents' sweaty bed until my mother has to get up before the cow bursts. But I like listening to the church bells from up our hill. On the first Sunday of every month they ring in the afternoon too. That's for the Gaelic service. My mother would like us to go to that but she's too shy to take us. Sometimes my mother helps me to say a wee prayer after she's tucked me into bed at night. It makes me feel all warm and safe.

Gentle Jesus meek and mild
Listen to a little child
Pity my simplicity
Suffer me to come to thee amen nighty by kitey now.

Is that you two up there playing with your emotions? My father says a poem instead. I like it too.

The image of Christ that thou dost see
Is my Christ's chiefest enemy
Thine was the leader of mankind
Mine spoke in parables to the blind

That's by Willie Blake. He was a friend of my grandfather's. I think. My father used to go to Sunday School when he was wee, but then he stopped. You don't have to go to church to have Proper Moral Values. Or to believe that Jesus was a Very Great Philosopher for his time. And look at all the evil which has been perpetrated in the name of Religion. He tells me a really good story about a wee happy black man who lived very peacefully very far away, speaking his own language and minding his own business, and then some white men came and taught him to sing *Jesus Loves Me* so's he wouldn't complain when they took all his land away from him. That's called colonialism. Did you know that, Mummy? That's bad. That's not like my daddy's Uncle Robert. He's in the China Inland Mission. He sends my brother stamps. He's a good man. And then of course there's Gandhi. He's a really good man. He doesn't send stamps though. My father doesn't actually know him. Well I don't think so anyway.

And then of course we have fights between good and evil going on inside our bodies all the time. Our cells. The phagocytes are fighting against the other ones. I forget their names. It might be stalagmites. But of course that's Physical. That's not Moral. There's a big difference you know. Like when my brother pulled the heads off all the flowers when he was a wee tiny boy and he told my father it wasn't him that did it. It was his Brain. Well that just shows you what a clever boy my brother is. I think he must have a very big brain. He can really concentrate. Not like me. I'm a Grasshopper. And my mother's a Physiotherapist.

Every single night my father sits up till two and three in the morning reading books about Religion and Philosophy and Psychology.

I love those long words. Philosophy, Psychology, Physiotherapy. I bet I can spell them. I bet you can not. Can sot. Can not. Is that you two still talking up there? Straight off to sleep now.

FOUR

The more you know the more there is to worry about.

My mother saw a dog in the street with its eye hanging out on a string. In *The Red Shoes* the girl had her legs cut off by a train — the legs went dancing away by themselves in their red shoes beside the railway line. My brother got chased by a horse, all the way across the field until it got him against the barbed wire, then it turned round deliberately and kicked him in the back. In my dreams I sometimes see my mother with her eye hanging out on a string. Sometimes with her legs cut off. In his dreams my brother sees big huge stallions coming towards him.

It frightens me when my father burns the heather. It makes a low evil sound and it sneaks along very close to the ground. When there's a proper fire the siren howls. Starts low and whining, works up to a high wail then trails off like a dying animal.

'A ha! The *tarbh-uisge*!' my father groans with awful rolling eyes.

He can't fool me. I know it's not the *tarbh-uisge*. I know it's people burning up — choking, screaming, dying. Like Joan of Arc, only not noble like her. God doesn't mean them to die. It's an accident. Though I suppose he could have stopped it if he'd really wanted to. Suffer the little children to come unto me, as the minister said when wee Lionel Thomson got his head bumped by the wind.

They say the further out of town the fire is the longer the siren goes: a sort of signal to the fire-brigade, who are all running out of their shops and businesses, throwing off their jackets and sliding down greasy poles. If it's very far away the people will all be dead before the fire engine gets there. Burnt legs, charred hair sticking to their bare skulls, black bones. I've seen the gnarled heather-roots on the hill in autumn. Like burnt fingers raised in eternal prayer.

The siren belongs to the war. Of course the war is long past but you can still see its effects all around. The air-raid shelters are still standing in our play-ground, crumbling red bricks that smell of pee. On our *dùn* there is still a round dug-out thing: on Sundays the big boys smoke and gamble in there, lying on their bellies flipping coins into the round hummock in the middle. My brother knows I don't like the dug-out. He tried to give

44

me a fright by saying it was made by a giant: he comes up our hill every morning while you're asleep — he ties his enormous goat to a stake in the middle of the dug-out, look here's where the stake goes in and here's where the goat wears the ground down running round and round in a circle. Oh yeah. That would have made me very scared a year or two back, but now I wish I could believe my brother. Giants better than wars I think.

The war worries me, even if it is long past. My brother makes mountains with books and an army blanket, and his soldiers all fire at each other over the hill. I don't like my brother's battle-ship. You press a wee lever and it all explodes and the soldiers fly out dead. I don't like my father's gun either. You have to have a gun if you've got beasts, they tell me, but I don't think my father would ever use his gun. Well, if he did use it I wouldn't ever forgive him so why bother to have it! He's not a murderer.

But then neither is my Uncle Donald and he went away to the war and got caught by the Japs and didn't get home for years and years, and someone in the prisoner-of-war camp had to have a hole in his skull mended with a bit of cigarette case. When Uncle Donald finally got home he found his house flattened and his wife dead of TB. And neither is my Uncle Ian. He got caught by the Germans but he escaped out of his prisoner-of-war camp and managed to get to Switzerland (was it Switzerland?) where he was hailed as a hero because of his contributions to medical science before he went into the army. Imagine if he'd got killed by the Germans. What a waste. What a lot of ill people wouldn't have got better without my Uncle Ian and the pills he invents. They made my brother better when he had the double pneumonia. Uncle Ian's hair turned white in the war. But he won't talk about it. And neither is my Uncle Colin. He was a Lieutenant Commander on a ship exactly like my brother's, sailing about with all those torpedoes waiting to explode him. I just can't understand any of it.

Donald, Ian and Colin are my mother's brothers. My father's big brother went to the war too. He is a piper. My Uncle Bob. He was in both wars. In his kilt. He pretended to be older than he was the first time and younger than he was the second time. You couldn't imagine my daddy doing that. He'd rather have gone to prison. If he'd had to. He doesn't approve of wars. Not like the English. I wonder what my grandfather thought about Uncle Bob and all his wars.

The day the sweeties came off the ration there was a queue from Hannah's right round to the gas-works. Liquorice toffee with white stripes, butterkist and gob-stoppers, aniseed balls, soor plooms and sherbet dabs. Nobody heard the bell that day and the teachers had to come out and drag half the children in with their pennies still in their hands.

But even that wasn't the end of the war. There are men in my daddy's hospital who've been there since the First World War. Hidden away. Like Joe. His face is all eaten away from frost-bite in the trenches. My mother can talk to him. She's used to him. She can understand what he's saying. Not many people can. One day her assistant's wee boy came in and walked all round Joe looking very hard at his poor face from all different angles. 'Joe's dot a funny nose,' he said eventually. Oh that's awful, Mummy. Poor Joe. Was he very upset? Och not at all, she replies. He was delighted.

'Well I have got a funny nose,' he said. 'Only most people don't dare to look at it.'

Uncle Donald comes up to have a holiday with us. I follow him about very quietly, wishing I could make it all up to him. He'll never have children of his own now. I take him over to the golf-course and help him carry his things. I've never been out on the golf-course before. I've never seen our house from this side of the glen. It looks very queer. There is always more than one way of looking at things. I'm beginning to learn that. Take the Hospital for example. We always called it the Hospital. The rest of the town took longer to think of it like that. Grown-ups usually called it 'The Rest' ('West Highland Rest' short for). Kids at school mostly called it the 'Poor House'. Your dad works at the Poor House. Oh no he doesn't. Oh yes he does. Oh no he doesn't. Shurrup. Sometimes tinkers got washed off the hill and had to stay in the Hospital till their tents (or their fathers?) dried out. They would come to the school for a few days and then disappear again: one of them gave my brother a bloody nose for being the Governor's son. Or rather for insisting that he wasn't.

My father was the Hospital Administrator, but it was a good while before people stopped thinking of him as The Governor. He had The Governor's old office. You could smell The Governor in the varnish, in the brown photographs of soldiers and clan chiefs. When he first went there my father saw them dumping the meals straight out of tin basins on to the trestle tables in the hall. The place had been fenced in like Colditz, the children were sent to school in brown uniforms to make sure everyone knew they were from the Poor House. My father saw an autistic child, baring its teeth like an animal, caged in a pen in the corner of a ward.

So they painted The Rest all over in lovely strawberry-coloured paint and called it the Dalintart Hospital. When the rain fell it made streaks of darker pink, like melba sauce on a pink ice-cream. But it never quite hid the old name carved in the side of the wall: old people still prayed they wouldn't end up in The Rest even after the gates were unlocked, the wards grew bright, the gardens exquisite with landscaped rose-beds and prize-winning vegetable marrows.

In Oban there was the Cottage Hospital if you got appendicitis; the County Chest if you got TB; the MacKelvie if you got scarlet fever. If you went mad or got hooked on the meths you went to Lochgilphead. But nobody in Oban was very sure what the Dalintart Hospital was for. Even if my daddy's office was there, and my mummy's department; even if he had to look after all the other hospitals right up to Glencoe, and she had to look after all the sore backs from here to Ardnamurchan. I got to know them all in the Dalintart Hospital. The epileptics, the simple folk, and the tall sensible woman with the pudding-basin hair-cut who took Turns every now and then. The smiling pretty young woman called Jean who spent her life in a pink bed-jacket fading away slowly surrounded by cackling and mumbling. The solid woman in calipers and her attentive white-haired boy-friend from Part Three: I think they got a house and married eventually. The mongol and her kind friend who would have been someone's mother if she'd been a hundred per cent all the time: they got separated for good when someone decided Their Relationship was Unhealthy. Part Three — big barracks at the back of the hospital, full of *bodaich* who chewed tobacco and peeled spuds and spat across the concrete: old bachelors, old widowers, old soldiers. And younger men — put away for some disability or handicap — who wheeled trollies, dug the garden, and went down the town on errands. Everybody was always pleased to see me, always ready for a blether. I had to learn how not to show it if I was scared or shy.

A lot of them spoke Gaelic. They were the best ones of course. A famous man with one arm came up from Edinburgh to the hospital to record some of them.

I am allowed to listen, so careful not to cough, so thrilled at the courteous lovely conversation, the one-armed man coaxing, caressing by bed-sides, beside armchairs. Afterwards in my father's office, drams in medicine glasses. My father tells the man I can sing a Gaelic song.

Oh Dad-dy!

But the man is courteous and coaxing. Trembling, I sing into the tape-recorder, my one Gaelic song plus gulps and swallows. After it's over I feel triumphant. One day I will have a tape-recorder. I will speak Gaelic and collect all the songs like the nice one-armed man.

If you stand in the yard you can see right down to the gate. The grassy hummock in the middle of the road dwindles to a point and disappears behind a slight incline. If you look at it upside down through your legs the colours seem brighter. The hummock grows high in the summer time and my father has to flatten it with a spade and fill in the puddles. It's always on his conscience. He gets irritated if Granny asks him when he's going to get round to it. This is usually if she gets a taxi home from the town and old Rankin complains about his chassis. I'll not be coming up this road again if it doesn't get any better he moans.

The postie comes most days and Coopers' van comes on Saturday afternoons with the groceries: ½lb Ayrshire bacon, 1lb Summer County Margarine, ¾lb tea, 1 pkt Rich Tea Biscuits, 1 pkt Digestive Biscuits, 1 tin Heinz spaghetti, ¾lb Cheddar cheese, 1 tin guavas . . . It would be far too much for my mother to manage on her bike. Otherwise we hardly see a soul. A car coming up our road is a real occasion.

Mind you, it's nice when we do have a visitor. It turns my father into a different person — very gay and smiling, humming under his breath. Even if the phone goes and it's for him you can see him changing halfway through the house between the byre and the front hall. He gets up from the table with a face like fizz. Who on earth is it? Can you not deal with it Mary? As he crosses the kitchen he straightens his shoulders and puffs out his chest. As he opens the hall door he starts whistling under his breath. By the time he reaches the phone you'd hardly recognise him.

Sometimes Hughie MacDonald comes to see us, for example if they've been to the Mart together. Hughie helps my father if he needs a loan of the tractor or the likes, but one night we heard terrible news. Hughie has fallen down the hold in the Lismore boat and broken his skull. Oh God please make Hughie better.

Occasionally people come from my father's past. I hear their voices downstairs in the kitchen, talking, talking about Scotland. No-one understands them except my father. No-one understands Scotland any more except them. They come here to be sad and ill, it seems.

First Uncle Hugh. Hugh Paterson: we've to call him Uncle Uisdean. He was a friend of my grandfather's. He could tell you all about him. Gentle and grey as a dove, his voice silver and Gaelic like the brooch he gave my mother. He's deaf — from the war I think maybe, or an explosion.

Then W. D. MacColl: we've to call him Uncle Uilleam. When Uncle Uilleam was younger he went to somebody's house just as they were finishing their meal. He sat down at an empty space at the table and started drinking by mistake out of the cup they'd been using for all the tea-slops — nobody liked to say anything, and he finished it all up, too polite to complain. Once he went to the theatre in London and there was a woman sitting in front of him with a big huge hat on; he asked her very politely to remove it, and when she wouldn't he sat there delicately tickling her big fat bare shoulders with his programme. You wouldn't think it seeing him now. Lying like a yellow skeleton in a bed ben the hoose, arguing with everybody as if his life depended upon it. He even argues with me if there's no-one else around. But Uncle Uilleam, hens aren't less intelligent than cows, they're just different. I like hens very much and I think if you got to know them you'd realise they can learn a great deal: people just don't bother to teach them. You can't prove anything about a hen just lying there saying it's stupid. Oh ye gods. Listen to her. A generation of vipers. Just like her father. None of them can bear not having the last word. I shall get out of here just as soon as I'm better. A letter comes for him in the post. Look at this Mary. Don't you be telling me I'm paranoid. See, it's been opened. Quite definitely opened. How did they find out I was here?

Then T. D. MacDonald: we've to call him Uncle Tom. He has a Gaelic name that he uses sometimes and lots of little children. He has come here with a pain in his heart: the world has turned its face away from him; no-one wants to listen to him, read the things he writes, accept the truths that stare them in the face. His wife doesn't know where he is. His fierce black beard trembles, his bony hands clasp and unclasp. I am scared of saying the wrong thing to him. Please let my father help him. Voices on the phone, speaking quietly so as not to wake us upstairs in our beds, reassuring, insistent: no, no, Mary dear, we'll take care of him, don't come, you've got enough to cope with. My father sits up all night with Uncle Tom, talking, talking. In the morning the ceiling is black with smoke and all my brother's home-made wine is finished, but they are calm and sober. I wished his wife had come up and brought all the little children. I learned their names by heart and played with them all alone in the hazel-house. When his sons come to take him home after he gets better they turn out to be grown-up and remote, but I go on playing with the girls: sit there Francesca and have a cup of tea till Theresa and Marsaili come in from the shops; no no Monica, I'll wash, you wipe.

Then one day I'm bouncing my ball in the yard when I see a car at the gate. Wow! A car! It's Uncle Paddy.

'Quick quick Mummy, tidy the kitchen, Uncle Paddy's coming up the road in his car.'

Don't be daft Anne. How can he be? We haven't seen Uncle Paddy since we left Stirling. You don't remember him do you?

Well no, actually. Not really. Just another name. But I can tell you he's coming up our road right this minute. You don't have to believe me if you don't want to.

Tyres crunch on yard-stones, the front door bursts open without a knock, and Uncle Paddy is in the kitchen like a tiny thunder-bolt, hugging us till we crack, hand-clasping with a grip to bring tears to my brother's eyes.

Oh ma wee tots come here to your Uncle Pattie an gies a big cuddleanakiss, no that way you big frostie-postie, a right cuddle an a right kiss. Mary ma lass you're bonnier than ever — and where's Granny? Come here you wee smasher. William ma laddie let's see what you're made of, aye — gies yer hand, aye that's champion ma laddie. Your Uncle Pattie didnae mean tae hurt ye. No no Iain Ah'll no hear of it — you'll need to take a dram oot o mine first. Noo a big kiss for your Auntie Ellen — come on Ellen lass come on ben — it's Anne and William — it's oor wee tots. Come on hen. There ye are noo. That's better.

Uncle Paddy's nose almost touches his chin: no teeth no teeth Mrs Tittlemouse. He takes off his trilby hat to reveal a little round baldie head like Gagool. Nothing has ever happened like this before. Everyone stands around not knowing what to say, giggling foolishly. How on earth did you know it was him Anne? Dunno. Just knew.

He has brought the biggest box of chocolates we ever saw — a mile wide. They're for Granny. He has brought soaps and stuff for my mother, and a tartan head-scarf. I got it made special for you ma lass up in the north. That's where you should be, Iain, no here in Campbell country. Ah'll no rest till I get you all away oot o here. It's no use at all. Don't say a word Mary your Uncle Pattie'll sort yous all out.

He has brought a bottle of whisky larger than a fiddle-case. And after he has given us another cuddle we find five-pound notes in our hands. Not ten-bobs. Not pounds. Fivers. I've never had one before. He won't take anything to eat but your father'll have another wee dram and Auntie Ellen'll take a wee cup of tea to get her pills down. Och Mary I don't know what I'm to do with her, she'll no eat nothin an Ah'm no satisfied wi what the doctors are saying aboot her at all.

He and my father go down the town in his car and on the way back they land in the ditch. Auntie Ellen is very quiet and her hands are soft and lifeless. Her eyes stare into the fire. Oh tae dash Mary never mind the car we'll get it out in the mornin. Come here ma lass till I get a proper look at you.

Reality is suspended till he whirls away again, leaving us breathlessly counting, re-counting his gems.

So Davy and me we goes tae the races, Ah'm just a laddie like, William ma son, juist like yersel, an ma mither's told Davy he's tae watch me an see Ah dinna get up tae nuthin. An we backs a right string o runners, an at the end of it a' we decides tae stay the night. In Ayr like. Well we stay in this hoose wi this big wumman and there's four ae us tae the one room an there's a po under a' the beds. Well Davy he's first tae get up an I hears him haein a wee piddle in his po an then back intae his bed. Then ma floatin kidney sinks an Ah'm up at ma po. Oh Mary ma lass you're lookin grand juist grand. But you're tired ma lass. That's no right Iain. Your lassie's lookin tired. Oh tae dash Ah'm goin tae get you away oot o this place. It's no damn good at all. Anyway, we're a' sleepin an then Davy's floating kidney sinks again — he's had a few pints like, Mary — an he gets up again an Ah hear him cursin away he's went an filled his po so he comes across an has a wee piddle in ma po. An the other laddies they've had a few pints and they're a' cursin away that a' the pos is fou. So Davy he gets up an goes tae the window an opens it an flings oot his po, goes tae empty it like, Granny, hen, but it turns oot it's no a window at a' — it's a damn wardrobe wi a mirror oan the door. Oh tae dash. A wardrobe, William ma son. Aye, Granny, ye're laughin. If you'd seen yon wumman. The size o her. Were we off oor mark in the mornin. Aw Mary, it's guid tae see you laugh ma lass. Dae ye hear that Ellen? Oor Mary's no laughed like that since she saw her Uncle Pattie the last time. Noo where's Granny? Come on ma lass an get oot your fiddle and Auntie Ellen'll gie ye a wee vamp on the piana. Come on ma hen.

Is it true, Mummy? Did he really play his accordion on the wireless? And was he really a boxing champion? Of all the miners? Was he a miner Mummy? And did he really knock out all the men in the pub and lay them over the grave-stones in the cemetery one by one? What happened when they woke up? So how old was he when he went to America? Just a laddie? Ooo Mummy you're beginning to talk like him. What does Prohibition mean? So what would he have been doing? And when he came back he was in the Hydro-electric — what's that? And what's a gaffer? Ooh that must have been hard, he said he was only nineteen — in charge of all those Irishmen. But is he not Irish, mummy, he's got an Irish kind of name? No I didn't think he'd be very pleased — he's certainly very Scottish. What's Barlinnie? What's black market? What's a bookie's runner? What's trotting? Why did they give the horse the pill? Why did they want it to run very fast? Didn't you like the bit about the horse running round Bannockburn with all the men trying to catch it? Which bit did you like best? Do you believe it about the fighting cock? How could it strip all the feathers off his granny's hens? Why's Auntie Ellen so sad? Does he have to look after her all the time?

Go to sleep dear. Take deep breaths and relax. Your Uncle Paddy helped Daddy a lot when he was at the Quarry. He and Auntie Ellen are our best friends. They were the only people at our wedding. Auntie Ellen was very lovely then and worked in the Arcade. But they've never had any children of their own, so you are their wee tots now. Oh dear I *am* beginning to talk like him. Now off you go to sleep. Nightie by kitey.

Sometimes Uncle Alasdair comes. He's quieter, more Gaelic. But he's good fun too. Daddy whistles when Alasdair's here, as he walks through to the byre to get a dram for them both. Uncle Alasdair takes his teeth out to eat his ham and eggs. His teeth are set in brick-red clay and they lie grinning on the table-cloth beside his plate. Nothing bothers Uncle Alasdair. Tell it again, Uncle Alasdair, about the County Council meeting in Lochgilphead and the wee councillor that had to share a bedroom with the Piscy minister — you know, about how the minister took the altar thing out of his case and put it on the dressing-table and the wee man sat on the edge of his bed and watched the minister lighting all the candles round the altar and shaking the incense bottle and kneeling down in front of the altar, and then the minister took out his cut-throat razor and started sharpening it on the leather strap and the wee man ran away out the room roaring in his night-shirt. Why did the wee man run out the room Uncle Alasdair?

Uncle Alasdair had a second-hand bike-shop in Ballachulish. In between being a Councillor. Santa Claus brought me a bike, but it was out of Uncle Alasdair's shop, painted over with black enamel. I saw the paint on my mother's hands. We went up to see Uncle Alasdair on the train, and they all went fishing in the Laroch and my brother caught an eel and they cut its head off and left it on the hook for bait, but I saw the body swimming away all by itself. Headless.

Then Uncle Alasdair died, and that was very bad of him. Who will look after my daddy now and see he doesn't get thrown out by the people on the Hospital Board? All the others have very long posh names. Except for Harry Carter of course. Harry is fat, and he's all right I think. He came rushing out of the bathroom in the hospital, roaring with laughter, right down to my father's office, buttoning up his trousers with one hand and brandishing a streamer of the new toilet paper in the other.

'Look at this Iain! Just look at this! Government Property! Government Property!'

Well at least he's got a sense of humour. Let's hope Harry Carter will see my daddy all right now Uncle Alasdair's gone.

One night my father said he wanted to do an experiment. He sent us both up to bed. We had separate rooms, so it must have been years later. He said he was going to think about something, down in the kitchen, and write it on a bit of paper, and then see if he could send his thought upstairs to us. Then Mummy would come upstairs and ask us what we had thought of. We weren't to worry, just clear our minds and see if anything came. No talking now. Just Concentrate.

I'm very nervous. I'm no use at this kind of thing. My brother can concentrate any time — you talk to him and he doesn't hear you, and he can look at a page and then make it come up in his head. That's one reason he's so clever at school. But I try. Try to clear my mind, but nothing will come — nothing except Uncle Alasdair, sitting outside his bike-shop in Ballachulish, the wee wooden hut with the trees behind. I'm not even sure that's what it looked like, it's so long since we've been.

My brother whispers, 'Did you get anything?'

'We-ell sort of. But it's not very good. Did you?'

'Yes. I thought of Auntie Jean's great hospitality in having us to stay in Whitby. What was yours?'

Oh golly I can't tell him about Uncle Alasdair and his hut: Auntie Jean's hospitality — wow, that's really brainy. I'd never have thought of that. I'd better try and think up something better. But my mother is already up the stair, talking quietly in his bedroom, coming in to me. I'm sorry, Mummy, I could only think of Uncle Alasdair outside his shop. I'm afraid it's not very good is it?

Then my father is up the stair, two at a time, cheek-bones glowing.

'Where did you see Alasdair? Where were the trees exactly — in relation to the shop? Was he sitting down? Now I don't want you to go talking about this with all your girls at school, giggling and gaggling about it. There are many things in heaven and in earth that are not dreamed of in our philosophy. Now off you go to sleep.'

Wow. Top of the Form. Hurra hurra hurra. I must be psychopathic, as the man said. Of course I shouldn't be telling you about it. That's typical of me really.

FIVE

There are all sorts of ways of describing people. Towns also.

One two three a leerie
I spy Mrs Queerie
Sitting on her bumbaleerie . . .

There really was a Mrs Queerie. Lily Queerie. It was written above the door of her wee shop in a hut on the edge of Lochavullin, just opposite the High School. Tiny wee nippy lady, with a bucket in her back shop. We saw her bumbaleerie all right, through her back window.

Across the road, on the corner of Miller Road opposite the Burgh depot, another hut: Joe Boni, round and overalled, and sons, tall and dark and Brylcreemed. The bucket in Joe Boni's shop shining aluminium took two to carry, to tip into the whirring round hole — waterfall of thick yellow custard. Some people got a single nugget. The big show-offs got a double nugget. But it was a waste of money really. The best bit was the ice-cream.

Joe Boni had been got at by my father, after I had to have six inches cut off my hair: 'Meester Geellies he say no bubble-gum for you — issa no bubble-gum.'

Issa no more squelch and tongue-flatten, tooth-frame, puff and nose-stick. Issa great shame.

Further down Soroba Road, the Pear Lady: Mrs Lopez. A nice pear for ze nice leetle girl — no no, a praisent. A pear, mind, soft rough skin bursting with sweetness down my chin and under my shirt collar. In return, my undying loyalty to her home-made ice-lollies — rows of watery fruit mushrooms, red and green and orange, stalks-up along the cold-counter, quick-dip into hot water to unmould it from its shell. You could suck all the taste out and be left with a white icicle on a stick.

Wright the Baker, fat polished cream buns hazy with icing sugar, cinnamon-flavoured dough-rings succulent with fat, sculpted wedding-cakes, birthday cakes, with other children's names in hard pink letters. For you a warm pan-loaf, wrapped in layers of tissue paper — crisp outside, soft as mallow inside: you pulled bits out and ate them like a weevil — if you didn't hurry up the road, you might eat the whole inside and land home to Granny with a crisp empty shell and a Good Smack Bottom.

The Wee Psstoffis for money marked out our wee brown books to buy balsa-wood planes and lucky-bags and stamp hinges. The Big Psstoffis for the family allowance, posh shiny table with leather inset, huge brass letter-boxes in walls, telephone directories and chained biros.

The Co for tins and Omo when you ran out mid-week. What's your number again, Anne? Oh yes — 726. The Poly for the papers. Tell your mum there's two weeks to pay. Hannah's for cinnamon sticks to smoke if she would sell you matches. The Tobacco Shop — the wee tobacco-man dipping and dancing from the waist, hissing with obsequiousness and smiling like a side-winder. The big tobacco-lady calm and huge-breasted: and how is dear Mr Gillies keeping? The tobacco lifted delicately from china Ali Baba urns, Mixed to Your Requirements and weighed on highly-polished brass scales.

Jackson Bros Butchers. Bloody overalls and raw red hands. Sawing and hacking and entrails on marble. We have three quarters of a pound of mince once a week plus a joint on Sundays unless Mother's planning to thraw a hen. After Daisy went to the slaughter-house we went without beef for months — just in case. Poor hens, flapping about dead on the floor of the barn. It wasn't all that fair if you think about it like that. Anyway, Mr Jackson subtracts the money for the eggs we bring in plus the rent-money for his sheep once a month: sometimes you hardly have to pay anything. It's dead embarrassing. People look at you as if they think it's daylight robbery.

An albino lady with quivering mauve eyes sells apples and bananas and things like green peppers and avocado pears that only come in now and again and that you've never tasted. A finely-manicured blonde fine-wraps men's shirts while his big auburn wife takes the money and rings up the till. Mr Douglas sells Scots song-books and tartan dollies, maps, moothies, chanter-reeds and every fiddle-string but the one your granny needs.

Boots the Chemists. I hand in the slab of lard bought in Jackson the Butchers and watch Dougie behind his glass partition, mixing in the salicylic acid, plastering, potting and labelling: 'Mrs Gillies: udder cream: for external use only.' Should really say 'Daisy: for external use only' — mother's udders OK. I think. Ha ha.

The joke on me the day the doctor gave me the prescription for my sore mouth:

'Och aye, Anne — it's nothing to worry about, nothing to worry about at all. Hand this in to Dougie, and if he asks, say I was definitely sober at the time.'

Behind his partition Dougie reads the prescription, glasses sliding down his nose in amazement. Comes out into the front shop, wattles wobbling.

'Hullo Anne. How's your mum? Aye, very good, very good. And your gran? Aye that's champion. Now tell me, Anne, you've been in at the doctor I see. Now the doctor, Anne, how did he - er - seem when you were in at him.'

'It's all right, Mr Bannatyne, he said to tell you he was definitely sober today.'

All the pretty white nylon girls giggling, pony-tails swishing. I get the package home — why were they all laughing, Mummy? Mother opens, reads:

'ARSENIC ANAL SUPPOSITORIES. Anne Gillies: dissolve slowly in mouth three times daily.'

My sore mouth gone after three sooks, and no apparent side-effects — death for example. Whew.

By the door in Boots the Free Samples. We take cartons of De Witts Pills when mother not looking and do beautiful bright blue wee wees in our white pots to surprise Granny.

One day my brother says I must have worms. Look at you — thin as a stick, pot belly, appetite like a pig. Worms. Definitely. I worry for days until I can get back to Boots. Nick a Free Sample of Worm Crystals. Force the whole tub-ful down with a teaspoon, locked in misery on the black bakelite toilet seat. It looks like demerara sugar, tastes like sweet bicarb. It puts me off Puff Candy for life. And all for nothing: fleas often (see hens, see fleas) nits once (see school, see nits) but worms no. Well, they never appeared anyway. You'd have seen them. Wouldn't you?

Upstairs in Boots, the Library. The lady always knows which murders dear Mr Gillies has read, can always find one he'll really enjoy. Rolls on the date with her little rubber stamp, flicks and flaps through the cards with lightning fingers.

Shops we couldn't afford: Walkers (coffee beans and bottled apricots) Chalmers (cashmere jumpers and deer-stalkers, mohair stoles and long tartan skirts) Wotherspoons (carpets, brass coal-scuttles and plastic three-piece suites) The China Shop (tea-sets and Dresden shepherdesses) MacLean's (gents' suits and school uniforms) The Bunny Shop (all the wee cuddly things you wanted) Laird Parkers (cameras and French perfume). And of course the Gem Box. Nobody in Oban could afford the Gem Box — a very Highland sort of shop full of Celtic designs and jewels with Gaelic names on white silk like in coffins and big lumps of jaggy amethyst picked up on the beach on some Hebridean island. The lady in the Gem Box is not Highland though. Quite the contrary. You should hear her. She called my mother 'moddom' the day we went in to ask the price of a brooch for Granny's golden wedding. After we'd made a right pair giggling at the lady's accent we went away home and built a Galley of Lorne out of cardboard and gold paint. That gives you an idea of the prices in the Gem Box.

When the *Coronia* (is that how you spell it?) moors out by Kerrera once a year the posh shops open on the Sabbath and put up all their prices. Just for the day. Well, the locals wouldn't go in on the Sabbath anyway, would they? One year we went down town to stare at the canary yellow Yanks. One of them was swinging out of Chalmers' plate-glass revolving doors with his new tartan tammy on his head and I heard him saying, 'Nadda bad liddle shack.' Ha ha. So much for Chalmers.

The tourists come in trains and buses. In the summer you can't get along the pavement for them.

The tourists go on the big boat to Iona and Fort William and on the wee boat to Seal Island and Heather Island and on the bus to Easdale to see the bridge over the Atlantic. If we have visitors we sometimes go too. We went to Iona and my Daddy promised he would come but he had to go into the office to check some papers first. Typical. I didn't know if he would really come anyway. My granny didn't think he would. And then I saw him coming, running along the Railway Pier, but he was too late. He missed the boat. Typical. The boat went off without him. We sailed away and he was left standing there all sad and lonely, getting weer and weer. It spoiled the whole day for me. I was so irritable it made me hate the tourists even more than usual.

You should hear some of the things they say. We were down in Easdale one day and we went in for our tea in one of the wee cottages and this Englishman was sitting there talking to the lady and calling her 'mother'.

'Do you do all your own baking, mother?' he said, and 'Can I have another of your delicious scoans, mother?' Scoans. That's what they call them. What's the matter with them? Why can't they say 'scone' like everybody else? They laugh at the names of all the places and pronounce them wrong on principle.

One day my brother and I decided the tourists must feel a bit cheated, coming all the way to the Highlands and then finding it so ordinary — so un-Gaelic. So we went up our hill when the train was due and took off all our clothes. Here comes the train!

We leap out beside the railway line and start dancing. Away down at sea-level my mother is frantically waving a dish-cloth at us. We wave back cheerily and get on with our dance, jumping up and down and making Indian walla walla noises till the train is out of sight. There — now the tourists can at least say they've seen a few natives.

Back down in the yard my mother is trying to be cross, twisting the dish-cloth in her hands. But her nostrils always wiggle in and out when she's trying not to laugh.

The tourists get guide-books that tell them all the places of interest and the history of Argyll. So-called history: Fingal and his magic boots all mixed up with Robert the Bruce and St Columba. No wonder they all look so bemused.

The tourists buy postcards of sunset over the bay and MacCaig's Tower. The tourists always call it MacCaig's Folly but I don't think MacCaig was foolish, do you? He wanted to provide employment for all the men who were out of work in the Depression, so he got them to build him a tower with lots of windows like the Colosseum in Rome. No doubt the tourists think it would have been more sensible for MacCaig just to sit in his house counting up his money while the men starved.

To me the town is a map of where people stay.

People at our school I mean, not the Catholic school. I don't know any of them. And certainly not the Piscies — I didn't even know they existed until they sang *Can Ye Sew Cushions* at a concert in the town: they were some singers, the Piscies — you would get two fingers between their teeth all right. Though I got to know them a bit better when I joined the Brownies — marching and wheeling and knotting and promising to do my duty to Godandtheking; running home every Friday afternoon to eat a bovril sandwich while trying to dig the Brasso out of the crevices in my badge, just in time to run straight back down again for five o'clock; walking back up the road in the dark with my torch picking out the blood-red eyes of the sheep that coughed like dirty old men in the ditch; saluting the County Commissioner and vowing to thee my country when it became Godandthequeen: we weren't much into all that sort of thing in our family. Still, fee-fi-fiddlie-ay-o you certainly met other girls round the toadstool. Fairies, goblins, kelpies and Piscies.

I classify folk in our school into four kinds: down the town; up-our-end; Miller Road; bus-ones. There may be more kinds, but I don't know them.

First the kids from down-the-town — Pulpit Hill, Ardconnel Road etc. They're in the A-class, they always put their hands up when the teacher asks a question and they have famous dads who drive about in cars — teachers at the High School, hoteliers, publicans, policemen, bank managers and chemists. They were the ones that said I had monkey ears and laughed the day of the school photographer. Helen was the prettiest in the class; her picture was so beautiful. Maureen's was nice too, and so was Sandra's. Even Janis's was OK. But they all laughed when the teacher held up my picture. Helen drew little monkeys in the margin of her jotter with arrows pointing at me. I want you to burn that picture, Mummy. Now. No I mean it.

Next the kids from up our end. A lot of them were in the B-class. They weren't so good at answering questions and their fathers weren't famous, though you knew if they kept their gardens good, bred budgies or took a good bucket. But their mums always said hullo when you met them out pushing the pram or walking the alsatian or taking a cup of tea at the station buffet. Some of them had big brothers in Barlinnie. Some of them came to play. Unasked, over the back fences, all ages. All boys.

Wake up cow-pokes mornin's breakin
Corn's on the cob and coffee is a-makin.
Bang bang you're deid Ah'm no playin.

The horse-tree, the plane-tree, the jungle-tree: Roy Rogers, Captain Marvel, Tarzan. Who they?

They put the cat in the water-butt, broke the rocking-horse that my Daddy kept for forty-odd years, squirted oil out of a bike-pump all over the kitchen walls, trampled down corn, left gates open, slashed my leg with a broken-off bottle stuck on the end of a stick. When the Burgh eventually put up a proper fence they called it The Iron Curtain.

They asked me to judge a 'what do girls look like' competition: they waited their turn in an orderly queue, strictly no conferring. They demonstrated wee plackets by puckering up the skin on their legs or arms. Am I right? Am I no right Anne? They took it very seriously. Judging was easy. They all knew what girls looked like, so I just gave first prize to the oldest, kindest one. I was in love with him. I went to his house all by myself in the hopes of seeing him, but he wasn't in. His granny was most kind and gave me thick tea and plain bread and jelly. Plain bread — wow! His Nana and me chatted politely and then I went home.

My brother's best friend stays at the end of Dalintart Drive. Well he used to be his best friend anyway, when his hair was ginger. He was a very nice boy, very polite. Now his hair's black with a D.A. and he wears a long black jacket and black suede shoes with thick white soles. He's a Teddy-boy, like Davey Crewcut in the song. We don't see much of him now, but he's still very nice and polite to my granny if we meet him.

Jim and Duncan live in the houses nearest to us. Jim's mother suffers from her nerves and her adenoids. We hear her shouting JIB! JIB! when he's over playing with us. Duncan's dad is dying of cancer. Duncan hardly ever comes to school. His mum doesn't know. We go down the road to school, he comes up it and away up our hill. After school is out he comes back down again, sliding past our kitchen window so's my granny won't see him. We feel very sorry for him. It doesn't solve anything Repeatedly Sending the Attendance Officer to Worry his Poor Mother. The attendance officer must be the most hated man in Oban I reckon. He comes up to check that we're really wheezing, his bicycle clips clicking with disapproval. My granny can deal with him all right. Well I'm just doing my job. You must admit they're both off a lot. I hope he gets a puncture.

There are a few girls my age up our end. When we first moved to Oban I got to know one of them because her big sister knew my mother at the hospital. I went over to her house in Mossfield once or twice. What a lot of people lived there. You couldn't work out who was who. You're welcome here any time at all Anne. But she had brittle bones and was always getting ill and after a while I never saw her any more. The girls nearest to us were out playing all the time. You'd hear Hannah Pearson's mother shouting for her at tea-time. She just stood at the door and yelled at the top of her voice: HA-NAAAA HA-NAAAA HA-NAAAA until she came home. You could hear her right at the top of our hill. Every night at the same time. You'd think they could have come to some other arrangement. My mother would die rather than shout like that. My mother never raised her voice in her life. Anyway they mostly went about in a big gang and I never really got to know them.

It was just as well anyway. It was always embarrassing when girls needed the toilet. It was easier for boys. Plumbing no problem.

One girl actually wet herself rather than do it in our toilet. Oh I couldn't I just couldn't. Now look at that I've gone and wet myself — now what are you going to do? She was crying. As if it was all my fault. Stupid thing. Don't worry. I'll fix it. Come over here by the water butt. Now pretend you're playing. She sits on the edge of the water butt and I splash her all over with water. Camouflage. Anne splashed me. Now what did you want to do that for, naughty little girl. I'm sorry Granny. I thought maybe you could dry it or she'll get heck from her mummy. Yes of course. Poor child. Just look at you. Come over here by the fire. You are a naughty little girl Anne. It was very boring all that. Why do girls have to be so boring?

'Oh Mr Gillies, Mr Gillies, I've just stood in a cow's bathroom.'

'Oh Anne, Anne, thon ram's following us.'

After school I walk home with Chryss. When she's speaking to me that is. She stays in Soroba Road just along from Joe Boni's. We take ages coming up the road, bouncing the ball all the way along the pavement.

Mother mother I am ill
Send for the doctor up the hill
Up the hill is far too far
Send for a motor car
A motor car is far too dear
Send for a bottle of beer

Along past the Laundry. The Laundry makes a noise like a ship's engine and one day we saw all the women come running out pushing a wheelbarrow covered in streamers. There was a woman sitting in it with a po on her head. They say she's getting married tomorrow. I've been into the Laundry. My mother sends the sheets there because they're too heavy to wring. I saw all the machinery. The sheets were lifted high up in the air by big mechanical arms. You could recognise our sheets at a glance — sides to middles showing up against the light.

When Chryss isn't speaking to me I walk home with Joan. If she's speaking to me that is. Joan stays up Sinclair Drive opposite the ice-factory where I burnt my fingers. One of the boys put a big lump of ice in my hand. Here hold this. What is it. It's stuck to my hand. Ha ha Anne Gillies burnt her hand.

One day I left Joan off at her close and went on up the road blethering away to myself as usual. I never noticed a big fat woman hanging out the ground floor window. Aye aye hen, talk to yerself and nobody'll ever answer you back.

Sometimes we all walk home together, if Chryss and Joan are both speaking to me. And to each other.

Sometimes I go into their houses. Chryss always seems to have neighbours in. You don't need an invitation and they have proper furniture — glass cases with china cups and plates in them and framed photos of weddings on top. Her mum makes wee cakes with hundreds and thousands on, and you have to peel off the paper without wasting the hundreds and thousands. They always ask you questions when you have your mouth full of cake. The wee girl from downstairs came in to show off her new party dress. It was snow-white paper nylon with frilly underskirts. It had ruffles edged with red embroidery. I was astonished. I didn't think people got white things because they would just get dirty.

Then there are the folk from Miller Road. None of them are in the A-class. Heather stays here. She's got a blank white face covered in black-heads. Sometimes she shouts loud sweary words. Once during the holidays I saw her and Alex MacMaster walking along the middle of the road at the head of a big huge procession of kids all shouting and screaming. The traffic was stopped for them. Alec was singing at the top of his voice as usual and Heather was dragging a bull's head by the horns along the road. It had blood and stringy things trailing out of it. I don't know where they were going with it.

Finally there are the ones who come in the bus — last to arrive, first to go. You can get one as a partner in gym when everyone else is taken.

Most of them stay in Dunstaffnage, but one girl stays at Pennyfuir. Imagine staying in a cemetery. I don't like Pennyfuir. I'd rather be in the Parish Church grave-yard. You could lie there and listen to the weddings and the *cèilidhs* and the folk gossiping on the way into the Wee Psstoffis or the Crofters' Supply. In Pennyfuir you'd really know you were dead. Your family would have to take a bus to come out and visit you.

And a boy in my class lives out at Ganavan Sands. That would be good. My mother always takes us on the bus to Ganavan at least one day in her fortnight off, however far behind we are with the hay. We always try to find a place up by the rocks away from everyone else. My mother makes tents with towels but they always fall off. Then away down into the sea to hide mummy's legs and try to swim. Granny waits among the sand-flies, unwrapping tomato sandwiches and plastic-flavoured tea. I make a castle. It's not very good. Mummy mummy, he's knocked down my sand-castle. I'll get you you wee liar. Then round to the Pavilion, pockets weighed down with shells to make a garden round the back of the house. Tea now being served by ladies we know looking odd in black dresses and frilly aprons. How are you Mrs Gillies? My my William's fairly catching up on you. And how's wee Anne? And granny — we've not seen you about lately? They lick their pencils, I twiddle with sand between my toes. Don't look now Mummy but that's Eric. He's in my class. Oh heck he's seen me.

On the way home from Ganavan we pass the cave where Alec MacMaster stays. And Dunollie Castle where the Clan MacDougall stayed. And Maiden Island where the poor lady was left to starve to death while her husband sat listening to her fading cries. Then the cathedral where Mrs Lawrie's priest stays. And the house where Anne Lees stays, where I had to come to do my Housewife's Badge for Brownies. There are ever such a lot of Annes in my school. Chryss says we must have all been named after Princess Anne but I says to her my Daddy wouldn't have any of that Royal Family nonsense. You're older than Princess Anne stupid — I expect the Queen called her after you. D'you really think — oh ha ha I see it's a joke, well very funny and I don't think. Mummy he hit me. I knew we shouldn't have sat them together, Mary. Can't you just be quiet and look out of the window. Your mummy's tired out.

And so we reach the town again. Off the Ganavan bus at the Linen Bank and onto the local bus that drops us off just past the High School. So now I reckon you know Oban as well as I do myself. Just about.

SIX

In Primary Four we get Mrs Innes. I know for a fact that she can speak Gaelic. But she doesn't. Not to us anyway.

She wears a green and black tartan skirt and a bottle green twin set and a silver Celtic brooch and rimless spectacles with a gold chain hanging from them. All very Gaelic, I think to myself. Even her eyes look Gaelic — brownish yellow with dark flecks, like Alan Breac's. Anyway, no-one else in my class seems to care one way or the other about learning Gaelic. I suppose we just have to wait till we get into the secondary school. What a scunner. I take down my grandfather's Gaelic books from the shelves and read them to my granny, pretending to know the pronunciation. What a clever little girl. She doesn't know any better anyway.

We start Primary Four with a geography test — to see what level we've reached, Mrs Innes says. A test! I can feel my brain getting hot and bothered straight away. It stops my ears from listening to what she says. Long bits of paper, torn out of last year's unfinished jotters and halved length-wise down the middle, are placed in front of us. The long unfamiliar thinness of them makes them look even more scary. As usual everybody else knows what to do. Everybody else has written their names at the top, so I write mine. Chryss, who is sitting beside me, puts numbers all the way down the edge 1 to 10. So I do too. But I haven't the time to get it finished before Mrs Innes starts asking all these questions. 'What is the capital of Canada?' 'Name the largest . . .' I haven't time to think about the first one before the second one comes, so I just copy down what Chryss has written: 'Montreal'. The same thing happens with the second, and the third . . . I'm not trying to hide the fact that I'm copying — I haven't time to worry about that. Anyway, we get different marks, because I haven't time to get all Chryss's answers copied.

Mrs Innes says I am a dreamer. She also says I should try and stop all these nervous habits of mine. I can't manage these new pens we've got. The ink runs up my sleeve and there is a dent in my third finger with holding it too tight. I get lots of extra pages to copy but I still can't do it. Wouldn't life be wonderful if you didn't have to go to school. You've already said that. So what.

As soon as I woke up I knew I'd done it at last. Managed to get really ill. I lay there for a minute very thirsty and a bit guilty — I must have wished it on myself. Then I decided that was just silly and I might as well enjoy it.

'Go and tell Mummy I've got pneumonia,' I said calmly to my big brother.

That took the wind out of his sails all right.

'Don't be daft. What are you talking about? Pneumonia indeed.'

I was feeling all sweet and Christian with the illness, so I didn't say all the sarcastic things I'd usually have come out with — about him always knowing everything and always having to get double pneumonia, wasn't single pneumonia enough, and things like that. I was also trying not to grin. That wouldn't look very ill would it? But my mother came up and took my temperature and said, 'Well she may be right' in an incredulous voice and then I'm afraid I did grin. Then the doctor came and said they would have to take very good care of me, and the flowers were all dancing about on the wall-paper and my chest was too sore to breathe, but I'm telling you, being ill is definitely better than other people being ill. I can be ill no bother. It makes me really nice. If I died people would be really sorry, remembering me like this — smiling bravely through the pain.

I love it all. Being important. Being Off School. Being read to. Reading and reading. The beady-eyed moth-eared monkey the doctor's daughter gives me as a get-well present. My mother sitting by my bed making a dolly out of pipe-cleaners. My daddy talking quietly. I get up for the first time, pale and pithless as grass under a stone, and the doctor comes. I am petrified he will say I can go back to school now that I'm up. But no — I have to stay off all term, I've to do just whatever I feel up to and no more. Wow! I can even take a wee walk down the town if I feel strong enough, wave at the Attendance Officer on his miserable bike and look up at the school with all the relish of a liberated convict. How empty the streets are and how warm the sun. My mother passes on second-hand tales of sports days and choir concerts which I hear with supreme disinterest. Mrs Innes has told her how much she misses me, what a shame it is I've missed so much this year as I am one of her very brightest pupils. She said what? You must be joking.

'So did Mrs Innes say who I'm getting next year Mummy?'

'You're getting Mr MacNeill, dear. The new headmaster. Mrs Innes says he's very nice.'

Oh no. A man. Mammy daddy.

I had seen the new headmaster before. Before I took the pneumonia. One of the days when we were all taken into my brother's classroom — that's my big brother, see there he is grinning with embarrassment, sit three to a desk children, less noise, settle down at the back there. The green partition with cloudy glass windows folded back to make room for the whole school. The infants come in, waddling, with their little round slatted wooden seats attached to their bottoms, everyone who has nowhere to sit use up the space at the front please — cross-legged if you don't mind, Anne Gillies. My legs must be an odd shape — if I cross them I can't get my back to straighten up. Anne Gillies, just look at you, are you deformez? This was where we came once before to hear a man called Roger Bannister running very fast on the wireless and we all got given a china mug that I had to scratch and scratch to get one of the ones off because she wasn't Elizabeth the Second she was Elizabeth the First — didn't the teacher know anything about history? This time we are here to meet the new headmaster.

The new headmaster is called Mr MacNeill: Good moooorning Mr MacNeill. He has a very shiny baldie head with a circle of hair like mince round the edge of a china plate. He is younger than Mr Penman who has retired. Or, for all I know, died.

But that was before I took the pneumonia.

You're getting the new headmaster next year Anne. Oh ho.

If my mother was worried about me getting a man in Primary Five she needn't have bothered.

He mo leannan ho mo leannan
Se mo leannan am fear ur
He mo leannan ho mo leannan

He is a Gaelic-speaker from south Argyll. He teaches us Gaelic songs. And my love's an arbutus by the waters of Lene: his eyes have a soft sapphire sheen too.

His name is Hector, name of heroes; a sailor returned from the sea is he. When his backside itches he scratches it.

He talks to us all the time. As if we are really worth talking to. He lets us talk in class. But we are well-behaved: the boys can smell his authority and respect his casual stocky strength. In return he makes no distinctions between us: no good ones and bad ones, no clever ones and stupid ones. Walter MacIntyre's story about the spider that came down his mother's plug-hole is as precious to Hector as my careful sentences. My sentences become less careful.

'When I grow up I am going to marry a man who is tall dark and handsome and always ready for fun.'

Well actually I'd have married Hector if he'd asked me, baldie heid and all. What would the Rev. MacKenzie have made of that, with his long black face and his long black prayers now boys and giggles let us bow our heads and lift up our hearts and glogify God.

Hector conducts the Gaelic choir. He holds us spell-bound with his watery blue eyes, mouthing the words with his thick lips and covering us with spittle. Mrs Innes goes over the Gaelic, dimpling and girlish in his presence. They take us to the *Mòd* in Perth. There are big girls in the choir, down from the High School, who know hundreds of Gaelic songs. While we are queueing up outside the hall waiting to go up on the platform we hold a competition with another choir to see who knows most songs. With Kay Carson on our side we win easily — *Eilean Fraoich . . . Thug mi Gaol . . . Moladh na Lanndaidh . . . Eilean mo Ghaoil . . .* she goes on and on. I pretend to know them too, to annoy Katharine Troup. We have a party in our hotel and next day Kay Carson's picture is in the papers in her pyjamas. I am sharing a single bed with Katharine Troup, and in the middle of the night I fall out on the floor. I'm lying in the darkness in fits laughing while everyone else snores. I'm trying not to wake anybody, but I keep going into paroxysms even after I've got back into the bed. After that I can't sleep a wink, lying giggling silently and counting the chimes every quarter of an hour. I keep hearing the song of the clock all the way home on the bus. I wish I could get white socks like the other girls.

Hector is a great drawer. He draws us, we draw him. We draw everything. He shows us how things look smaller in the distance and how shadows always go the same direction and how you can't see all four sides of a house at once even though you know they're there.

He likes poetry, and lets us choose the poems we like best. It's no bother learning them when you like them yourself. Him and me like the Scottish ones best: Come in a-hint ye wannerin tyke, did ever buddy see the like, and Wee sleekit cooerin timorous beastie, o what a panic's in thy breastie, and The Laird o Cockpen he's prood and he's great, his mind's taen up wi the things o the state.

He reads to us, one cheek perched on the lid of someone's desk, acting it out with his voice: exciting stories, making it sound as if he's been there.

I am sitting at the Pole in all the snow, hearing the huskies bay, crying over poor Mr Oates who went out and never came back, never bothering with Joan who is waving the sharp end of her pencil at my eyes. (It must have been her turn to be not speaking to me that week.) Hector suddenly swoops on her, hardly pausing in his tale except for a brief 'I've been watching you for some time now, young woman.' Still reading, he takes me up the back of the class to sit beside the tall, timid country girl, just arrived from Kilninver (who's she? they say her daddy's dead). Her name's Anne. Anne my love, my friend. Tall and fair and sprouting beneath her yellow aertex tee-shirt. Unafraid of cows and geese, laughing with me feeding hens or turning hay, picnicking on liquorice sweeties and bruised apples, courteous to parents, clever with hands, sensible and kind. The mother in a nylon overall, tall as a haystack, hands to shape pastry and smooth cushions; the fair sisters flocking round her, opening ovens, kissing kittens, peeling onions, making light of adversity and a country home out of a terraced boarding-house. The dead father, the lost life, behind them yet colouring what they are. Anne, whom I know without trying, so different from the shop-keepers' kids, the bus-drivers' kids: the Town kids.

I am getting clever in school — bringing home good reports signed Hector MacNeill. Especially considering she missed so much last year. My friend Anne can run, knit, sew, bake, do cartwheels, ride her bike with no hands, iron and tame animals. I can do history, geography, writing, reading, drawing, spelling, singing — even, gradually, arithmetic.

Hector has just one rule in the week: Friday morning, a Test and Strictly No Talking — while he checks and signs the registers. Well, he's the Headmaster, don't forget. He has to do all that too you see. We help him. I am the class messenger this week, have been all round the school collecting up the registers. I come back into the class feeling all important and self-satisfied and mature. I smile at Hector and go and sit down, wondering why it's so quiet.

'What are we meant to be doing?' I ask Anne. She frowns at me warningly.

'Come out here Anne Gillies. You know you are not allowed to talk during the Arithmetic Test.'

I walk towards him, disbelievingly, as he opens his desk and takes out the heavy leather strap. His eyes are on me, bulbous, beseeching.

He turns me round to face the class then puts himself in between me and them so they can't see. He raises the belt sharply over his right shoulder. I hear it whack against his shiny jacket. 'I'm so sorry. I'm so sorry. You know I have to do this,' he mutters, head down.

'Yes sir,' I sigh, as pain and betrayal snake upwards from palm to wrist to heart. Holding my breath I go back to my seat. Watching fat tears roll down my nose, staining the desk, I sit very still all morning, cradling my hand in the folds of my skirt, making no attempt to work. At play-time he silently gives me a huge white hankie, but says nothing about my going out to play. The others walk out and come back in again very quietly, finding I have not moved. At dinner-time I walk slowly home and bury my face in my mother's lap. My brother has told them what happened. They know. No-one tells me to buck up or suggests I should go back to school that afternoon.

At half-past five Hector comes up our road, flying over the bumps in his wee grey car, sitting incongruous in Grampop's chair with the wings. My mother gives him tea, my father gives him a dram, and they talk quietly while I sit listlessly in the swing outside feeling my face tight with crying.

Poor Hector. He's very upset.

'It's all right. I understand. Yes of course — I'll come back to school on Monday.'

Things are becoming less frightening now. So you invent things to frighten yourself. Nature abhors a vacuum.

My friend Anne is sensible. Far away, the other side of town. So Chryss becomes my Sancho Panza. Together we tilt at windmills, box shadows, run up the dark street pursued by whispering crisp packets, hold our breath from one lamp-post to the next, till washed up, peching at her close-mouth. Yawning, black, draughty, it creaks and sighs. On the step we clutch and giggle and procrastinate. A sudden cat slits open the dark tunnel with its claws, flying loud as a Zeppelin from the back garden, across the close and away into the street. Oh mammy daddy I nearly died.

I'll get you up the road.

Are you sure?

Aye — well, I'll get you half-way up the road.

Och well if you're sure.

My cat's eyes steer her over ruts, place her feet on gate-rungs, link her across crunching lemonade factory glass. Running a stick along the corrugated iron frill of the Games Ground to frighten away dirty old men, I guide her delicate through a mine-field of cows' pancakes. Don't be daft. That's just a sheep. And that's just a tree. Probably. By our gate we clutch and giggle and procrastinate. A sudden owl rips apart the dark silence, cracking open a bush with wings like gunshot, through the branches and away up into the sky. Oh mammy daddy I nearly died.

I'll get you back down the road.

Are you sure?

Aye — well, I'll get you half-way back down the road.

Och well if you're sure.

Cough of sheep, sough of reeds, bough of trees, rough of road, yough of slugs, we reach the main road again, blinking at Bed and Breakfast signs in yellow light. If the road was straight we could see your house from here, Chryss. Aye if the Burgh Depot wasn't in the road. Burgh Council getting in the road again. Ha ha. I don't know what it means. I heard my daddy say it. Och well I suppose I'd better be away then, well cheerio then, see you tomorrow. What day is it tomorrow? The day after today. Ha ha. Have you got the time? Aye but not the inclination. Ha ha. I don't know what it means. 'You heard your daddy say it.' My cousin in Glasgow says two hairs after freckle. Ha ha. Cheerio then, are you not gone yet? Not yet, has thon woman left her washing out all night? Why are you whispering? I am not, you are sot, not, sot, I amny, aye y'are, aye ah'm no, have you done your reading yet? Oh I forgot, I'd better away then, you've been away for a long time if you ask me, ha ha very funny.

Wind glissandos on telegraph wires. The pupils of my eyes have shrunk and my path is impenetrably curtained. Something scrapes on the High School wall. Oh mammy daddy.

I'll get you back up the road . . .

Doomed to eternal night-wandering we totter back into the darkness, Siamese twins in navy raincoats. Past the lemonade factory, round the corner of the Games Ground, towards the black gate. Swing on the gate for a while. Shhh. What's that? What's what? That. A cigarette glowing, footsteps crunching, a heavy sigh. A Dirty Old Man. Oh mammy daddy.

We turn and run. Footsteps run too, catching up on us swiftly. The end is nigh. Dreamed of, feared, longed for. A hand on my shoulder. Oh mammy daddy mister dinny harm me.

'For heaven's sake Anne. What are you two sillies up to? Giggling and gaggling at this hour of the night. Chryss MacArthur your mother's worried sick. She's been phoning up wondering where you are this last half-hour.'

O mammy daddy. Ah'm gonny get mauled.

Deflated we walk each side of my father. Now the street is flat and grey as a B-picture. We're sorry Mrs MacArthur. It was partly my fault. I am lectured all the way home. Familiar sensation, uncomfortable, comforting, like having your back scratched with a loofah.

And then there was the time we decided to walk to Ben Cruachan.

Well we were up our hill this day after school, poking at puff-balls with bracken stalks and maaing at the sheep. Come on I'll show you a secret. What secret? It's called the Cathedral of Trees. You're not allowed in there. I know but they canny stop you.

The Cathedral of Trees is our special place. It's in the middle of the forestry. The nave and apse are made out of yew-trees, the stained-glass windows are the colour of sunshine or moonshine filtered through pines, the roof is painted with rainbows and clouds and stars. The man for whom it was made lies up at the altar in a grave carved with a poem that weaves the wind into words. You don't walk there except on tiptoe; you don't talk there except in whispers; you certainly don't come there giggling and gaggling with Chryss MacArthur.

Also you have to know the way. I've never been there on my own.

We cross the burn, climb the dyke, jook under barbed wire, scramble up the sheep-track, clamber another dyke into the forestry. Cross pools of grub-like grass, coo at ring-doves, reel at swaying tree-tops, come inadvertently upon the Big House in its purdah of rhododendrons and run for our lives from a barrage of barking. Emerge, scratched, in an ocean of ochre moorland.

Cruachan was right in front of us rising out of the foreground like a Chinese water colour. You could almost touch the snow.

There's Ben Cruachan. Let's go there instead.

Oh I knew fine how far away it was. Maybe she didn't, but I had been on a family walk through Glen Lonan, how much further now daddy? Shoulders back and heather-step and pull your socks up and fill your lungs and I'll blow smoke on you to keep the midges away and March March Ettrick and Teviotdale — whining and scratching and wheezing and blistering all day long until we reached Taynuilt and caught the last service bus home. It'll do you all good. You'll see. You'll sleep tonight.

But this evening Cruachan was just over that hill. Just keep walking in a straight line.

If it wasn't for the barbed wire and there's a bull it's definitely a bull and I've gone over my shoes in the mud and I want my mammy and where's Cruachan it's disappeared and I'm telling on you this was all your idea.

Come on now Chryss heather step and shoulders back and fill your lungs it canny be far now. If it wasn't for the bogs and the hills and I've got a stone in my shoe and I want to go home and it's getting dark and we'll fall in Loch Nell and get drowned and nobody will ever find us. Don't be daft Chryss. Loch Nell's nowhere near here, it's OK we're going home it's good for you you'll sleep tonight.

We tumble down a bank onto a road. It's that way home. No it's definitely that way. I know the way. I am lying in my teeth. I am not half ready to go home yet. It's not often I get the upper hand. Suddenly an oasis of light in the distance. It is dark right enough. Maybe we should go up to the door. I chap the door. Davey Balfour at the House of Shaws. But the lady at the door is more like Auntie Isa than Uncle Ebenezer. I put away Stevenson and take up Blyton.

'Please excuse us bothering you at this hour of the night but we are two poor little girls who have wandered all the way from Oban. Perhaps we might come in for a little to shelter from the cold before setting off on our way again.'

Kindly she keeps her face straight, gives us tea and biscuits, makes us phone home. They send a taxi. The journey is surprisingly quick. I savour in advance the tearful reunion. Get Granny frost-white with rage sitting over a cold grate. Mummy and Daddy have gone out. You made them quite late with your carry-on. I was looking forward to an early night myself.

But Mummy and Daddy never go out. Well they have. How could they? I might have been lying drowned in Loch Nell. Huh says my brother and goes back to his book. I got mauled says Chryss the next day. But she bears me no ill-will.

But I'm still dead scared of the geese. Don't be silly, says my father. He won't bite you. Not unless he thinks you're scared of him. Stand completely still and look him straight in the eye.

I am standing completely still looking him straight in the eye.

Mummy Mummy Molotov bit me. He did not, says my brother. Did sot. Look. A round white mark, crimped like pie-crust, just above my sock. Oh help. Phone for an ambulance. Rabies. Hydrophobia. Foaming at the mouth and dying in agony.

Be quiet Liam. Don't tease your sister. I keep telling you. You have to stand completely still and look him straight in the eye. Come along now. I'll show you.

Father stands still. Goose hisses and waves ugly neck.

Molotov: Angry hiss.

MOLOTOV! Doubtful hiss.

Now keep looking him in the eye. Show him who's boss. *MOLOTOV!!!*

Hiss of defeat, dignified retreat, bum-wagging, tail-shaking, back to where Tom waits to console.

There you are now. What did I tell you.

Overheard over the fence:
Hey did you hear what the farmer said to thon goose?
Naw. What did the farmer say to thon goose?
Bugger off!
He did not!
Aye he did.
Oooh that's terrible. I'm tellin my mammy on him.

SEVEN

My mother is ill a lot. I think. She always tells you after she's better and you feel guilty for not realising before and giving her peace.

Her hip hurts sometimes, and she hirples with a bent back for days on end, up and down the road to the hospital like a half-shut knife to put other people's backs right. She coughs and coughs every morning, shrieking coughs that sometimes end in sickness. The surgeon told her she had farmer's lung. It made her very angry. What was the point in telling her that anyway? What was she supposed to do about it? Go off and live in Switzerland I suppose.

Sometimes she stops smoking. I get up in the morning and find her pacing up and down chewing match-sticks, muttering to herself. I beg her to start again. I will never ever start smoking. Once she stopped for weeks on end, till the day she fell off her bike. I was coming down the road outside the school when I saw someone on the ground on the pavement opposite with a man bending over her. It was my mother. What was the man doing? I ran right across the main road without looking, screaming 'Mister, hey mister, that's my mum,' tearing at his coat to drag him off her. He brushed me aside summarily. Well then you can push her bike for her, hen. He took her to the hospital with me following, shaking, the pedal tripping me, skinning my legs; staring at the hankie she was holding up to the side of her head, blood-sodden. Is her eye out, mister, is her eye out? Please tell me mister. Is her eye out? After the sister had stitched her eye-brow she gave her a cup of tea and a fag and she was away again.

Once she was so ill my Auntie Jean had to come up to look after us. It's all the Worry. It makes her glands go funny. Her eyes are starey and her neck is swollen. It is terrible. I go upstairs to talk to her. My father's in with her. They don't see me at the door. She is crying and crying.

'Good Lord child, whatever's the matter with you? You look as if you've seen a ghost.'

'I'm fine thank you, Auntie Jean.'

My mother's wrists get sore and her hands get blue — milking, rinsing, wringing in cold water. She has to boil kettles for everything and sometimes folk wet their beds and she has extra. Sometimes she brings the clothes off the line frozen solid, like skeletons in shrouds, and they melt and drip and steam all round the fire, and fall into the raked ashes if we're not careful. We often aren't.

I pick up her stockings out of the ash: watch out for heaven's sake, you'll ladder them, my father says. I'm surprised how rough his voice is.

She has to do her washing on Sundays, hoping the People in the Houses won't see she's been Breaking the Sabbath. She gets very angry when my father cuts the hedge. Now they'll be able to see everything we do.

My granny blames my father for everything. Bringing her Mary to a Place Like This indeed. This does not Improve the Atmosphere in the house. I am very sorry for my mother, but I wish my granny would get off my daddy's back. I hate my granny. How dare she speak about my daddy like that. My daddy is a wonderful man and he has things to worry about too and my mother likes Oban very much and she wouldn't live anywhere else. Especially now that the peewits have come. They must have followed us after all.

Sundays my father cleans out the byre, or digs a huge trench to empty the Elsan into, or mends fences, or fills in potholes, or puts slates on the roof, or sweeps the yard with angry swishes of his metal brush. He always goes to sweep the yard when he's feeling miserable. Like on Christmas Day. We wait and wait for him to come in and give out the presents. Why can't we just get on without him? No, no, I cry — we can't do it without Daddy. One Christmas my mother cried and said a bad word. It sounded so odd it made her laugh. But I was paralysed. Still he always comes in eventually, straightening his shoulders and whistling to make himself feel jolly as he washes his hands in the sink in the byre. You see I told you he'd come. Huh.

My mother calls me 'mummy's little peace-maker'. She writes 'Blessed are the peace-makers' in my autograph album. But I'm not blessed. I can't help it. I shake all over when there are rows. I can't bear it.

As we get older we can help more. But often don't.

Into our lives for a while comes Nichol. Up the road from the Hospital to help with the cows, to help feed the hens. He used to live in Half-way House, half-way from Dunstaffnage to Oban. The house where they looked out the window and saw the poor man nearly dead of the cold wandering along wearing nothing but tar and feathers: been out all night like that, trying to get home; he never made it to his wedding, nearly never made it full stop; never married anybody after that; great night, great joke ha ha. Some place Oban.

Nichol in his cloth cap, moves slowly, doesn't say much, smokes peacefully. One day his pocket went on fire: pipe smouldering away against his hip. Nichol getting too old to help now.

Then Iain John comes, lithe, pucker-faced. In the town they call Iain John 'The Dummy', but I can talk to him — I can do the dummy alphabet. One day my father told me to go out to the field and tell Iain John he was spreading the manure too thick. I went across the field towards him, smiling. He can't smile, but he makes explosions in his throat that say I'm smiling. I start to sign 'Too Thick', but only get as far as the first letter. Iain John explodes happily in all directions, throws the graip like a javelin into the ground and goes bounding off to the house for a cup of tea. A cup of 'T'. Get it?

One day Iain John went into the stable not knowing our Scottie dog had puppies. The dog chased him out of the stable, across the yard, up the hill, round the back. We nearly died laughing. Sheila is tiny, timid, down-trodden, creeps under my mother's skirt of an evening. Iain John is tall, strong, agile, dangerous as a bull with his noises, his red neck, his thick twisted lips. But how his tackety boots fly, twig-splitting, mud-splattering, as the little dog screams with primeval smeddum, and we cry with laughter. Iain John can't hear us. Just as well. He stomps off back to the Hospital nursing his pride. You shouldn't laugh really. I bet Iain John could talk if somebody had ever taken the trouble to teach him instead of shutting him up in the Hospital. Not only that. I bet he could talk Gaelic.

We don't have any aunties or uncles around to help out. Our relations are all south of the Border.

Why could we not at least have relations in Lewis or Dunoon, like other people? Even a granny in Poland like Chryss's would be OK.

But England . . .

Everybody knows that England is second to none as regards imperialism and colonialism, second only to America as regards capitalism and materialism. Christmas is a good example. Very materialist. Not at all spiritual. Not at all Scottish. Anglo-Saxon paganism parading as Christianity for Purely Commercial Reasons. But all the kids I know have Christmas. Aye more's the pity. It's only a very recent thing. We sit miserably as usual, waiting for That Man To Make The Effort Just Once A Year For Your Mother's Sake, wishing Granny would stop poking the fire. Then relax as he comes in and lights the wax candles on the tree and Granny settles down with a bowl of water on her knee ready to save us all from Kingdom Come.

I am torn. Christmas is all right by me. Christmas rustles when you move your legs in the bed — a mince pie, a tangerine, a celluloid vanity-set with silver-paper mirror, an ocarina, water-flowers to grow in the wash-hand basin before anyone else is awake. Christmas is stuffed with chicken and chipolatas, brussels sprouts, crackers, and a floorful of presents from our English relations. The best are from my Uncle Donald. I find out years later he sends money and my mother chooses something special that she wouldn't have been able to afford. Dear Uncle Dondy, thanks a million for my teddy bear. I've called him Shampoo because just now he's so clean he looks as if he's just had a shampoo and when he gets old he'll look as if he needs one.

Other presents chosen specially for little Scotch girls by distant aunties: hand-knitted fair-isle tammies with pom-pom toories; a dolly dressed in tartan; toffee in boxes with pictures of Loch Lomond. Dear Auntie Joey, thank you very much for the lovely toffees. The picture of the Highland cow was very nice as were the toffees. We had a lovely Christmas and I hope you did too. Mummy and Daddy send their love, as does Granny. Well I'd better close now. Thank you again for the lovely toffees.

These children get far too much. In my young days we made do with far less — but were we any the worse for it? My father is pleased when Christmas is over. Gives his presents — bottles of whisky to people who have helped us, e.g. Hughie MacDonald for the loan of his tractor — a week later. Hogmanay: pure Scottish. A time for reflection. For celebration. Thanks giving. Resolutions. That's more like it. Even when no-one comes to first-foot us.

Auntie Cissy comes to stay. Granny's little sister. Tiny as a wren, with little tarnished claws; the cigarette hanging from her bottom lip stains her moustache yellow and bounces up and down when she speaks. Her imperious English voice makes me cringe:

'I need my spectacles. Get them for me, there's a good little girl. They're in my reticule on the bed. Trot along. Do as you're told now.'

Then they tell me to play for her. Do as you're told now. Oh heck. Despondently I find music, loll on the piano stool waiting for them to listen, hoping they'll forget and start talking about something else. Right. So what's it to be then Anne. Ah good. I like *To a Wild Rose*.

I expect the usual vaguely encouraging adult response before conversation is resumed with relief all round. But Auntie Cissy is full of surprises.

'Well child, you certainly make up in musicality for what you lack in technique. Thank you for your music. Now I will play for you.'

My mother peels the canvas skin off her cello, tunes, rosins. Smiles in the irritating adult way that says I know something you don't know.

'Shall I get out the music-stand for Auntie Cissy?'

Mother is shaking her head and frowning warningly: poor old Auntie Cissy can't see to read music any more. Well, how was I supposed to know that?

The cello is as big as her. Her little claws creep round it, cigarette bobs as she wriggles her skinny buttocks on the seat to draw the huge instrument in against her bony chest. How can she possibly play it? Poor old soul. Let Mummy play instead. I stare at the floor in embarrassment. It's a shame.

And then without warning the room is filled with a dizzying scalade of music — mischievous, joyful, thumbing its nose at age, arthritis, blindness. The bow bounces across the strings of its own volition, leaving Auntie Cissy free to grin and squint at me round the neck of the cello: what d'you think of that, then, little girl — perhaps a little technique would not go amiss eh?

'You should have seen your face. It was a picture.'

'But oh, isn't she wonderful. And then when she played the Saint-Saëns — I've never heard anything so beautiful in my whole life. I wanted to cry and cry. Oh, I mean I love it when you play it, but . . .'

'Yes, darling, I know. Auntie Cissy is a *real* cellist. It's such a tragedy that she's getting so frail.'

'Mummy, can I get piano lessons? I mean real piano lessons. I mean Granny's not really a pianist is she, and nor are you. I'll need to learn to play properly.'

'We'll have to see what we can do.'

My father doesn't think much of the way my granny and Auntie Cissy were brought up: all music and no education. I suppose he's right. But it would make life much easier if my father felt differently about music. He talks indulgently about Your Mother's Music as if it's some irrational wee treat she deserves now and then after all her hard work. But I don't think he really believes that some people actually can't do without it — any more than he could do without his books. That some people would actually rather go blind than deaf. Sometimes we wonder if it would help if we got him something to play himself — a melodeon, maybe, or a set of drums: he's good with the knife and fork when Scottish Dance Music's on, and he's a good singer, though he only does it for mischief — histrionically *basso profondo*-ing his way through 'Praise be Rory Og O'

Mor for sending loons to Hades' or 'The Dook of Argyll was troubled with the Bile'. But proper music seems to get caught up in his brain before it has a chance to reach the other parts of him — like his ears or his heart or his imagination or his stomach or his thighs. The places it gets me anyway.

'All this bourgeois sentimentality,' he says. 'All this imperialist cant. Where's your sense of history? Where's your understanding of politics?'

My father listens to Elgar and hears the British Empire. He won't allow Wagner because of Hitler. He could forgive Beethoven, but Brahms . . .

'Oh Ia-in, really. Listen to that melody . . .'

I want both my parents to be right so I have to divide myself up. Part of me is male: the strong-minded, energetic, spiritual, honourable, hard-working, thrifty, left-wing part that thrills to folk-music — Celtic, Negro, Slavonic — *Scottish*. Part of me is female: the decadent, artistic, intuitive, romantic, self-indulgent, sentimental, bourgeois part that wallows in classical music — German, Italian, French — *English*. Ambivalent, I skip through Mozart, languish with Chopin, then have indigestion like an overdose of sweeties. You'd be better off practising your scales young lady, says my thick-skinned, one-track minded granny, whose technique is so good she never had to be nervous: just took off her glasses so's she couldn't see the audience and got on with it.

Female, I sit quietly in our kitchen, cramped with metal stands and tattered scores and leather cases, when my mother has her musical evenings, inwardly swooning or exulting; or turn pages, pulse racing, eyes devouring the notes, anticipating the next great swell, the heart-melting return of a beloved theme, the next stomach-turning key-change. Watch with satisfaction the science teacher's hands (deft for Bach, neat for Haydn, strong for Brahms) passing tea-cups and pouring milk like in a proper house.

Male, I revolt against the flashy selfishness of the violin, against the perjink science teacher pecking at a biscuit or genteelly milking cake-crumbs from his English beard. Am captivated when the silence between two movements of a piano trio is broken by divine comment from the ceiling above. A terrible rumbling, beginning *sotto voce*, crescendos to a roaring climax then fades in a long, teasing reprise. The science teacher sits bolt upright, alarmed. 'Whatever is that dreadful noise, Mrs Gillies? Should we go outside and check the roof?' Valiantly Granny attempts to distract attention. 'Haven't the daffodils been nice this year' and 'Anne did such a lovely drawing in school today, why don't you show Mr Kay your drawing Anne.' But no soft pedalling can damp the exquisite naughtiness of my daddy standing upstairs, straightlegged, po on the wooden bedroom floor, peeing from a great height, making his own chamber music for devilment. For sheer devilment Mary. Dear me I never knew such a man. Right in the middle of the Gypsy Rondo. What must poor Mr Kay think of us?

If my granny would go to bed at night it would help a lot. My mother and father never get a chance to talk. And my father has so many worries I wouldn't know where to start telling about them. They're not all my granny's fault I know, but that doesn't stop me feeling I could pinch her black and blue.

Then one day comes Mrs Lawrie through a hole in the fence and things take a decided turn for the better. Mrs Lawrie speaks Gaelic and can milk cows and is kind and very mischievous.

O Dhia gam shàbhaladh, why didn't yous ask me before, Mrs Gillies *m'eudail.* Here I've been sitting all these years looking across at the beasts and feeding them over the fence and talking to them and wishing I could come across and help yous all. *O Dhia nan gràs,* I was after missing the beasts since I came to Oban. *O Dhia Dhia, na beathaichean na beathaichean* (Oh God, God, the beasts, the beasts).

Mrs Lawrie, tall stately body wrapped in layers and layers of motley clothes — six jumpers *m'eudail,* six jumpers — are you not believing me — see, one, two, three . . . they're all full of holes but the holes is all in different places. Six jumpers and a huge flowery cotton overall and black wellies, a wrap-around tweed skirt and safety-pins, head-scarf like a turban and rolled-down stockings held by knotted knicker elastic above each enormous knee. They call me Kate but my name's Catherine. We called her Mrs Lawrie. Nothing less would have done.

She transformed all our lives. Protesting loudly when my mother paid her (Oh Mrs Gillies that's far too much I wasn't wanting the likes of that I'll bring yous a soda scone in the morning) cackling with raucous, risqué humour, tears running down the little purple river-beds below her old elephant eyes, wiping them off on the corner of her overall ready for the next good laugh. Her hair was iron grey, her cheeks apple red. She must have been nearly seventy even then.

We didn't have to apologise for ourselves to Mrs Lawrie. We lived the way Mrs Lawrie's people lived at home. Her brother still worked the croft. I had never met anyone else who lived like us in all my life. I thought nobody in the world lived like us. Mrs Lawrie's favourite joke was the one about the man from Uist who went down to the Royal Garden Party in Edinburgh and came back and told his wife '*Tha iad gu*

math neònach ann a shiod — bithidh iad ag ithe muigh 's a' cac a-stigh.'
('They're very queer folk down there — they eat outdoors and shit
indoors.') I'm saying he said to his wife *'bithidh iad ag ithe muigh 's a' cac
a-stigh'*. Ha Ha! Oh Mr Gillies I'm a terrible woman I'm saying I'm a
terrible woman, *O Dhia Dhia.*

Once she laughed so much her safety-pin opened and her skirt
unwound around outsize pink drawers — unwound slowly, tentatively, as
if it wasn't sure it dared, while we all watched spell-bound until at last it
collapsed, with a wee sigh, around her wellies on the floor and that made
her laugh all the more.

O Dhia gam chuideachadh Granny yous is after making me do a
struptease.

Once her and me were clowning about and she cut her arm on the latch
of the kitchen door. From then on she would roll back her sleeve every
now and then to show me the scar — wordlessly, as if it bound us in
blood.

When she got frights she would say lovely naughty things she'd never
have dreamed of saying in English. Well she wouldn't have known them
in English anyway would she? *O mhic na galla!* and *A mhic an diabhail!*
('Oh son-of-a-bitch!' . . . 'Ah, son of the devil!'). We could make Mr
Thomson sit up all right if we came out with some of that in the Gaelic
class once we got into the secondary school. Shiver his respectable Lewis
timbers.

She was always getting frights. Like the Christmas my brother showed
her the cheese under his new microscope — *Dhia gam chuideachadh na
biasdagan, na biasdagan!* (God help me the beasties, the beasties!) She
never ate cheese again. Or so she said anyway. Like the time Angus was
down at the fish-market and brought home the lobster when she was out
and she met it coming towards her when she opened the bathroom door.

Like the time my father had a couple of drams at the Mart and bought a
daft wee black calf by mistake. He made a temporary pen with an old gate
propped up in a corner of the hay-barn and then forgot to tell anyone it
was there. He was sitting indoors grinning away at his boiled egg while
they finished the milking and Mrs Lawrie went to the barn to get some
hay . . . Imagine her as she crossed the pitch-black yard, bats swirling
round her bobbing storm-lamp. Imagine her as she pulled back the barn
door and something black leapt out on her and danced away into the
night on cloven hooves . . . *'O Mhoire mhàthair, Mhoire mhàthair, Dia
sàbhail mi Mr Gillies Mr Gillies chunnaic mi an Diabhal fhèin san t-sabhal!'*
(Oh Mother Mary, Mother Mary, God save me Mr Gillies Mr Gillies I
saw the Devil himself in the barn!)

Like the starry night in 1957 when we took her up on the hill with a telescope to see if we could see the Sputnik: you're not believing all that nonsense Mr Gillies *m'eudail*, it's just something the papers has made up, they can't go round the moon *m'eudail*, the moon's far too wee I'm saying the moon is far too wee. And then the moon went behind a cloud. *O Mhoire mhathair, Riùisianaich na galla, chuir iad as dhan a' ghealaich* (Oh Mother Mary, Russians of a bitch, they've gone and put the moon out!). Dear Mrs Lawrie. Who was she kidding?

She clattered and clanked and milked and fed and strained and scalded and sined out the cloths and sang tunelessly and talked to herself and sighed and shook her head. *Tha mise falbh a nisde.* (I'm away now). I'm saying *tha mise falbh a nisde Mrs Gillies m'eudail.* I'll be seeing yous in the morning. If we're all spared. Aye that's the way, that's the way. *Shin agad sin.* We never know what's in store for us Granny dear, I'm saying we never know what's in store for us. If we're all spared. Aye aye.

She told us all the Oban gossip — her own rich versions in which amusement, incredulity and disapproval never quite added up to condemnation of anyone or anything.

'And his wife not cold in her grave, Mrs Gillies, is that no terrible. Aye aye poor soul. Not cold in her grave. Ach well, that's what they're saying anyway. If you believe what you hear you'll eat what you see. I'm saying if you believe what you hear . . . That's what they're saying anyway. But I'm thinking he had a hard time with her. She was a fine woman all the same. *Shin agad e.* They're saying he had a good dram in him at the time poor soul. Not cold in her grave. You don't know what's round the next corner. Is that not right what I'm saying Granny. The next corner *m'eudail.* You just watch yourself Anne. You keep your nightie down about your knees when you grow up. Ha Ha!'

She told us about working at the gutting — she'd been away down in Yarmouth and all over. She told us about her first job in service, kitchen-maid in a big house full of big posh kilted boys that teased her and tormented her and threw bits of scalding mashed potato at her that stuck to her arms and neck and burnt them red. She told us about the night Angus brought in the fish suppers and she took out her teeth and laid them on the newspaper that was wrapping them and the priest came to the door and she was so ashamed she put the chips back in the wrapper and threw the whole lot in the fire — teeth and all. She would tell you she was just a silly old *cailleach* that didn't know nothing. My father didn't like that — just making a mockery of herself. Putting herself down all the time and making a mockery of herself. That's what they're all coming to nowadays.

She thought we knew everything. We wished we knew half what she knew.

And yet, Mrs Gillies *a luaidh*, the funny thing is, all these clever people with all their book-learning and they haven't the *Gàidhlig*. Aye.

Her husband Angus, little mainland sergeant-major with a waxed moustache and no Gaelic. Marching at the head of the pipe-band, marching to his work straighter than a ram-rod, tipping his cap to the tourists whose bags he wheeled on his barrow from pier to pier, station to hotel. Queen Victoria would have appreciated Angus: John Brown's body lies a-mouldering in his grave but his soul is marching up the Railway Pier in Oban.

Angus playing the Jew's harp: no-one has ever played the Jew's harp like Angus, not before, not since, sitting in our kitchen in his British Railway trousers, snuffling down his moustache, humphing in his throat, playing the music of the *piob-mhòr* on half a crown's worth of base metal.

Angus knew everyone and everything. He was everything Mrs Lawrie thought she couldn't be — clever, articulate, worldly-wise. Angus would know what to do, Angus would fix it, Angus would look after her. When Angus proved vulnerable, retching up pints of black blood, it shook Mrs Lawrie to the core. When he died she never recovered, though she lived on for many years, bringing some of her fears over to us, laying the rest on the doorstep of the priest's house.

EIGHT

'Bring me back a monkey,' Mrs Lawrie said.

I feel like the wee girl in the joke: God bless Mummy and Daddy and my wee brother and the cat. Well now, God, I'm afraid you'll not be hearing from me for a fortnight as I'm going to England on my holidays. But I'll be in touch again when I get back. Amen.

The old leather case is on the bed. My mother is folding things and putting them in the case and my father is telling her that none of you people know how to pack a case, and he walked all the way from somewhere to somewhere else with a whole fortnight's supplies in a rucksack including a kettle, and taking all the stuff out the case and starting again making the Best Use of Space Provided. It's all a matter of Dynamics. We grin and wink at each other. Let him get on with it.

Auntie Jean is my father's sister and Uncle Alex is the Town Clerk of Whitby. I know the Town Clerk of Ballachulish. He's called the Wee Toon and he sings Gaelic songs. But Uncle Alex doesn't sing Gaelic songs. He's English I suppose. Except that he's got a Scottish name. Ross. Oh heck. My relations are all very confusing.

We sit in opposite corners of the compartment looking out at darkness. Six o'clock in the morning. Daddy promised. Och yes, my mother says, but you know what he's like in the morning. Don't be too disappointed. But yes! He *has* woken up Mummy. He *has* remembered. I told you he would. Far away in the blackness a tiny glow-worm. My father with the storm-lamp waving from the *dùn* as we pass by in the train. We watch and watch and wave and wave. It's funny seeing things from the other side. It's usually us down there looking up at the railway line. Get out the way. I can't see. It's not fair he's bigger than me. Can Daddy see us Mummy?

Then my mother wipes smuts off our faces and tells us about not fighting and not hanging out of train windows. Then she goes off to sleep with her mouth falling open.

It's getting light now and we've eaten all our sandwiches already. And then the train goes into a long black tunnel. Oh mammy daddy. Don't you take any notice of him darling. He's just a big tease. When it comes out of the tunnel we are in Glasgow.

We have to hurry to the other station. My father has gone over it and over it — not much time in Glasgow, no hanging about looking in shop windows. Turn right out of George Square and then straight down Hope Street. It's easy. Look here on the map. But my mother still isn't sure of the way, so we queue up and get into a taxi. Central Station please.

But the driver tells her we'd be quicker walkin hen, *sa mairch oan ra day*.

We soon find out what he means. We can't cross the road. Pounding and roaring and shrieking and swearing and fifing and drumming and screaming of bagpipes, they spew down the road in an endless, impenetrable stream: royal-blue banners, golden tassels, twirling batons, braided uniforms and trailing leopard-skin, with waves of music that well up, climax and merge into the next great arrogant wave they come upon you, pushing their crazed foul-breathed faces into yours, daring you with their mockery, their flicking flags, their strutting war-dances. We cling together, buffeted by yelling running boys. What are they Mummy? I'm not sure darling. An old woman looks at us amazed, pitying. 'San Orange Walk hen. Billy Boys. Battle o the Boyne annat.' By the time they have gone so has our train.

The man behind the window says we will have to go via Edinburgh now. We will have to go all the way back to the other station and get the train to Edinburgh. Oh dear. What will daddy say? You People Will Waste Time. Better phone ahead to warn them we'll be late. All those connections. My mother's hands shaking as she presses pennies into the phone-box.

We seem to spend all day changing trains. Carrying our case over one iron bridge after another. My mother's mouth hangs open in corners of compartments. Whistles blow. Accents grow English. Stations are grey with dark-green paintwork and you lay your hand flat on a steel plate, put in your penny with your other hand and wait for the little steel pins to pop out and read your palm, tickling you from wrist to tip to wrist till they send you out your fortune written on a card the colour of Yeast-vite. We should have done this before we left home, Mummy, it might have warned us about the orange men. Yes dear.

As we reach Whitby (smell the sea, smell the sea) our faces pull themselves up into clown-smiles, involuntary as a dog's snarl. We try to hide them from amused English bystanders. Silly Scottish smiles. Hullo Auntie Jean. Mary how lovely to see you again. Alec's got the car waiting. Oh you must be tired. What a journey. What a journey. Shhh everyone's looking at us.

My mother is to go back tomorrow morning — now you be a good girl and help Auntie Jean all you can — all the way back she came, mouth open in a corner. What if she sleeps past her stop? Misses her connection like the day she went to Gleneagles by mistake and had to stay the night in a hotel after a day's shopping in Stirling. What a feckless lot you are. What if the orange men are out again? What if — but she's gone. No tears now Anne. Come along and see what Uncle Alec has got lined up for you.

The house in Whitby is not at all like our house: tall and thin instead of square and low. Carpets instead of lino; ornaments instead of books; a table with polish instead of oilcloth; chintz chair-covers with hand-embroidered linen cushions; sharp-edged window-sills, dry, no flies, no mildew; electric lights with silky fringes; a cooker, a refrigerator, a bathroom with shiny taps and a lock on the door; hearth-rugs and brass tongs and a poem in a frame on the wall:

Life is mostly froth and bubble
Two things stand like stone
Kindness in another's trouble
Courage in your own

I get Uncle Alec to write it out in my autograph album.

Out the front is very neat. People paint their walls in pastel colours, and have jigsaw paths and little wooden gates that click shut. You don't see pebble-dash or corrugated iron or old bedsteads here. The hedges are low and flat and you can see over them into little front gardens with sun-flowers and hollyhocks. Little fat men with short-sleeved shirts and wobbly brown wrinkled arms stand out on the pavement clipping the hedges all afternoon and calling out to each other about the weather or the Test Match — then they brush up the shavings in a dustpan and put them on their compost heaps at the back. Beside their greenhouses. You can go for a walk through the corn-fields along a neat little path with flag-stones all the way to Robin Hood's Bay. You meet people dressed in flowery summer frocks like we'd wear for best. They're out walking their dogs. Gosh. You can't walk in corn-fields in Scotland or you'd flatten the corn. Not that that stops some people, mind.

Round the back is shady and private with huge trees and redcurrant bushes and you can hear the schoolboys playing cricket in the field beyond the trees — clop the bats go, clop . . . clop . . . Birds sing politely, low down in branches: no pine-trees or peewits or spacious firmament on high here. Clop . . . clop . . . Polite applause ripples across the birdsong.

From inside the cool dark house you can hear the wireless playing cricket too, its ripple of applause, its commentator talking in an endless straight line, and in the distance the hum of lawn-mowers while Auntie Jean shells peas into a colander. No tinned peas here. The West Indies are playing. They are beating England. I think. Oh joy. Uncle Alec is not amused. It's all very peaceful.

But then we go up on the moors to visit Mary's school, driving across a grey hillscape like Argyll with its top cut off. It's spacious here all right — bleak and grey, and we pass miles and miles of bleak wire, punctuated with bleak signs: DANGER and FIRING RANGE and MINISTRY OF DEFENCE and KEEP OUT. I imagine guns in the bleak heather: guns where black-faced sheep should be. This is the land I've read about in books. *The Secret Garden. Wuthering Heights.*

We hardly see our cousins. The boys come home in evenings to drape their long trouser legs across the sofa. Mary comes home only at weekends. But we are kept too busy to miss them.

Sometimes it's Auntie Jean who takes us out. To Scarborough, where a wide-mouthed boat hurtles down a waterfall on wires to hit a pond with an almighty splash, making everybody scream and queue up to go back down again. I watch and watch, but you wouldn't catch me going up there.

'Quite right, my dear,' smiles Auntie Jean. 'I feel just the same way about it myself.'

She used to be a teacher. I wish I had a teacher like her. We talk and talk — and she builds me a new Daddy — a delicious Terrible Boy who hung spiders down from his bedroom window to frighten his little sisters and did the dance of the seven veils with a towel in the front garden. She likes my Lovely Scottish Accent: and how's my little blether the day then? Bu' she doesn't like i' when I drop my t's. Which seems inconsistent to me: tha's jus' the way we say i' up in Oban, Auntie Jean.

She takes us to a swimming-pool where I cling with skinny fingers to white china and look down at my squint turquoise legs. To Harrogate, dripping rhododendrons and soggy custard-tarts: Uncle Alec always has to have his custard-tart when we go to Harrogate; a mad old Scottish lady scuttles along the pavement glorifying God at the top of her voice: Harrogate's full of them apparently. To a church hall where a man can tell there is someone in the audience called Cecil who has a key, a bus-ticket and a packet of Pontefract cakes in his left pocket: Am I right, Maisie, could I be right, could Cecil please identify himself? My goodness me, Auntie Jean, what a clever man — do you think it could be a trick? To the picture palace (we just call i' the pictures, Auntie Jean) and to the church to hear the new vicar (we call them ministers, Auntie Jean) and the funny old man who shouts ay-men and halleloo; Uncle Alec asks us if we have enjoyed the sermon and Auntie Jean says ay-men so I say halleloo.

She lets me have a real bath — not like the zinc tub in the kitchen and Granny guddling about with kettles of boiling water. Auntie Jean looks in at me through the steam:

'You'd like some help wouldn't you, my dear, you're not such a great big girl yet are you?'

We-ell — I'd quite like to be left to enjoy myself, and no-one outside the family has ever seen me all bare before. But I don't like to hurt her feelings. So she washes me all over with a soft sponge and scented soap. When I come downstairs my uncle pretends not to recognise me, now that I'm clean. Who is this clean little girl coming in? Do I know her Jean? It's a joke. I hope.

Sometimes it's Uncle Alec that takes us out. Uncle Alec has two wives. One is Auntie Jean, and we see a model of the other one in the Town Hall. I didn't know ships had husbands, did you?

He takes us fishing in the slippery slime underneath the pier: in England people go to wee stalls with stripey roofs to buy their bait in cardboard tubs instead of digging up worms or collecting mussels. I think I saw someone eating bait, but surely not, it must have been something else. My brother catches a fish. I don't.

He takes us bathing, jumping into crashing, rolling waves. You know, Uncle Alec, many people believe it's much colder up in Scotland than it is in England, but actually we have a Gulf Stream. I shiver. Uncle Alec puffs and blows:

'Reuters reports a whale basking off the Yorkshire coast at Whitby Bay earlier today,' he says, and then we bury him in sand.

He takes us up on top of the Pavilion where only town officials are allowed to go. You can't hear the music up here, and you have to shout to make yourself heard above the wind, but you can walk right round and look down through the glass dome and see the orchestra playing. I'm pressing my nose against the window, pretending it's my grampop conducting, when Uncle Alec starts poking me in the ribs and pointing, heaving with laughter. He tells everyone about it for days: one of the fiddlers was sawing away when he suddenly stopped playing, took his music off the stand, got another piece off the floor and started again. Heaven knows what it must have sounded like, him playing something different from all the others for the first two hundred bars. Gosh, you never know what will make other people laugh. Especially adults.

When Uncle Alec laughs he keeps his mouth shut and his face straight, as if he's pretending to be doing something else. The effort makes him go very red and his specs slide down and he has to wrinkle his nose to get them back up again.

He makes us climb up a hundred steps and then down again: I'm scared coming down, makes me feel as if I'm going to fall, and my knees shake. But I don't let on to Uncle Alec. Then we go to look for fossils — the remains of the snakes Saint Hilda banished over the rocks. They're ammonites, not fossils, stupid. My brother finds some, I don't — but who cares.

He takes us to watch Yorkshire playing. Uncle Alec is wearing a hankie with knots in it at each corner; nothing much else is happening, but wee boys on ladders keep changing the numbers on the board, and people clap, and the umpire seems to be wearing more jumpers than Mrs Lawrie, and Uncle Alec gets cross if we move about in the batsman's eyeline. Sometimes one of the players lets out a yell and old men round about us call out in deep unintelligible voices. I like the bowlers best — they do rude things with their balls. That's the kind of thing that makes me laugh. But even my brother is pretending not to notice.

We look everywhere for a monkey for Mrs Lawrie. We saw a real monkey down by the shows on the pier — a wee manky thing with a face like a prune, arms like dried bananas, the fur under its oxters dusty and scuffed. It dances miserably in its red felt jacket beside the stripey sugar walking-sticks and the bare electric light bulbs — scorch-red, sick-yellow, grease-green, while a sexless nasal voice wails ceaselessly: 'Swanee how I love you how I love you my dear old Swanee'. But Mrs Lawrie wouldn't want a real monkey even if we could rescue it. Anyway it's full of germs. Don't you go near it, Uncle Alec says.

Further away from the sea the streets narrow. Glass shelves blaze with plaster and feathers and bakelite, taking my breath away. Laid out on your bed your precious purchases seem miserly as a match-stick in a grate. 'Oh I wouldn't worry dear,' Auntie Jean says. 'It's the thought that counts.' But there are no monkeys anywhere.

Then suddenly, on the very last day, I see what I'm looking for. It is palest green glazed china, its neck encircled with pink rose-buds.

'Eeee, we'll ave to wrap im oop well woant we then dearie. Goin aallway to Bonnie Scotland are you then, little moonkey? E's a raight naice little ornament is that, Missus. I didn't even know we ad im till t' little lass pointed im out oop there.'

That is because he was a miracle. Mrs Lawrie understands things like that. Her life is full of miracles. Rainbows. Saints.

That evening my father comes. He's going to take us home tomorrow.

Familiar dun-coloured raincoat emerging from the train; tartan scarf flapping, heather tie, check flannel shirt, lovat-green pullover, Harris tweed jacket, grey flannel trousers, brown brogues, shiny domed head bouncing along the platform head-and-shoulders above the wee cotton English. Delivering his ticket with a magician's flourish — you expect him to burst into song. People are smiling at him, but not mocking. He is all conspicuous gaiety and nonchalant pride. He is Scottish.

He starts speaking before he even reaches the barrier: 'I never heard such a lot of nonsense as those people talked all the way from Middlesborough. What they do fill their heads up with, these people nowadays — on and on about their hotel rooms and the weather and the price of clothes. As if there was nothing more important in life. Ah there you are then Jean' as if he had just popped out to buy tobacco.

'He doesn't change, your Daddy. He kept us up all night long arguing.'

'What nonsense. Alex didn't let me get a word in edgeways.'

'Oh I-ain!'

The journey home is very different from the journey down. My father isn't sleepy. There is too much to Learn. We run from side to side of the compartment, craning to see the things he points out. They weren't there on the way down. Dark satanic mills, scenes of battles, glacial shifts, the Border, the ghosts of Edward the First of England and Bonnie Prince Charlie and Hadrian and Saint Ninian.

This time we go to Edinburgh deliberately — not by mistake but because we want to. My father wants to show us our capital city.

Ghosts of John Knox and Willie Wallace, Davey Hume and Donnchadh Bàn. Smell of breweries, sound of cannon, French Impressionists in a Greek temple.

He takes us to the High Street to see History. Real History, not your tourist mumbo-jumbo. Royal Mile indeed. Not down to the Palace, not up to the Castle, but across the cobbled road and straight up a dank close. Tiny windows so close together they squint, grey washing on poles out windows, disease and overcrowding and pride and stone walls do not a prison make. Poverty like a princess goes in my land.

'Dad-dy! Come away. This isn't History. This is people's houses. Come on. There's still people living there.'

But he is unrepentant. Unabashed. Ghosts of Thomas Muir and Robert Burns, the Tree of Liberty and the soo's tail to Geordie. Gardyloo!

Then we stand waiting to cross Princes Street. The cars coming both ways stop for him as if he was the Prime Minister. Of Scotland of course. There you are they've stopped. He waves his raincoat expansively in acknowledgment as he strides between the cars. A celebrity. Down from the Highlands.

'Dad-dy! Don't be daft! The traffic lights changed!'

He doesn't care. Isn't he funny. We rush along, laughing, scandalised, trying to keep up.

We go on a tram, bumping and jerking. He talks loudly to us, to the world at large, sitting bolt upright across the passage: the Union of Parliaments and Sir Walter Scott and George the Fourth and the birth of the New Town. Why doesn't he keep his voice down? But the other passengers are listening with amused interest, as though to a slightly eccentric tourist guide. This is yet another Daddy. He's not like this at home. Is this what he was like when Auntie Jean knew him? When he was young? Dancing naked on the lawn? Jumping over the flower arrangement and off the platform and straight out the Camden Town Hall when the London Gaelic Choir started singing God Save the King? When his father was alive?

Then the tram stops. We're at Waverley. He and my brother jump out. The tram moves off.

I cling to the wheeling pole, crying with terror. My number's up.

But the pair of them run along the pavement, laughing heads bouncing parallel to the tram. At the next stop I fall into his arms, rub my tears into his bristly cheek.

'Now now, what's all this,' he says loudly, cheerfully, for the benefit of the smiling, kindly, sympathetic, nosey Edinburgh folk all hanging out the tram. But he holds me very tightly and whispers in my ear: 'You didn't think Daddy would lose his little love-bird did you?'

When we get home everything looks very wee and shabby and dingy. And lovely.

NINE

In Primary Six we are moved out of the main school, down the brae, to the Hall.

The Free Church stands like the heavenly gates up at the top of the brae. Pech all ye who enter here. You need a life-line to pull you up when it's icy. Or perhaps faith. The Free Church Hall squats down at the bottom opposite the public urinal. But still very church-like inside. Huge brown varnished beams and arched windows. Plain glass of course. They don't like pictures in the Free Church. The hall is on loan to the school — to cope with the post-war bulge. I wonder why the Free Church needed a hall in the first place. No *cèilidhs* with a dram and sugar-sprinkled dumpling in the Free Church calendar.

Two classes occupy the hall, separated by a fraying pressed sawdust partition that doesn't reach halfway up to its celestial ceiling. You can hear the B-class through the partition, taught by Miss MacIntyre, my brother's teacher last year. Two years with the A's, two with the B's: crop rotation. My brother's class is up in the High School now. Gone but not forgotten. Oh no indeed. An excellent class. Particularly high standard. We'll have to pull our socks up if we're not to be put to shame.

Miss Hope invites Miss MacIntyre in to look at Willie Gillies's wee sister.

'Well if she does half as well as her brother you'll be very pleased.'

Some hope, Miss Hope.

For a long time my brother haunts me irksomely. Your brother would never have, your brother always did, this is almost as good as. Occasionally — very occasionally — it's well seen whose sister you are.

We are the Pre-qualies. Things are getting serious now. A lot of the time we spend going over old intelligence tests to prepare us for the Pre-qualy Exam. It makes me very nervous.

We get marks for everything, tests in every subject. Every sling and arrow is reflected in the weekly move around the class — everyone out to the floor with your school-bags, top marks at the back, starting on the right. Anyone visiting the room can sum us all up with one glance. Katy Troup and I sit together at the back, one desk along from Hamish McGhie and David Crawford.

'Oh boys, boys, the girls are giving you a showing-up. What are you going to do about it eh?'

You can't move in the desk without elbowing your neighbour. You mustn't speak except to the teacher. You may not speak to the teacher without putting up your hand. You dare not snap your fingers at the teacher or you will be treating her like a dog. We have to speak proper English too.

'What is this wurrd you are using, Alec Smith? Burrrd? I know of no such wurrd. The wurrd is not burrrd, Alec Smith. The wurrd is birrrd.'

We read out loud around the class. Us clever ones at the back rolling up our eyes while the poor readers stammer and mumble. Us reading *molto espressivo* while the folk at the front scowl and mimic behind their hands. I like the story about the people who never took any exercise and so eventually their legs shrivelled up and they had to have wee wheels to get them around. It's a parable of course. A moral tale to make us all go out and take lots of exercise. Based on the evolution of the species. Of course nothing's quite as simple as that in real life. Remember the cartoon my father showed me of the psychologist peering through a hole in the wall to observe the monkey, with the monkey on the other side peering out to observe him.

The *Radiant Reading Book* tells us stories about children of other lands: children with different coloured skins. I know about that too. Mendel's Law.

'Please Miss, my father told me a poem about that.'

'Very nice, Anne Gillies. Let us all hear the poem.'

There was a young lady called Starky
Who had an affair with a darky
The result of her sins . . . CRASH!

Miss Hope brings down the lid of her desk.

'That is quite enough. I am sure Mr Gillies would not dream of any such thing.'

'Tell Daddy what you said to Miss Hope, Anne.'

'Oh Mummy. No. He'll be cross.'

But I am made to tell.

'That was a little unwise,' he says in a silken voice.

'I was going to explain to her about Mendel's Law, but she didn't give me time.'

'Well perhaps it's you who should take time and think before you utter — keep your unruly member in check.'

But their eyes are dancing with mischief.

I still find it difficult to write with the scratchy brass-nibbed pen — my middle finger is still furrowed, and ink still flows against gravity up past my knuckle. But I am getting to be a dab hand with the adjectives and adverbs. Miss Hope collects them like butterflies and displays them to the class: weeping piteously, autumnal chill. Well done as usual, Anne Gillies. As the year goes on Miss Hope becomes easier and easier to please, forever sending me in next door to show off a composition or a picture. But I don't think much of Miss Hope and so am unimpressed by her praises. I know perfectly well I'm not half as clever as she thinks. The Pre-qualy will tell the truth. Our IQ. Our intelligence, stripped of teacher's preconceptions. You can't fool the Pre-qualy. It doesn't know who your brother is. It doesn't approach your work with High Expectations.

On the day of the Pre-qualy we are led up to the school and into the gym hall. We pass Hector and smile, but he is strangely formal, serious. There are single desks out in the Hall, all separate. Some of the girls have brought mascots. Jennifer Hendry has brought a real rabbit's foot. But that won't help: the Pre-qualy defies good luck charms.

We have to work out hundreds of questions on a printed paper. Which is longer, how many different patterns, underline the odd man out. The problems are good fun to do, lots easier than the test papers Miss Hope's been giving us — though I don't admit that to anyone afterwards.

'Ooh yes, wasn't it terrible,' I say. 'Did you get that one about the squares?'

I also don't let on about the girl in the desk across the passage.

'Show me your paper if I get stuck. Please, Anne Gillies. You're clever. You won't let me go into the F-class, will you? Please. I don't want to go into the F-class.'

'All right,' I say uneasily, just to get her to shut up, wanting to say no.

She is pushing her paper across the desk, casually tapping with her pencil on one of the sections, pretending deep cogitation, but her eyes say please, please, Anne Gillies. But this is the Pre-qualy. The Truth. I can't interfere with The Truth. What if I help her and she gets the wrong IQ. She might get into a class higher than she should; she might get into one lower than she deserves. Either way it would still be wrong. Feeling very guilty I feign concentration and pretend not to see her. Later though, as I check through my answers, I take care to sit well back in my desk, innocently holding the pages at arm's length, passing the buck from my conscience to hers. I angle my head away, not wanting to see how her conscience decides.

They never did tell us how we got on in the Pre-qualy. I feel very uncomfortable about this. Miss Hope is walking about knowing more about me than I know myself. Your intelligence is the most important thing about you. Without it we would all still be swinging from the trees. We ought to be told. It's not fair.

When someone asks Miss Hope about the results she purses her lips.

'The Pre-Qualifying Examination merely confirms what we already suspect. I do not need examinations to tell me who is using his brain and who is not. Next year you will sit the Qualifying Examination and then we shall find out for certain who intends to do well and who does not.'

Down the front heads hang hopelessly. Still, there's a whole year before the Qualy.

But towards the end of the term we are sitting doing needle-work (girls) and handwork (boys) — no more pressing worries than how to get knots out of raffia or the elastic past the seam of coarse pea-green knickers — when two people are summarily called across to see the headmaster: one boy, one girl. There seems to be no common factor to explain the summons. She big and motherly, oldest in the class, slow of speech and writing but always on the scene to comfort anyone who falls over. He feckless and vacant with missing teeth and troubles at home. When they return to their seats the girl is crying quietly, the boy grinning blankly.

News spreads quietly round the class. They won't be coming with the rest of us into Primary Seven. They're going straight up into the High School. Into 1F. Doomed for all eternity.

Their heads are posted up as a terrible warning to backsliders, renegades and all those of a nervous disposition.

In Primary Seven we are moved again, this time up to the High School. It's much quicker for me to go home from here, but that's a mixed blessing: I'm on my own now — nobody else goes this way home. Across the playground avoiding the pounding big boys playing football with schoolbag goals; right foot finds the crack in the concrete, left foot swings over (hey hey show a leg!) sit astride the wall for a moment feeling hot face, cold thighs, long to be brave enough to turn my back on them and launch off forwards into the five-foot chasm below but end up scrabbling down facing them, scraping knees delaying my release from their expectant grins. Up yer skirt! Then across the field, through the gate, and I'm home. Granny and I wait disconsolately for my mother to come home and colour the chilly house.

Sometimes I go into the Hospital and knock on my mother's door. Just to avoid going home. She never seems annoyed to see me, however busy she is. She puts me into her waiting-room (no-one is ever waiting there but me) and I wallow in a bubble-bath of *Woman's Own*s and *Readers' Digest*s: Dear Mary Grant life's like that. I read avidly to discover what real people do and say. Sometimes we go down town to buy something for the tea. We have to hurry before the last of the shops shut. I can't hold her hand any more now, but sometimes I link her arm after we get off the street and onto our road.

The High School is built around a large hall with a brown pitted wooden floor. The cleaners empty their tea-leaves onto it to get the dust up. Large wooden boards with Noah's Ark tops and golden writing to tell who has been killed in the war and who has been dux of the school. Dux — geese — hee hee. It's Latin stupid. He doesn't bother telling me what it means and I am finding it increasingly hard to ask people what things mean:

'What, you don't know what prejudice means? Where's your Jane Austen?' says my father.

'I'm surprised at you not understanding an easy question like that, Anne Gillies,' says Miss Hope.

'Anne Gillies can't do her long division,' says Hamish McGhie.

Stupid, says my inner man.

All round the hall runs a balcony with a polished balustrade. Rooms lurk behind: all you know of them is frosted glass and a brief surge of interesting sound when someone goes in or comes out. The doors swing shut quickly; it's none of your business what goes on in here, they say.

It's hard to fathom whose business we are: our room is one of three tucked away in a backwater off the hall, 7A to the right, 7B to the left, 1F across the passage. 1F! The end of the line! Good-bye world! Mrs MacKay is so good at finding things to occupy them. Just primaries, we come in the side door, funnelling into the cloakroom straight ahead, slink along the wall past another frosty door and round the corner to our lair. Be quiet there you young ones. People are trying to work in here. The best thing about this school is the inside toilets.

We are disorientated now: from being the oldest we have become the youngest — school appendix; inessential organ next to the back passage. Miss Hope, white-haired and wattled, is a junior here, gownless in Gaza. Even Hector, not here to defend himself, is cut down to fit the new scenario:

'Mr MacNeill is not the headmaster here. You will kindly desist from thinking of him as such. Mr MacLean is our rector.'

Curiouser and curiouser. I know Hector is still away down there, still at the helm, teaching some other lucky class. People don't cease to exist just because we can't see them. But some other person, up here in a study at the top of the stairs we're not allowed to climb, is in charge of us now. I do not like this revelation at all; am glad to hear Walter and Joe muttering their disapproval, affirming their loyalty to Hector whatever *she* may say. I am not predisposed to this rector. Mr MacLean. Whoever he is.

One day he comes to visit Primary Seven. All the way from his study. Big deal. We should be so lucky.

'All stand. This is Mr MacLean, our Rector. You will kindly bid him good morning.'

'Good mooo-rning Mr MacLean.'

He is going to run a spelling competition. We will all keep standing and spell words round the class. When people get one wrong they will sit down.

The ones at the front are soon sitting — glad to get the weight off their feet. But I am not going to sit down. Not if it takes all day and all night. I'll show him.

Soon just me and Katharine Troup are standing, while the others watch us idly, turned round in their seats, glad of the rest. But for once I am not competing with Katy Troup: I am locked in head-on combat with this man who dares to set himself up against Hector.

'Through, thorough, trough, bough.' He goes on and on. Me and Katharine Troup go on and on till at last the dinner bell rings.

'Well done girls. But we must decide this yet: I shall come back in the afternoon and we shall discover who will be the victor.'

'Great stuff, Anne Gillies. Keep going and we'll not get any work all afternoon.'

Don't you worry, Alec Smith, I'll not be beaten by *him*.

In the afternoon it soon becomes just him and me. He must know it's a fight to the death, otherwise he'd have called it a day long ago. My feet are getting sore and my back sags. But I am not going to give in.

'Infinite, statutory, aristocracy.' Oh aye, Mr Rector, it pays to increase your word-power: the Gillies family has played the Spelling Game every tea-time since I was six. 'Antecedent, pendulous, catastrophe' — why don't you ask me eliomosynary, or boudoir: I'm not sure what they mean, but I know how to spell them. 'Hierarchy, myopic, benign' — he is a salmon on the end of my line — with his chestnut hair and his long Gaelic vowels. 'Psychological, attorney' — pardon — 'attuuuuurney'. A-T-T . . . ('goooood . . .?') A-T-T-U-R-N-Y. Aha. Got you at last. Well done Anne Gillies. Give her a big hand boys and girls.

Got me. With his long Gaelic vowels. His chestnut hair. Sorry Hector.

I was furious Mummy. What a silly word. He told us it was something to do with lawyers in America. He says American lawyers always work in their shirt-sleeves. He doesn't approve of that at all. No I don't know who he is Daddy. What, that nice man with the one arm who came to the hospital to record the Gaelic stories? Oh I remember him all right. And Mr MacLean's his brother? A scholar — Gaelic and Greek? And his other brother's a Gaelic poet? Sorley MacLean? That's different isn't it. I didn't know that did I. Och well, he seems quite nice himself. With his long Gaelic vowels and his chestnut hair. Sorry Hector.

Most of the time, though, is spent preparing us to sit the Qualifying Exam. The Qualy will decide the rest of our lives: our Educational Future; our station in Life, even our friends. Will we Take Advantage of the Chances our Parents Never Had — or leave school at fourteen and become message boys and mill-girls and scaffies and shop assistants? The Qualy hangs over us even at our play. At night I wake up lying in a puddle. If I stay very still in one position it usually dries out before the morning.

Every day we struggle through yellowing past papers, taking them home to finish. The more you finish the more you get to do. I am almost back to 1930. Every evening I weep in despair over boys putting apples into average baskets in average orchards; thick men filling square swimming pools with round buckets. Rods poles perches; miles furlongs acres of questions to fathom; ounces pounds stones hundredweights tons and tons of worry. I chew the insides of my cheeks, bite my finger-nails, tear at the skin till I bleed to the quick.

'Look at her, Mary. If you keep doing that no man will ever look at you,' my father says. 'Tell me what the question is and I'll show you how to think it out properly.'

'You shouldn't worry about these old papers,' says my brother. 'It won't be anything like that. The real exam's much easier.'

But my brother's really clever. And my father won't be there to help me to think it out properly. And Miss Hope doesn't know anything anyway. Why does she keep telling everyone how clever I am? They'll really crow now if I fail the Qualy.

'Don't be so silly darling. You're not going to fail the Qualy,' says my mother. 'Look how well you've been doing. You're my very clever little girl.'

But what would she know about it? She won't mind what class I go into. So she says anyway. But I will. So will my father.

One day, for a bit of light relief, Mrs Stewart comes across from her hut to give us an Art Lesson. Miss Hope thinks Anne Gillies is the bee's knees at Art. O ho. Now we'll see.

We are to paint a tree. Now what kind of tree shall it be, little ones? Perhaps a stately pine casting long thin shadows, its branches stiff, its needles sharp, its sturdy trunk tapering to a point that seems to pierce the sky. Perhaps a hardy oak with ancient twisted arms, or an apple-tree heavy with fruit or blossom. Ah! an apple tree. I do hope someone will paint an apple tree. I want to smell the blossom; taste the apples. I want to hear the wind whispering in the leaves; I want to feel the rough bark, the smooth apples, the soft blossoms. Or perhaps you will paint me the tree of your dreams, in some tropical jungle, entwined with sticky creepers and hissing snakes. Or a palm tree on a desert island, its feet touching white sand, its leaves reaching out to the bright blue sea, shading it from the hot yellow sun.

I cannot wait to get started. Sit with pencil poised, waiting for paper.

'Ah no. No no no no no my little ones. No pencils. Trees are not edged with black lead. Trees are edged with light. Trees grow from the ground, free and alive. Paintings grow upon the page, free and alive.'

Oh golly. No pencil. No 'clever Anne Gillies so good at drawing'. We all begin as equals growing trees upon a page. Nervously I dab and paint over, trying to guess what will please her. My tree will not grow. She flits about, encouraging, suggesting. No 'this is exactly what I'd expect of the likes of you Joe Wright'. No 'I'm looking forward to seeing what Anne Gillies has done'. I curl my arm protectively round my picture to stop her looking. She smiles and passes on. Now make sure your names are on them my darlings. I'll be back next week and we shall all talk about our trees before beginning on another painting.

I lie awake every night for a week re-creating my hated tree in my mind, hoping vainly that Miss Hope will give them out during the week so that I can try and save its miserable face before the Art teacher comes back. On the night before the Art lesson I hit upon a desperate plan. She will give out the water, the paints, the pictures. I will turn with interest to admire Katy Troup's tree and knock my water all over my painting. 'Such a pity, Mrs Stewart,' Miss Hope will murmur behind her hand. 'Anne Gillies is our most promising artist.'

But Mrs Stewart arrives with our paintings in her arms. Holds up each one in front of the class. Now whose is this fierce tree? This is a tree in darkest Africa, I think. See how the big leaves hang down. What lurks there? A snake perhaps, or a black panther waiting to pounce? And here — oh here is a happy tree. A tree in a bright sunny garden, I think, where flowers love to grow and children love to play. Am I right? Whose tree is it? She finds something cheery to say about each one. She likes them all. One of them is mine. I don't recognise it. She reads out my name and I go out to collect it wonderingly. It's not like I remember it at all. It's not that bad really. I begin the next painting free and alive. But Mrs Stewart never comes again and we go back to our sharp pencils and our careful chalks.

Comes the Qualy and my brother is right. No rods poles or perches. The problems are easy. Good fun. Logical.

I write a composition. A snowy day. Plenty of opportunity for adjectives and adverbs, crystal snow-flakes lowering sky hung tenuously around a story of a lamb lost in a snow-drift.

I am to be in the A-class. So are most of the others in my class. The B's next door scattered between B and F.

'You are an old silly. You never expected not to, did you?'

I suppose not. Not really.

I try to console Anne, my friend, who can turn heels and sew from patterns and bake from recipes and work out in her head how much change we should get from ten bob. I try to console myself. Tell her it won't make any difference to our friendship what class she's in. Tell myself it won't. But it clouds our summer. As if we already knew that after these last few weeks together our paths would diverge further until at last I would hardly know her.

Oh aye, it's a great thing, the Scottish Education System.

TEN

The house and I are growing up together. In fits and starts.

Long fallow periods when nothing happens, then something triggers off a period of such intense activity that you begin to believe this time we'll both be finished, the house and me. But it never quite works: the impetus is never maintained, and we both sink back, adapting to our piecemeal alterations. Some of the alterations are obvious, superficial, some are inner — more radical.

A visitor from my mother's past gets the house whitewashed and roses round the front door; the Elsan brought into the cupboard under the stairs and the grass in the middle of the road levelled down at last.

A pigtail pulled once too often, and the imminence of the 7A Class Prize at the end-of-term presentation in the Playhouse, propel me into the hairdresser's in High Street. First time I've been inside. Veined black and green marble mingling with chrome and plastic, with fishy-smelling pink bakelite and peroxide, perm lotion and floral nylon.

'We would like a proper grown-up hair-style for a big grown-up girl please,' says my mother, who hasn't been at the hairdresser's since Uncle Donald's wedding.

I go into a cubicle and yellow swathes fall on lino. Smell of rotten eggs, smart of chemicals, screw of paper, grip of curlers, stifle of hairdrier.

'My bahoochie's getting sore, Mummy.'

Shhh everyone can hear you, she writes on an envelope, giggling. That's funny. I can't hear myself. Don't shout, she mouths desperately.

I sit very still. You really have to suffer if you want to turn into a swan. It's only afterwards we discover how you turn the heat down with a knob.

'Dear, dear, that's a nasty blister on your neck. Why didn't you tell your mum it was too hot?'

But I have not turned into a swan. I am not grown-up. I am not even me. Above new grey-flannel suit (ordered from J. D. Williams for the prize-giving) pokes tiny head, eye-brows pulled up in shock of tight curls. Luckily the perm doesn't take long to fall out. Then I return to my old self with a new straggle of ragged hair falling across my left eye: combing it back with fingers of right hand swells list of Nervous Habits.

Poison barbs from Granny, sighs from Mother and long-awaited planning permission all help to empty the byre, floor over its concrete runnels, plaster-board over its cobwebbed beams, partition it into kitchen, bathroom, corridor. Then the house yawns lazily and fills up the unplumbed stainless steel sink with egg-boxes, the unwired linen-cupboard with weed-killer, the waiting bathroom with zinc tubs and dirty washing. After storms, eels still come down the one working tap, and the tin box on top of the Valor stove still burns the bottom of my mother's toad-in-the-hole long before the batter has set.

I am learning not to Over-react when my brother teases me. His body is growing too hard to kick or bite, so I tickle instead.

Cootchy cootchy tickle tickle, he collapses on the grass. I avoid his flailing knees, trying to get a leg across his stomach.

'Stop that at once Anne. Get up immediately and pull your skirt down. You're getting far too old for that sort of silly horse-play.'

I run into the house, stung by my Granny's voice: he's two years older than me — why is it me that's getting into trouble? That night my mother says to my father: 'It's time Anne had a room of her own.' Lying in bed I mentally explore the house, sceptical. Our room, Granny's room, my parents' room, the living-room (which we still call the kitchen), the kitchen (which we still call the byre). Will they build me a tower like Rapunzel's or a leafy bower like Aucassin built for Nicolette? Will they let me sleep, like Heidi, in the hay-loft, or are my dreams true that tell of other rooms hidden away through cupboards or behind wainscots, waiting to be re-discovered and inhabited? In the morning I go round the back of the house to check the outside walls again: no sign of hidden extensions. I haven't done that for ages.

The following Sunday my mother empties away the rubbish from the upstairs landing — outgrown toys and clothes, mildewed memories — and my father builds a hardboard partition across the top of the stairs parallel to the bannister. There's just room to get by and into my brother's room. Tucked in under the sloping ceiling there is just room for a small bed and a chest, a shelf for water-jug and books, a rag rug for me to squat beside the bed. Daddy will make you a door when he has time, meanwhile we will hang up a nice curtain. It's still there I think — Miss Haversham curtain, cream and shiny with red poppies and blue corn-flowers in the boarded-up house.

J. D. Williams sent a pink nylon eiderdown — it lay clean as marshmallows on top of grey army blankets.

My room. A most precious room.

Even though plaster sometimes falls in a musty pile, heavy on your sleepy legs, and water drips, staining the pink marshmallow — rain and melting ice and condensation and more rain.

Even though I can't lock my brother out when he comes reiving my treasures, or stop the spiders from spinning their way across from the skylight to tickle my blind face in the night.

Even though I have to keep my elbows in, my head tucked down, while I sit on the bed to read or draw, and once I knocked my lamp down into the bed-clothes. I crept backwards up the bed and crouched on the pillow, hypnotised, as oil snaked across the cover — blazing between me and the narrow curtained doorway. 'Daddy, daddy,' I whispered softly, desperately trying not to startle the raging beast further: what, then, brought my father running up the stairs to beat it out before it could consume me?

In my room I read and wrote and dreamed and drew and thought and read again. Began each year with a secret diary and brave new resolutions which I never kept up past January. Copper-plate platitudes. What Katy did.

Mind's diary more vivid, more — secret.

Today a gang of us were playing down by the ice-works. Charlotte climbed up on top of a shed. I saw her pants. White as snow and soaked with blood.

Today we went to Stirling to do some shopping. On the way home the train was nearly empty. The ticket-collector told my mother he'd take the weans off her hands and show us the front of the train. He bought my brother a ginger-beer in the buffet-car:

'Now you sit there, son, we'll be back in a minute.'

See if you stand up on this seat there's this wee hole and you can look through it and see the engine. Nice wee navy-blue man with silver buttons, helping me up and holding me tight so's I won't fall. And slipping his hands round the insides of my legs and putting his finger into my private-place. I daren't move or it will be even sorer. Then he is sniffing his finger, and helping me to get down, because my legs have gone all wobbly with fear and pain and disgrace. He wants to shake hands with me.

'Come on, lassie, you're all right. Don't you worry. I'll not tell on you. I'll not tell your mammy on you. Come on, we'll shake hands on it. All right? Our secret. I'll not tell your mammy.'

'What a kind man. Did you see the front of the train?'

'U-huh,' I say irritably and bury my face in *The School Friend*. I'm sorry. I'm sorry. I didn't mean it.

Today the others flew up into Guides. I watched. When I became a man I put away childish things.

Today we decided to drown the kittens in the water-butt. We were only trying to help. My father should have done it ages ago and their eyes'll be open soon.

We hold them by the scruff, firmly but gently, under the water — mourning but sensible: some things have to be done. 'Life is made of joy and woe and when this you truly know then through life you'll safely go.' Willie Blake.

But the kittens will not die. They swim and swim with tiny webbed paws, struggling on and on. We are humbled by their obstinate life-force, panic as we reach the point of no return. I am crying. I never thought.

Don't be stupid. You can't take it out now — you'll only prolong its agony. Oh God forgive us, please. 'I'm truly sorry man's dominion has broken Nature's social union, and justifies that ill opinion that makes thee startle at me, thy poor earth-born companion and fellow mortal.' Robert Burns.

Pinky calmly goes off to get pregnant again. 'I think I could turn and live with animals, they are so placid and self-contained.' Walt Whitman.

Today a boy from Miller Road followed me all the way home. He said he wanted one of our kittens to buy. I take him across to the hedge where they're playing, and while I am trying to catch one of them he comes up behind me and rubs his slimy thingie along my bare leg. What's the matter with you? You like it, don't you? Come on, don't kid on you don't like it. You'd better not tell your dad or I'll tell him about you. Oh God, what have I done now?

Today Maureen Ferguson spoilt my autograph album.

When Anne was wee it was toys toys toys
But now that she's older it's boys boys boys.

Oh come on darling, it's meant to be a joke. I'm sure she didn't mean any harm by it.
I think it stinks.

Today I started *Jane Eyre*. Can't wait for tea to be over. Read the Cerebos salt tin and the Robertson's jam jar to make the time pass more quickly.

Today we got sex education in school. We had heard Miss Hope always did it on a Friday afternoon, just before the end of Primary Seven. Girls one week, boys the next: 'Take the football, boys, and line up by the door.

You will play nicely for one quarter of an hour. I shall be watching from the window. Now, take up your knitting, girls.'

Positioning her stool near the window she hoists herself up and folds her hands. Sunshine haloes her hair, white as swans' down; her plump pekingese jowls glow with rectitude; her lips pursed away years ago, with her hopes of matrimony. What can she tell us about sex, eh?

In a few weeks' time you will leave the Primary School forever, girls. You are growing up fast, and there are certain things you must understand as you stand upon the threshold of womanhood. In the years to come you will no doubt wish to develop friendships with boys — friendships which may develop into attachments of a more permanent nature — marriage, a family of your own. I need hardly impress upon you the importance of marriage, of the lasting benefits which it brings both to yourselves and to the community as a whole. For the Christian, marriage is a commitment for life. Girls who forget this golden rule bring shame not only upon themselves but upon the parents and teachers who have done their best to bring them up with proper Christian values.

Here in the safe haven of the Primary School you have been protected. But now you are going out into a wider world. From now on there is no knowing whom you may come up against. I trust, therefore, that you will carry this little talk with you always as you make your way through life. It is imperative that you choose your friends carefully from among boys whom you trust and respect, who will trust and respect you, to whom you would be proud to make such a commitment.

Girls, there are two kinds of boy in this world. There is the Protestant, and there is the Catholic. I hope you will choose wisely. That is all girls. You may resume your knitting.

Today the boys were pretending not to be scared about the ducking everyone says they'll get in the boys' toilets when we go up into the Secondary. I'm glad I'm not a boy — for once.

Today is the first day of the summer holidays. Hector comes to take my brother and me out in his sail-boat.

I have looked forward to this for so long, but now I can't enjoy it, however much I try. The sun shines, painting the world in sharp picture-postcard colours. Hector is like a wee boy, showing off. I lie, eyes closed, one arm trailing in the water, half-listening as he and my brother laugh and talk and fish together.

I feel like Wendy in Never-never Land.

I long to get home to Mr Rochester.

BRIDGE: GLASGOW, 1989

I was scared to read all that through again. It seems so long since I wrote it. So much has happened in the meantime. So many changes. I'm quite a different person now.

I think.

Well, I must be, mustn't I? Passed my driving test, got a Ph.D., a mortgage . . . Seen the kids grow into people, my father die, my marriage break up . . . Got a proper job, resigned from the proper job . . .

Not that they didn't warn me. You're far too young to write an autobiography. Floruit circa Sandy the Seal and the Satchel Club. You'll go on developing and be stuck with something wholly embarrassing or irrelevant.

Anyway, they whispered, why on earth are you writing it at all? Not being a philosopher or a mystic, a survivor of historical upheaval or a victim of personal trauma. Haven't achieved anything very startling in adulthood — the Scottish climate's not conducive at the best of times. Well, I mumbled, I thought maybe I was representing the woman's point of view. Och that's old hat nowadays. Women are people now, or hadn't you noticed? Well, the child's point of view, then: I did try to recapture the child's vision as it tunnelled along pragmatically underneath the adult surface; tried to avoid exposition along some subsequently learned set of parameters. Yeah yeah, they smiled, it has been tried before you know, Anne. So then I pointed out how instructive I'd found the writing — cathartic to say the least. Very nice, they whispered, very therapeutic, but does that make it literature? Best just to forget about the whole thing. Put it back under the bed till it acquires a patina of age; and/or you get wise enough to reappraise it objectively; and/or throw it out and get on with looking after the grand-weans. Thank goodness you never signed that man's contract, eh?

Abandoning it was a relief in lots of ways. There were definite drawbacks.

Not least the nightmares — lurid, unbearably elusive: raw, untamed essence of the memories impaled on the page. By day, groping consciously for an idea, I come across flat paragraphs of prose. Catch myself quoting my own half-truths in mid-conversation, recalling only those segments of myself that I have chosen to record. Will this pass in time, or have I already become a bore, like the holiday-maker who brings his edited memories home on video, to re-run on winter's nights?

And then the guilt.

Maternal guilt. Re-creating one's own childhood experience, re-discovering forgotten joys and needs, requires concentration, metaphorical flat stone on stomach. A most paradoxical excuse for depriving one's own children of the vestiges of their mother's attention.

Uxorial guilt. As above. More or less.

Filial guilt. My father slowly fading before my eyes, both of us still avoiding each other's fumbling, non-synchronous advances despite the growing urgency. He completely taken up with recording his own last testament in handwriting which grew smaller and smaller until, at the end, almost illegible without a magnifying glass: his own father's life-story — its lessons gradually fading with him?

'She'd better just not mention my father in her book at all, Mary,' he said. 'I won't have her writing some half-baked nonsense about him, compounding all the other rubbish that's ever been written, before I can finish sorting out all the papers and recording an authentic version of the times we lived through, his philosophy, his political vision.'

'But why doesn't he let me help him, then?' I asked her. 'This silly book of mine can be written any time. I've got the word-processor. He can just throw stuff at me every day. I'll type it up, return it to him next morning and he can make all the changes he wants. Doesn't he understand how simple it is with the computer?'

But no. That was very kind of you, but your brother's going to help him whenever he gets time to come through from Edinburgh.

And so, on holiday near Dumfries, home of his paternal ancestors, he made sure my brother knew exactly what was in his mind and where all the references could be found. And when he had got all that in order, on the day after he got back to Glasgow, he suddenly felt very strange.

'Quick, Mary, bring me a pencil and some paper. I want to write down how I'm feeling.'

But, head slumped forward on the writing pad, pencil falling from his fingers, he was not quite quick enough to record the final venture. Couldn't even wait for me to bid him godspeed, crashing gears through the pottering Sunday traffic, let alone to see me finish my thesis on Gaelic education three months later. Haunting me palpably throughout the writing-up, questioning my every premise from beyond the grave. Closer to me then than in life. I don't think he ever thought I'd finish it. Never understood why I'd started on it in the first place. Well, I only really understood it myself after he'd finally foiled me. Bleak graduation.

And then of course the marital break-up. No-one could be expected to write an autobiography at a time like that, could they? Dangerous, even if you had the energy, to look backwards through such a dark glass. My father, in his last weeks, shedding familiar pearls: has she considered all the relevant factors, Mary? Does she really appreciate the strain a job like that puts on a man, Mary — the effects a split will have on their finances, his career? Thank God I knew him well enough to be sure I had not killed him.

And then, of course, there was the Cause. High stakes to play for. The language, the culture, now at the most critical phase in its long history; winds of change fanning its embers after long centuries of stultification. For me, a Proper Job. Justifiable on philosophical, on altruistic grounds. Following in your grandfather's footsteps — almost. Not like that self-centred show-business, that singing to indiscriminate galleries. But, if I were to contribute my full bob's worth as a Gaelic educationist, not only a pledge of time and energy, but also an appropriate profile to establish and maintain. Not as easy as you might think.

'C'mon, Anne, now gies a song!' shouted the Strathclyde councillor after the Education Committee agreed to the principle of free transport for all Gaelic Unit pupils.

'I heard a really funny rumour about you the other day,' said the man from the Strathspey and Reel Society. 'Someone told me you were doing a Ph.D. You are doing a Ph.D.?! Good Lord! You fairly go up in my estimation!'

'We have had a well-researched paper on the Gaelic counting system from Anne Lorne Gillies,' said the man from Highland Regional Council. 'A most valuable paper — unless of course it was her brother that wrote it for her.'

'Your speech on the current situation in Gaelic education was the best thing I've heard from you yet,' said the vice-chairman of the language development agency. 'It finally proved that you can be objective, instead of relating everything to your own experience all the time.'

'Actually, I thought your speech was pretty tame,' said the Scandinavian speaker. 'Knowing you, I'd expected something with a lot more balls.'

'That Scandinavian woman was a complete waste of time,' said the man from the Gaelic College. 'I mean, what on earth was all that stuff about colonialism and women's rights to do with Gaelic?'

Passion? Creativity? Soul baring? Forget it. 'Tis a long and hard, straight and narrow furrow we plough in this line of business. In this careful wee country.

But then, one day, just when I most needed a steady income, a Cause to hang onto, I found myself parting company with the Job. You must be mad, whispers the worm in my gut. You have so much to offer, writes the Scandinavian woman. Oooh dear, says my loyal, worried mother, who has heard her mother's, her husband's songs fade in their time, but who still hears the tread of the Sheriff's Officer. But, feeling myself to be in some real but indefinable danger, I let go.

For a fortnight I sweated, staying close to the carpet, jobless, fatherless, husbandless, afraid to go out the door in case I floated away altogether. The Minister, passing by upon his way, offered the usual anchor. How we both wished I could grasp it. Go back to primary school teaching meantime, he counselled. Thanks, Rev, but I was hoping to find my voice again. And so I woke up one morning, becalmed, exposed, but free to turn the Calvinist ethic upon its head. Three hungry babes to feed solely by the singing of this (and other) songs. Anything considered. All guilt gone. Whoopee.

Pathetic isn't it, in retrospect? Never mind. God works in mysterious ways. March march Ettrick and Teviotdale. The Publisher surfaces serendipitously after two years' silence. Yeah, I'll see if I can pick it up where I left off. I've already read it through. Actually, I quite enjoyed it.

God will provide, I tell the children cheerfully. Mum's finally flipped, they tell each other cheerfully. They don't mind what songs I sing as long as their friends don't have to hear them. I encourage my son's ambition to go to Art College — he decides to try for Oxford. All's right with the world.

'Oooh, Mum,' says my perspicacious thirteen-year-old viper, peering over my shoulder on a Friday afternoon. 'You certainly wouldn't be able to publish your autobiography if you went in for that job!'

The Publisher crosses his fingers and sends another contract. Mind you, I still haven't signed it. The girls want rooms of their own. The mortgage rate shows no signs of going down. You're not getting any younger and there's a recession just around the corner.

Aye aye, now perhaps you're beginning to realise what it's like to be a man. A man with real responsibilities. You will learn the hard way, all you people.

Shh. Rest in peace.

ELEVEN

Right. I'm twelve years old and I live with my parents, my granny and my brother, who is fourteen.

Officially my hair is fair and my eyes are hazel, but in actual fact my eyes and my hair are the same colour. If they were coats or blankets you would call them khaki. My granny says my hair is like rats' tails. My mother says perhaps I should have another wee perm — it can't be good for me to be squinting like that all the time. My father says I should use bitter aloes on my hands — in his young days children did as their mothers told them, and how can I expect to grow into an attractive young woman if I never listen to a word of advice.

My worst habit, apart from biting my nails and sucking my thumb, is giggling. Double entendres for example. Lycid-arse, or when Auntie Bonnie said, 'I see you've got all the cocks up already.' (Hay-cocks, silly.) Just knowing it would be inappropriate to laugh is enough to set me off. This girl from Mull hasn't spoken to me since the day I laughed when she told me how Mr Thingie from Tobermory had come in from his work and sat down in his chair by the fire and died. And my mother wasn't too happy either the day I set her off when Uncle Paddy went wrong in the words of 'Bless this House': 'Bless these walls so firm and stout, trouble in and trouble out.' Dead right, Uncle Paddy. My mother's nostrils started trembling, and he still had all the high throbbing bits at the end to get through. We're all as bad as one another, my father says. He's twelve years older than my mother, which explains a lot, I think. Her giggling and gaggling like one of the children, him saying she never imposes proper discipline, my granny trying to protect her from him and us and the world at large. My father's always telling her she needs to stand up for herself and stop being a door-mat, but he'd get a fright if she did. So would I. I've only ever seen her angry about twice and it frightened the life out of me. But I think that if I was her I'd be angry a lot of the time. Especially with my big brother. And my father. And my granny. My mother just wants peace. She's always saying that if we can just get through this next crisis everything will be all right. I'm not going to be like her when I grow up.

I used to want to be a bus conductress when I grew up, then a physiotherapist. But now I have no idea whatsoever. Mostly I'd like to be pretty, though there's not much chance of that. My mother doesn't give two monkeys what she looks like. Other women look awful all week, with their hair in curlers under their head-scarves, and bare white legs in camel-coloured pom-pom slippers. But it makes them look all the better when they get done up on a Friday night — take out the rollers, put on the war-paint and the nylon stockings. My mother has had the same hair-style for thirty years (water waves were fashionable when she was young), has never possessed make-up or jewellery, and automatically buys the biggest size in everything because of her big bones. Everything she wears is brown, and she just takes whatever shoes will go on her feet. When you're younger you don't really look at your parents. Now I'm beginning to notice things. My mother's skin is yellowish and full of wee holes. She has singed bits in her hair, from re-lighting her cigarette dowps. It's very embarrassing when she leaves her Playtex off in summer and you can see her bottie squidging underneath her dirndl skirt, not to mention her tartan legs. She has enormous knees, while my father is forever pulling up his trousers to show off his shapely Gillies legs. He says we get all our bad habits from the Cathie side. That's his little joke. I'd better not tell you what the habits are.

Sometimes, when I catch sight of myself reflected in bus windows, I think I look like my father. When you can't see the superficial details, I mean, like you would in a proper mirror. High forehead and hollow eyes. Alas poor Yorick. Ha ha. Of course it would make me very proud to take after the Gillies side, but I can't honestly say my father is very pretty! I look at myself a lot, just to see how I'm coming along: in mirrors, in shop windows, the backs of spoons, the water-butt. Vanity vanity all is vanity. You could hardly accuse my mother of that. I expect that's what attracted my father to her in the first place, though you'd think he might lay off me a bit about my hands. If you look at yourself in the back of a spoon it gives you a very solemn expression like a weasel. Also a large nose and small ears, which is not a bad thing in my case. My mother sometimes puts bandages on my ears at night, if I've been particularly upset about them that day. In the morning they are flat for a moment or two, but then they crunch out again, which is quite excruciating. Not to mention discouraging.

My father is a few inches taller than my mother. One day Mrs Lawrie saw my father's shiny head bouncing along Dalintart Drive. 'Here comes your father,' she said to me. It turned out to be the negro-man you sometimes see in the town. Mrs Lawrie was terribly embarrassed but I think my father would have been flattered. I think he would consider it very worthy to be mistaken for a negro. Not that you could expect Mrs Lawrie to understand that. My father says his hair is bound to grow back in again if he keeps using the Pantene. It is my job to rub it into his head once a week and count all the hairs that are supposed to have grown in the interim period. Who's kidding who? It's quite funny considering how scathing he usually is about proprietary brands. Pink shampoo in wee metal sachets from Woolies, or my granny's Zoflora. Corrupting the economy and polluting the atmosphere. Carbolic soap, elbow grease, the starving millions in China and all that. Of course he's right — as usual. The Zoflora stinks the house out and the wee metal sachets won't melt and they blow about the yard when you empty the ash-can and if the cows swallow them they will choke and then where will we all be? Mind you, that doesn't stop you buying them, and trying out hair-rinses to see if they will make you beautiful.

My father uses his face flannel to scrub his head every morning in the sink in the byre, and my mother gives him a shampoo about once a month, pouring water over him with the aluminium jug. It is a terrible palaver of wailing and fussing. Almost as bad as when he cuts his toe-nails. My mother cuts his hair with wee silver nippers she keeps in a special velvet-lined box. Nip nip nip nip nip nip nip, they go, straight up the back and start again in rows like a hay-field. Mind my ears, he wails, in his wee boy voice that he always uses when anything bodily is happening to him. I got him a back-scratcher for his Christmas last year, but I might as well have saved my money. He'd rather have my mother doing it for him.

We've got the planning permission now for the bathroom. Did you know you're not allowed to build a bathroom next to a kitchen? You have to have at least two doors in between cooking and you-know-whatting. My father has put up the wooden frames for the doors, but he never seems to get round to doors. My mother strings grey army blankets up to keep out the draughts and to hide the muddle down by the back door. The preserved eggs and corn scoops and all that. We've got blue marbly linoleum on the byre floor now, with funny wee rugs here and there to catch the dust. They are made by my granny out of rags — you can say hullo to my old tartan skirt and my brother's short breeks and my father's sports jacket down there, before they get too dirty to distinguish. My father can't finish plaster-boarding the ceiling over till we can afford to get the electricity men in, so you can look right up into the rafters and see the dish-mop my brother chucked up there to annoy my granny. You should have seen my brother's face. It was a picture. A mixture of 'Oh help, what have I gone and done now?' and 'Oh hee hee look at that, what're you going to do now, eh?'

Occasionally (usually on a Saturday evening) my father decides to wash the dishes. This is another huge palaver. None of you people know how to wash dishes properly. Everything is set out in neat piles and the food scraped off neatly into the sink-tidy while the kettle is heating up. He talks all the time, explaining his strategy. Organisation, that's the secret: the least greasy things first, then the more greasy, then the most greasy. It's a wonder we haven't all died of food poisoning. He never puts the dishes away after he's finished. That's menial work.

At the moment we have the usual plethora of cats, a budgie called Jimmy and a collie called Sine (pronounced Sheena, which is Gaelic for Jean). My father loves the budgie. He's always whistling at it — 'The Campbells are coming o ho o ho' — and trying to get it to speak. It came down from the sky one day when my brother and I were out playing in the yard. It was the most unnatural-looking green and yellow colour when you saw it against the hill — a sort of divine mistake. 'Oh look,' I shouted, pointing in astonishment, and it came right down and landed on my finger. Nobody claimed it, so we had to go to the Wee Pstoffis for a cage and cuttle fish. Sometimes we win goldfish at the Shows, but they don't usually last. There is something most depressing about coming down in the morning to find that the goldfish has died in the night. We bury them in ant-egg boxes.

My cat's name is Pinky, because of her pink nose. I love her so much I could eat her. When I call her you can see her white bits streaking and bouncing over the green hummocks from wherever she's been away up the hill. She has lots of kittens every year. We don't keep many of them, but Howler, Wowler, Yowler, Fowler and Skite keep down the rats and mice in the barn. Skite is a most peculiar cat. He makes a horrible eldritch noise for a miaow and pees unashamedly without digging. When it's sunny he lies flat out on his back, turning the front half of himself around to survey the scene now and again, elbows on the ground like the Sphinx, while his back paws stay sticking straight up in the air.

My granny once had so many pekingeses that she had to call them Doh, Ray, Mi, Fah, Soh, Lah and Ti, and one of them hid in the oven and came out half-baked with its eye-brows all singed. Lucky for the dog it was meringues and not roast beef that day. My granny likes Yowler best of all the cats. Just to be perverse, you understand. Just to annoy me because Pinky is my cat. She says Yowler is no name for a cat, and she calls her Maggie, short for Magpie, because she's black and white. She tries to get Yowler to come into the house, but Pinky won't have any of it. Neither will my father. My father hates all cats. CATS! he yells as he comes in the door of an evening, and Pinky screeches away out between his legs and waits on the window-sill till he's had his tea. Mind you, something very queer has just happened. I haven't seen Pinky for a day or two, which is not all that unusual. Well, actually it's more like a week. I go out and call her every day, Pinky Pinky Pinky Pinky pusspuss-pusspuss, but so far she hasn't come back. Maybe she has kittens hidden somewhere. I wish she would come, though. Anyway, tonight Yowler suddenly came into the house for the first time. Without being invited. Drank the milk I'd put out for Pinky and sat herself down in the chair beside the fire. Just you wait till her mum comes back. Maggie indeed. Her name's Yowler. Stupid-looking cat. Pinky Pinky pusspuss. Where are you?

We got Sine from Hughie MacDonald when she was just a puppy. I will never ever forget that day. My mother had answered the phone about tea-time. 'Oh this is kind of you, Hughie,' she had said, 'but of course I shall have to ask Iain. Yes, we'll phone you later.' Then we had spent the entire evening waiting for my father to come home from his work, getting more and more excited about the thought of a puppy, more and more depressed thinking how he was sure not to let us have it. Then when he eventually came home he wanted his tea and he didn't want us all talking at once and he couldn't understand how important it was to phone right away in case Hughie went to bed early and gave the puppy to somebody else in the morning. And when he eventually went to phone Hughie he wouldn't tell us what he had decided. So we had to sit without breathing to hear what he would say, and when it sounded as if Hughie might have persuaded him to agree our faces were splitting across, and me and my brother and my mother were all hanging onto each other and trying not to make too much noise, while my granny grinned and clucked her false teeth and her knitting pins in the corner.

And when the puppy came I have never been so happy in all my life. She was the most beautiful wee thing I have ever seen. She could sit on your hand then, with her wee black nose snuffling up your sleeve, and on the first night she cried and cried loudly all alone down in the kitchen and I thought it would break my heart. I could hear my father humphing away in the bed and making my mother feel guilty about ever having asked him to let us have the puppy in the first place. I was getting really desperate about the poor wee thing, it being so sad and lonely without its mummy or its brothers and sisters, and so was my brother, but my parents just lay there and said we weren't to do anything or we would spoil her and never get any more peace at night. Then suddenly she stopped crying without any warning and we never heard any more from her. She must have gone off to sleep. There you are — you see: a bit of discipline. I told you she would soon learn. In the morning we found out why. While we were all upstairs wrestling with our consciences my granny got up quietly without any fuss and went through into the kitchen and took the puppy into her bed. What an old devil, eh?

Sine has silky black fur with white patches and a beautiful face like a seal and she lays her head on your knee and fixes her brown eyes on your face and pulls back her ears and sighs with love and devotion, which almost certainly means she likes the smell of what you happen to be eating at the time. My brother and I are training her to fetch a ball, to sit, to lie and to come to heel. When we play tennis in the yard we have taught her not to touch the ball, as she makes it all slaver-y. She lies flat along the ground, screaming with excitement down her nose and twitching her eyes from one side to the other as the ball goes back and forth over her head. But if the ball goes into the hedge among the nettles we send her in to get it out. She takes the opportunity to have a good chew of it before dropping it reluctantly at my brother's feet, and then when you hit it, the slavers stream off it for about five minutes. It's just getting dry again when one of us hits it into the hedge and the whole thing starts again.

My father is training her to fetch the cows, to leave the sheep alone, and to take chocolate drops politely from his trouser leg without snatching. My Uncle Paddy says we'll have her ruined, she shouldn't be allowed into the house at all if she's to be a working dog. My father says that when she dies he is going to have her stuffed. So much for him not wanting a puppy. And as for Uncle Paddy, Sine is so intelligent that she can already get the cows with a bit of help from my father, and she never looks at the sheep, and soon she'll be able to do it all by herself. She has had her first heat, which was terrible. She is very perjink about doing her wee-wees etc in front of anyone: at the best of times she goes and hides behind a clump of reeds and looks innocently round the edge of it as if to say, 'I'm just sniffing these flowers, I'll be with you in a minute.' So as you can imagine, on the first day of her heat she just went on and on walking and wouldn't do anything, so eventually I had to let her off the lead. And right that very moment along came a horrible looking dog from the Houses and I had to chase them for miles and I only just caught up with them in time and had to hit the dog with a stick to get him off her. You could see his nasty thin pink thing nearly tripping him up as he ran away. After that Sine just had to learn not to be so demure about her wee-wees.

It's a shame she can't have puppies, though. She's got this terrible habit now of pretending to have pups. If she finds a beetle, for example, she plays with it for hours, patting it with her paws and throwing it up in the air and poking it with her nose. When it gives up the ghost she gets really disappointed and pokes it to try and get it back to life. But the worst thing is when there are chicks or goslings. She loves them. If you let her get the chance she will steal one. You might think she was being blood-thirsty, like a fox, but she's not. She will carry the wee thing about for hours, looking very guilty and holding it very carefully in her big mouth with its wee feet sticking out the side; putting it down now and again to lick and nuzzle with her long nose. You can't just take it off her because she might crunch it accidentally in her desire not to relinquish it. But it always dies eventually anyway. You can tell how sad she is when it dies, and she doesn't eat it, just lies whining with it against her whiskers. You can actually see the fight going on inside her at times like that: behaving furtively because we've told her it's bad, but proud as punch because she's got a chicky (or a beetle, or a vole) of her very own. A bit like my big brother when he chucked the dish-mop up into the rafters. Not at all like a hunting dog. She is a very sentimental dog.

But this summer something awful happened. We went back for another holiday in Whitby. This time my mother took us down to Glasgow and we did the rest of the journey on our own. My mother found a nice respectable-looking compartment full of nice respectable-looking old fogeys, and asked them to keep an eye on us. It was terribly embarrassing. One of the fogeys was travelling with her grandson, who was about eight years old, and she took it upon herself to tell us about the dangers of looking out the window in trains. Why do adults have such a thing about looking out the window in trains, I ask you? I had this smashing book to read and I had no desire to go anywhere near the blinking window, even if you could get near it with the other two fat old fogeys, who had reserved window seats. But the old wifie went on and on and on in this terrible Glasgow accent about tunnels and headless bodies falling back into compartments and all that. The poor wee boy looked very embarrassed about it all, and the other two fogeys, who were much more genteel, buried their noses in the *Glasgow Herald*.

Anyway, to cut a long story short, the guard came round and said that luncheon was being served, and the fogeys at the window got up to go and have their dinner. 'Aha,' said the other old wifie, 'Ah'll get a seat at the windae noo,' and sat down in the window-lady's seat. I noticed that the wee boy was grinning to himself, but he never said anything. He waited for ages, about half an hour I would guess, and then he looked up:

'Hey Nana,' he said, with a beatific smile. 'You're si"in' on a tama'a.'

The wifie leapt up and sure enough there was the window-lady's tomato, half of it squashed into the seat and the other half of it stuck up the old wifie's bum. I laughed all the way to Whitby. That would be about six or seven hours. Every time I thought about it I started again. 'Hey Nana . . .'

We had a great time in Whitby. More on our own than the last time. You had to be very careful. Neil was winching, and you kept walking into rooms and finding them in clinches. My brother was determined to be outrageous. Just because we weren't at home I suppose. When we were going swimming he stuffed his towel down his tee-shirt to make himself look pregnant, and then we could laugh at all the silly wifies giggling as they passed, looking at the innocent children. And once, when we were at the market, he squatted down on the edge of the pavement and held out his hands going 'baksheesh, baksheesh'. I told him to stop it or I'd go away and leave him, which was a joke, because it was him that knew the way home. We took part in a sand castle-building competition, but neither of us won, and we went to see a beauty contest that anyone could try for, but nobody suggested I should try. And I made my mother a sun-dress on Auntie Jean's Singer, out of a pattern in the *Woman's Own*. I bet that's the best holiday present she's ever had, eh?

Anyway, why was I telling you all this? Oh aye. Sine.

We'd been down in Whitby a week when we got a letter from my mother. It started off with the usual stuff about having a nice time and helping Auntie Jean and then it told about how they had been in the hay-field and this boy came along with a shinty-stick and threw Sine's ball up in the air. Sine went to catch it, the boy went to hit it, and the boy hit Sine instead. Right in the mouth. Broke her jaw right through. It was just hanging off. My legs had gone so funny by this time that I had to sit down, and Auntie Jean ran away into the kitchen for sweet tea.

Well, anyway, this letter went on and on about how Sine went to the vet's, though he didn't see much hope for her survival, but he wound gut round and round her muzzle like a parcel just to see if it might knit. You couldn't really concentrate on any of it because all you wanted to know was *was Sine still alive or not?* But you had to keep reading, otherwise you'd never find out. Skimming over all this stuff about her lying as if dead in the vet's surgery, and him taking her home in his Land Rover to keep an eye on her overnight with a view to putting her down in the morning if necessary, and him and his wife being woken in the night with her up licking them in the bed. But it still not being very clear whether her jaw would knit permanently. And the boy who hit her with his *caman* being terribly sorry and not having meant it. Is she going to be all right, Auntie Jean? Can you make out? Oh dear dear, what a one your mummy is, keeping you in suspense like that. Yes, I think she is going to be all right, but you will have to finish nursing her when you get home. There there now, no need to cry, you old sillies. She's going to be fine.

Her jaw did knit, much to the amazement of the vet, and she went back to have the gut taken off. He didn't think she would need anaesthetic since it was not actually sewn, but it had got embedded in her gums between her teeth and removing it was very sore. Instead of giving her a jag he got two men to hold her down while he unwound the gut, and she got terribly upset. And ever since then, if you're not careful, she gets upset if you touch her round her jaw. Not every time, mind you, just sometimes. You can never predict. You can be hugging her and fussing round her ears and kissing her between the eyes and smoothing the velvet along the top of her nose as usual and suddenly you feel this deep rumble in her chest and you look down and see her top lip pulled up in this mean wee snarl with all her teeth showing. It is the most upsetting thing. It makes the backs of my hands go all tingly. Not that I think she would ever bite me, but I am so hurt that she should make faces like that at me when I love her so much and wouldn't hurt her for the whole world. It's much worse when someone you really love is nasty to you — have you noticed that? That's something you can hardly bear.

TWELVE

In secondary school the days are divided into white squares, all the same size and colour — as yet. Untried, unknown, unpredictable. In days to come forty minutes turns out to be as variable as people. Bilious with fear; blood-red with sarcasm; hodden grey with boredom. Mind-seducing as a kaleidoscope; short as holidays; colourful, day-dreaming, exciting, peaceful. Meanwhile teachers drill and hack their ways through a jungle of names, a camouflage of sexless striped ties and brand-new blazers. Summer still glistening on their cheeks, and us still trailing faint clouds of innocence, they wait and watch. Send us a sign oh Lord. Which of these hast Thou sent to visit their wilful ignorance on this Thy unworthy servant, to fill her days with insolence and Askit powders? I am lucky. They remember my name quickly. Ah yes, Willie Gillies's wee sister, such a clever boy; Mrs Gillies's daughter, my hip miraculously cured and does she still play, where does she find the time? Others are less fortunate. Dolina. Ah yes, and you're from Connel aren't you? No? Taynuilt? Well done Dolina from Taynuilt. Now you can show us how good the Taynuilt folk are at their long division. Hughena? You must be Duncanina's sister? Didn't your parents ever get lucky, eh? A girl's name is Lemon. Two m's? Huh. You'll be lucky. A boy comes from Och. Pardon? Och what? Och, *sir*. Och aye the noo. Sir has made a joke (again). We are allowed to laugh (again). A girl from Seil is like a ripe peach. No, a damson — rounded, blooming, downy, and bursting with rude health. One of the teachers cannot leave her alone. The Bemax Queen, he calls her. A boy has a speech impediment. 'Amo amas a man a mouse.' Class howls with derision. He smiles and smiles. Vaguely we hear about a terrible accident — house burned down, parents burned up. No. Not really. Are you sure? We are sorry then. But he is Mousey for life. Smiling amiably to make up for it all.

Most of the First Year pupils are new — the train ones, the digs ones, the hostel ones, some of them dumb and hollow-eyed with home-sickness. By comparison I am an old-stager, helping them to find their feet, a whirligig of assumed self-confidence. At four-ten (magic hour) they go their ways and I go mine, and the confidence drains with the setting sun.

Nightmares are set in that great school, that yawning time-table, the unfamiliar, ever-changing staff. Endless night-straying up and down stairs, along corridors cold as a morgue, outsize blazer rubbing neck, hot breath melting knees and stomach, walkontherightsinglefilenorunning-theregirl. The wrong jotter. The wrong paragraph. The wrong room. The wrong class. Lost. Fallen behind. Doomed. Detained. Disgraced. Belted. Och rubbish. They don't belt girls in secondary. Just boys. They only belt girls in primary.

The Gaelic class is tiny. Nobody I know from primary at all. Everyone else is away down the Modern Languages corridor doing French. They can go on and learn German if they want to later. Gaelic is different it seems. You can't go on and learn German after Gaelic. Gaelic is not a Modern Language it seems, even though a lot of the people in the Gaelic class actually speak it all the time at home. This makes me very nervous on the first day. I will be miles behind them. I won't be able to understand what's going on. But it turns out that the Gaelic teacher speaks to us in English all the time, and he teaches us all the grammar, which I can do no bother because it's quite like Latin. The Gaelic-speaking ones are mostly from Ardnamurchan and places like that, and most of them are not doing Latin, so they don't know what he's on about with his vocative and genitive and dative and all that. The teacher's always telling them they should be ashamed of themselves and look at how well Anne Gillies can do it without their native advantages. I expect I'll be first in Gaelic: all the brainy ones in the A-class take French.

The Geography teacher has been there so long her gown has turned green. And she calls the boys rogues. 'You rogue! you vagabond!' she screeches. You never know if she's angry or not. She screeches with rage, she screeches with pleasure, and she's hopeless at remembering names. One day she asked us what was the name of the highest mountain in Africa and Helen Lemmon said 'Helen Lemmon' out of sheer habit. It was a shame. I mean she's not *that* big. This day we had to draw an artesian well and the teacher was all over me, screeching. It was awful. '*What* a lovely drawing, Anne Gillies, a lovely artesian well — and isn't it pumping beoootifully!' I mean, it wasn't that good. What exactly's an artesian well for anyway, Mummy?

My father recoils from my gabbling, his authority usurped by classroom potentates. Look — I've drawn a picture of Galgacus at Mons Graupius. Mr Murray says the Scots were never beaten by the Romans. 'How many times have I told her that, Mary? She's just never listened.' But my father's not a *History Teacher*. He doesn't know what you have to do to pass your Highers. No time to regret — let alone understand — his irritation, I persevere with my Latin verbs, reap praise for my neatly drawn bunsen burners, learn my dates. The science teacher introduces expansion with a film about railway lines in winter; but the darkened science room is foetid with suppressed giggling and I can see this film's just a time-waster before we get on to the real science. Gillian Munro is crying. She has a sore stomach. 'I'll take her out to the toilet sir.'

First principles fade inexorably before the minutiae of staying first in the class. Food, clothing and shelter, my father sighs: but what has that got to do with jam and jute, I moan. Only in maths, where I'd have been better off without them, do my father's tenets rear up perversely to mock and flummox me. But what *are* logarithms, Willie? How do they make them? 'Why on earth can't you just use them, Anne? They save time, that's all.' Do they? I don't see why. I can't use something if I don't understand what it means in the first place. And what about this Pythagoras? I can prove the theorem OK but I can't see the point. What's it *for*? I can see why we do algebra — that's logical. You can apply that to other things. But what's this pi? Where did it come from? How can you use a formula if you can't prove it? I know you 'just have to learn them' but I can't. I can't just learn them off by heart without knowing what they mean. My father gives me a book called *Mathematician's Delight*. But I haven't got time to read it.

I win a thruppeny bit from the maths teacher for being 'the Second Most Popular Girl in 1A.' The Bemax Queen gets sixpence. I go along with that. I voted for her. But me? Popular? That's a laugh. Probably means the girl with second least enemies in 1A, I say to myself cynically on the road home.

It was a secret ballot — the votes counted openly. Put into piles on the front desk: Girls, Boys. Very Popular, Quite Popular, Not Popular. Demeaning, if you ask me, her doing that in front of everybody. And giving us money for it. You should get money for being *un*-popular. To cheer yourself up, like. But that would be just as bad. Imagine. You've come all the way from Morvern only to discover that you're unpopular. Or you go away home to Ballachulish thinking nobody likes you. Still, I'm glad some people think I'm OK. They say the maths teacher's husband won't go to church with her. I suppose that's the cross she has to bear.

In general I like the country people better than the town ones. But you can't really get to know them, disappearing away off on buses and trains, or down to the hostels poor souls. You hear stories about the hostels — especially the girls' hostel. If you say you're ill she gives you cascara before even taking your temperature. That way nobody's going to

Musical Sisters:

Granny and ...

Great Auntie Cissy

Grampop's orchestra,
Pier Pavilion, Llandudno

The Cathie family: Granny, Grampop, uncles Donald,
Ian, Colin, Baby Mother and ?

Grandfather Gillies   *Grandmother Gillies*

The Gillies family: Grandfather and Grandmother, Uncle Bob, Father, aunties Maureen, Jean and Sheila

North Third Reservoir: Father,
Auntie Cissy, Mother and Baby Anne

Anne and Granny, Townhead

Anne, Townhead, 1948

William and Anne, Townhead

Dalintart — the hayfield and the hill beyond   *Dalintart — the yard, the geese, the hens*

Oban Bay and the hills of Mull, from up our hill

Sìne

Grampop, William and Anne

Gillies family on a dyke

Snapped by the town's tourist photographer:

Granny, outside Chalmers, and ...

Anne, desperately seeking the wee blue salt sachet

Angus Lawrie and Father and midges

Mrs Lawrie in extreme old age

Granny's 80th birthday

Lockfield Gaelic Choir, with Hector and Mrs Innes

William and Anne, Whitby

School prizes

Anne, Mòd *silver medallist, 1958*

"The house and I are growing up together in fits and starts ..."

Aged 16, wearing Mother's tweed coat.

pretend to be ill for no reason. Imagine you've got the flu, or measles, or an abscess — and then she gives you the diarrhoea on top of everything else. And they're never allowed out — you hear them complaining about that. An hour up and down the street after school, once a week to the pictures, once a week to the church, and that's it. And if they misbehave they get gated altogether.

But to me the worst thing would be to be stuck with people around you all the time, whether you liked it (or them) or not. I try to imagine what that must be like. I heard about one hostel girl who stuffed hankies in her bra before the school dance and someone saw her and told everyone else. She was one of the most homesick ones, even before that happened, even though she came into the school in Fourth Year. Everybody felt sorry for her, right through the school. She cried for a whole term. That didn't stop them laughing at her about the hankies. Imagine not even getting peace to stuff hankies in your bra if you really wanted to. Not that that applies to me yet.

I like to choose what to do and when. I take hours over my homework, sometimes because it's difficult, more often because I'm enjoying doing it. If the Art teacher wants us to design a soft toy I can't wait to get started, and I'm going to make a brilliant soft toy even if it takes all night for a week, using all the wee bits and pieces in my mother's box. If the English teacher asks us to write about the seasons I'm going to find examples from poems out of all my father's books and write a fair copy illustrated with drawings. I expect you all think I do it to sook up to the teachers. Well, you can think what you like. But this is me sitting at the shoogly round table in our warm kitchen, my mother washing dishes in the byre, and my granny raking out the ashes under the fire, curtains drawn and the wind howling outside. And I'm adapting illuminated Celtic lettering out of my father's *Guth na Bliadhna*'s to go at the top of my composition; singeing my history essay carefully over the oil lamp to make it look like an ancient manuscript; poring over my book of Beardsley drawings to see all the different sorts of lines he uses before starting on the portrait of my mother (what is this Anne Gillies? are you trying to be smart? where is your shading?)

And this is me up the stairs now, and my mother's up with a drink and a wee tomato sandwich and hadn't you better be thinking of getting some sleep now, and I'm telling her that I can't possibly because I've got to memorise *Westminster Bridge* and I still haven't learned the second declension and if I don't get it before tomorrow Duffy'll murder me; and this is her hearing my poem and then going away and letting me get on with my Latin.

Imagine someone saying, 'That's it, girls, prep time is now over, pack away your books and line up for your cocoa.' Imagine trying to finish your work in the dorm with a whole lot of smart alecs peering over your pillow and saying, 'Poor wee Annie canny dae her homework' or 'teacher's pet' or 'swot'. Or being in digs with a family of five all sitting in the one living-room, and having to go down to the High School every evening to do an hour's prep in a room with no books and a fed-up teacher supervising and dying to get home to his wife. No wonder the Oban ones do well at school.

All in all First Year is quite comfortable in ways you don't really appreciate until you get further up the school. You're too young to be going down the street after school, giggling and gaggling on street corners as my father puts it. And First Years don't have a Christmas dance, they have a film-show in the canteen. So generally speaking nobody notices if you don't get pals, or a boyfriend, or a Valentine, or your two front teeth, or high heeled shoes, or a bust. Getting good marks is a perfectly good substitute in First Year, and you can do well and get first in the class and still be the Second Most Popular Girl. Even when you don't deserve to be First — like in Gym. (It must have been because of Scottish country dancing — first position, girls! first position! Anne Gillies has got it right — as usual! Show them the mark on your sock, Anne Gillies, where your heel has been. There now, you see. That is first position.)

Mairi Sheena Buchanan is Second in Gym — resigned but still perfectly friendly: 'Och Anne, I wish I could have beaten you in Gym. I could put up with you beating me in Art, but I really wanted to be First in Gym.' I agree whole-heartedly. Mairi Sheena the double-jointed — the lithe, supple, fast, graceful, sprint-starting, long-jumping, hand-standing, crab-crawling, horse-vaulting, spear-hurling, goal-scoring, eager, fearless, peerless warrior. Anne, the stookie, the craven, cowardly, skinny bunny-jumper, hiding behind the ample navy knickers of Anne Lees in time of hand-standing, knee-trembling in time of leap-frogging, pleading asthma in time of winter hockey-playing and summer field-lapping.

It was in Second Year the trouble started. Getting really bad by Third Year. It's hard to explain. People suddenly started getting stupid. Girls, I mean. Not all of them, but enough to be really irritating. They seem to do everything for an audience. Look at me, they seem to say. They talk to you, humouring you, pretending to be interested in what you say. But all the time they are looking over your shoulder to see who's watching them. Boys, I mean. One girl keeps pretending to scratch her back so she can stick her chest out and look down her blouse at the front. She told us she was dancing with her father in their living-room the other night and

singing 'Don't you rock me daddy oh.' Wasn't it funny, she says. Was it?
The boys that have repeated down from last year pull out the girls' bras
from behind. Ping. Gerroff. Ah'll get you Harry Dunn. Giggle giggle
wriggle.

One day I tell one of them that I've got a big brother. A really old one
— twenty-two, in the Navy. I make him out a mixture of Laddie (out of
my favourite book) and Uncle Colin (in New Zealand). All right so what's
his name? His name's Lan (after the son of one of my mother's Gaelic-
speaking patients). It goes round the class like a heather fire. They don't
know whether to believe me or not, but they look at me with new interest.

Normally I just get on with things. After all there are still plenty of nice
girls — especially the ones from down Easdale way. Most of them have
got bras too. But they don't make a song and dance about it.

Every Sunday I get hysterical. That's what they call it anyway. First of
all something makes me laugh and laugh and then it turns into I'm crying
and crying. For no good reason at all. I start telling my mother that
nobody likes me and I have no friends and nobody talks to me and even if
they did I wouldn't know what to say to them and I don't want to be
friends with them anyway they're so stupid and I just want to die and I
certainly never want to go back to that stupid school. It worries her I
know, and she has all her washing to do and the cows to milk and
granny's not been well and the hens are full of fleas, but I can't help it.
And it's not really true, what I'm saying, anyway. Yes it is. No it isn't. I
don't know. Did you ever feel like that, Mummy? I don't think she did,
whatever she says. My mother went to an all-girls school in London run
by two eccentric old ladies. The history teacher looked like Attila the
Hun. She was standing there describing the Huns — long faces like a
horse, with big high foreheads — and the whole class was in kinks
laughing because she was describing herself. That makes me laugh for a
minute or two, and then I start crying again. There must be something
far wrong with me. No there isn't. Yes there is. I don't know. But at least
my mother's sympathetic. My poor father can't make head nor tail of it
all.

I don't want to go to school tomorrow. Please can I stay off. Can you
not write me a note to say I'm not well. Friday nights are wonderful. The
whole weekend stretches ahead. Saturday is long and busy and bustling
and biking. But Sunday morning comes with the bitter taste of tomorrow
on it. The homework I used to love lies like a heavy stone on my brain. I
leave it longer and longer. End up in a panic at ten o'clock on Sunday
night. If you'd just get it out of the way on Friday evening, darling, you'd
be able to enjoy the rest of the weekend. No I wouldn't, I sob, Sunday is

horrible anyway. You might as well have homework to do as well. I can't
sleep on Sunday nights. My mind churns round and round. On Monday
morning I drag myself back to school. It's never as bad as I thought it
would be. There you are, darling, didn't I tell you. Now what were you
worrying about.

People I hardly know say, 'Don't worry it may never happen,' as they
pass by me in the street. I wish they'd mind their own business.

The science teacher can't keep order in class. On his cupboards are
musical instruments he has made — to illustrate the laws of physics sez
he. He organises school concerts, arranging baroque music for recorders
making me play all the silly bits: percussion on home-made leather tabors,
bird-calls on sopranino recorder, Mozart arranged for tuned beer glasses,
Vivaldi on miniature pipe-organ with herring box frame. Count a
hundred and six bars and go ping preferably without giggling. Still, at
least he didn't pick me to sing 'Oh Mother Mary hear my bean.' It's
bene. Bene doesn't scan. Mother Mary hear my bean indeed. That would
have finished me off. In class I am detached from him and his problems.
Watch dispassionately the two boys who sit making funny noises all the
time. The science teacher can't stand it any longer. 'G'rout!' he screams,
holding the door open. 'What us sir?' the boys ask, all injured innocence.
'G'rout!' the science teacher screams again. They stand outside the door,
making funny faces through the glass, freezing into patient caryatids
whenever the science teacher looks round. They fail to hear the Rector
padding round the balcony. 'What is this? You two again.' The Rector
brings the boys back into the class to apologise to the science teacher.
'Now I don't want to find you boys outside this door again do you hear?'
They hear. The science teacher hears. They sit for the rest of the double
period, heads down, punctuating the science lesson with a chorus of
'g'rout! g'rout!' — very accurate and just audible.

This year's register teacher belts the boys all the time — six thwacks,
half of which miss, snorting and shedding spittle like a good-humoured
war horse. They don't hold it against her. She often comes late for
registration, her enormous bosom heaving; holding up her powder
compact to mop her brow, comb her fine hair; frilly nylon blouse hanging
out of tailored tweed skirt. Tactfully we conspire to get her organised for
the rest of the working day, smiling affectionately as she dusts face-
powder and spittle from her desk with a neat paper hankie. She loves us.
Especially the boy in the front seat. Absent-mindedly she dusts him too,
as if he were an extension of her desk. She gets us to correct the first
year's geography exam papers for her — it'll be useful revision for us.

The Rector comes in without warning and forty exam papers disappear inside forty atlases. 'So what are you learning about today?' the Rector asks indulgently. 'Er — Russia, sir.' Forty atlases are hastily turned to the map of Russia. 'Ah, Russia, Russia. An aaawfully interesting country.' After he has gone the teacher takes out her paper hankie again, folds it into a neat pad, mops her brow and neck. She says nothing. Doesn't need to.

Someone in my brother's class had to leave school. She was pregnant.

I join the Scripture Union. There's a nice wee enamel badge and you get a book to record how much Bible you've read. I am going to do it every day. But I keep forgetting. And at the SU meeting I look out the window and wonder if my mother will let me get bobby socks. Doesn't she know that you have to get them. Everyone has them. I mean, it's not as if I'm wanting these fluorescent socks. Bobby socks are OK — you can wear them to school and the Rector doesn't mind and you know how funny he is about the girls' clothes. And hair. He made one girl go into the cloakroom and take down her French roll. Wasn't that odd. You'd have understood if he'd been asking her to put her hair up, not to take it down. I get bobby socks and they catch on the brambles at the side of the road and wee snaky-bits of white fluffy nylon poke out and spoil them. I stop going to Scripture Union at the end of term. For all the difference that made either.

My first school dance was when I was in Second Year. That was before things got really bad.

It's very hard to get anything to wear in Oban. The shops never have anything — except for the blue sparkly dress my mother saw in the Co window and my father went away down the street and bought it for her just like that. To everybody's amazement. Even though he couldn't afford it. Even though she didn't have anywhere to wear it. But that was the exception that proved the rule. That just left J. D. Williams catalogue — and you can't really be sure what they'll turn out like. So my mother and I go to PT's when we're down in Edinburgh at the Festival. We get a dark red nylon dress with a net underskirt and black squares of velvety stuff stuck on, a bit like the wall-paper in the One-O-One Club that my mother took me into by mistake in Glasgow on the way home, thinking we'd get a wee cup of tea before the Oban train. In the train I sit with the bag on my knee feeling the velvety stuff under the tissue paper.

Now wrap up well Anne. It's raining cats and dogs and you'll catch your death of cold.

I hope someone will dance with me.

They do. I hardly sit out at all. It's really good. Colin Campbell's band and we do the Pride of Erin and the Eightsome and Strip the Willow.

I hope Kenny will dance with me. But he doesn't. John dances a lot with me and takes me up for the supper dance. That means you have to parade across to the canteen with them and sit beside them all through the sausage rolls. Thank goodness somebody took me anyway. I don't think much of John. Not after the way he sang 'Tammy, Tammy, Tammy's in love' at the register class *cèilidh*. Puke. In the last dance he asks me if he can get me home. How on earth can he? He lives away down Easdale way and he'll need to go on the bus. But I say OK if you want. Just to see what he'll do. I go into the cloakroom to get ready. My cardigan and my school scarf and my raincoat and my wellies and my head-scarf and the rainmate over the top. Maybe he'll be away by now. But no. He's standing by the girls' entrance. He says he can't get me all the way home or the bus'll go without him. OK I say.

I think I'd better not make him climb the wall. He's not used to it, and anyway it's difficult to get a toe-hold in wellies. So we walk round the outside of the Games Ground. When we get in the dark he holds my hand. I try not to giggle. He keeps going in puddles with his good shoes. Well I know where they all are. Then suddenly he peers round the edge of my rainmate and kisses me splat on the mouth and then he's away back down to get his bus. I let out all the giggles that I've been storing up and run all the way home splashing the puddles and laughing into the wind. Oh ho. My brother rolls his eyes. Oh ho. Wait till next year.

Next year I'm more prepared. Have had a whole year to think about it. Now I'm praying I won't be left out at the supper dance. Now I hope to goodness someone will ask me to get me home. Just so's I can say they did on Monday.

My mother and I go to the Edinburgh Festival again. We see the ballet. It's *The Firebird*. I have never seen anything so beautiful in my whole life. All the *corps* are dressed in different colours of flame chiffon: red and orange and pink and burnt umber and ochre and all shades in between as if someone mixed them in a paintbox. Afterwards we go to PT's for tea and to buy my dress. But I want a dress like the ballet dancers. Och I doubt we'd get that in PT's. But couldn't you make one, Mummy. That's what I really want. Well I suppose I could try. We go to the material department and buy lots of different colours of chiffon — red and orange and gold and anything else vaguely like *The Firebird*. And some orange lining material to go under it. I mean you couldn't have all the boys seeing through you, could you.

Well my mother tries. She tries and tries, cawing the handle of her sewing machine, pinning and trying on and unpicking and starting again. But it doesn't work out. It's just an orange dress that hangs and stretches tight across my flat chest. Still I mustn't let her see I'm disappointed. Maybe it looks better on than I think. You can't really tell in that mirror.

The night before the dance I decide I want my hair like the *corps de ballet* too. To go with the dress. It's not long enough to put up in a tight scrunch like they had theirs. But I get my granny's setting lotion and saturate my hair in it. Then I brush it all back hard and stick kirbies in it all round to make it set back instead of flopping forwards over my face as usual. In the morning it's stiff as a board and almost black instead of my usual fair. But I go to school, hoping they will like it. There is a horrified silence. What have you done to your hair Anne Gillies? But generally they don't say too much. You can tell it must be really awful or they'd say something really rude and you might be able to believe they were just jealous. So when I get home I wash it all out and dry it quickly in front of the fire. My usual floppy straggle is back.

'I hope you're not thinking of going out tonight after washing your hair?' my granny says, sitting playing halma by herself on the kitchen table. 'You'll catch your death of cold.'

Don't be daft. Of course I'm going out. It's the school dance tonight. They're all mad, Mary. She'll catch her death. And you're not going in those shoes? Where are your wellingtons? Don't be ridiculous Anne. You can't go down the road in those shoes. Here, you'll wear these galoshes over them or not go at all. So I squelch off again, stuffing my rainmate into my pocket on the way, leaving the galoshes hidden under a bush behind the school wall. Well that hair-style's better than the last one anyway Anne Gillies. At least we don't have to look at your monkey ears all night now.

I sit out a lot. Nobody takes me up for the supper dance and the teachers have to pair off the ones that are left in the hall. Nobody asks to get me home. I might as well have worn my galoshes right onto the dance floor for all the difference it would have made. I don't want to go to school on Monday. Please don't make me go Mummy.

My brother says I shouldn't worry about the dance. That's easy for him to say. Boys can ask girls up to dance. The ones they fancy. We just have to sit and wait and hope we get asked by somebody half decent. Or, in my case, by anyone at all.

'Ah, but wait till next year,' he says. 'Things will be better. Lots of nice new boys will come from Islay and Jura and Tarbert and Ardrishaig and Coll and Tiree, and you'll be fighting them off. Just you wait. They'll all be sailing up our ditch in their gondolas to take you out to the pictures.'

Wasn't that nice of him. He can really make me laugh when he feels like it. He should know, anyway. He's after Seònaid Anderson. She's from Islay and has lovely Islay Gaelic and big dark eyes.

One day we get taken to the canteen to see a film about sex. You see a man and a woman and two children in silhouette like the cardboard dollies you can dress in paper clothes that they sometimes give away free in the *School Friend*. The children get taller and hair appears on their bodies, then he grows shoulders and she grows breasts and then her waist goes in and her hips come out. Then you see a picture of a womb emptying and filling up with blood every month like an egg-timer. A wee egg, and a wee sperm coming in the bottom to meet it, and then becoming a baby. It's very boring. I know all this already. My mother told me when she was on holiday from her work last summer, sitting on the bothy door-step. That's not what I want to know about. I want to know about love. You get more idea out of the *Woman's Own*. Some of the girls get *Red Letter* every Saturday down at the Station bookshop, but I'm not allowed to get rubbish like that. Peg's Paper, my father calls them. Filling your mind up with all that rubbish. I start reading Colette out of my father's book-case and Françoise Sagan out of the library. You get quite a good idea out of books like that too.

At the end of Third Year Mr Thomson says he thinks I should go to the Gaelic Camp in Tain. Me and Bibby are going. She's a native speaker, but I'm too scared to go to the Native Speakers' Camp. So she comes with me to the Learners' Camp. I'll have to get a bra, I tell my mother. Everybody will have one. Och you old silly, what do you need a bra for, she laughs. But she compromises. Finds an old one she got for Uncle Donald's wedding. She's never worn a bra before or since. It's faded pink lace with rusty hooks and it hangs off round me. I keep it on all the time at camp. Every morning I have to go to the toilet to pull it round from the back, then creep into the dorm to pull on my jumper, knees up in the bed.

The camp is a waste of time as far as Gaelic is concerned. All the other kids are from Glasgow and they can't even sing Gaelic songs right, far less speak it. Every morning they have classes which Bibby and I are allowed off. We help the grown-ups with whatever happens to be going on. In general we have quite good fun, going around on bus-trips and going into the town and playing games — except on Sunday. I thought one of the teachers was going to have a stroke when he looked out the window on the Sabbath morning and saw the boys playing fotball. He's quite nice actually. He said to me one night, 'Don't be sirring me, call me Alec.' It sounded very funny in his neat wee Gaelic voice with his neat wee pursed up lips, above his neat wee legs underneath his neat wee green kilt. In the evenings there are *cèilidhs* which are OK. Also it was very interesting to meet one of the teachers because she stole the Stone of Destiny. I think about that every time I look at her. It's funny to think that she's actually a Domestic Science teacher. At the end of the camp they give me a silver cup for the best at Gaelic: they explained to Bibby that she couldn't have it because she was really a native speaker. She didn't want the thing anyway. Neither did I. I wish we'd gone to the Native Speakers' Camp now, even if it had been a bit scarey at first.

Bibby stays with us for a night after we get back from Tain. I like Bibby. She's really nice. Then she goes away home to Morvern.

P.S. My father says Miss Matheson didn't steal the Stone of Destiny. You can't steal something if it already belongs to you. Can you?

THIRTEEN

Once upon a time everything was still. Once upon a time I sat like a stone thrown into the middle of the world, and regarded the ripples that radiated out from me. Once upon a time I worshipped the deep purple velvet of a pansy and fell, like Alice, into the yellow tunnel at its heart; translucent aconite, filigree of frost, mosaic of dew-drops on a withered leaf; mystery of holes and boles and moles and winding brown paths stained with sun-spots. Tickle of water boatmen and streak of stickle-back. Sitting still, the world danced gently around me and I tasted the air with my tongue's tip.

Och well.

Once upon a time I wormed my way reverently into every hole, anointed myself unthinkingly with pollen and snowflakes, mist and earth, spores and spawn. Shrink and creep, wraith-like, cat-like. Feel all around with your blue-bottle eyes. See with your cat's whiskers, your pink mole's snout. Shield your eyes from the buzzard's swoop. Spend whole days in a temple of icicles, heart singing to a continuo of bells, trying to imagine the moment when the water's humdrum movement congealed. Until thaw or boys with sticks destroyed the cathedral and made barley-sugar of its spires. Boy-like you break off the last icicle and suck its tasteless tip. Thrown spear-like, it makes the biddies jump and squawk.

What the hell.

Now my big feet crash through the bracken, flattening the speedwells and the woolly bear caterpillars, and my entire life seems to be spent going somewhere. School. Back. Town. Back. Piano lessons. Back. Dancing. Back. School. Back. Now the seasons are as follows: welly-season; laces-season; sandals-season; welly-season.

On Saturdays I pushed my bike to my piano lesson up on top of a high hill beside the Lighthouse houses, woolly chin-itch under navy raincoat, and then abseiled back down the other side, back-pedalling, no brakes, landing, in a heap of dust or damp leaves, against a gate at the back of Lochavullin. Katy Troup went to Someone Else in the Town — a Proper Piano Teacher, who made her do scales and arpeggios and put her through Associated Board Examinations, grades One to Heaven knows what, with Distinction of course. I went past Troup's house up the Pulpit Hill to the beardy science teacher, and we laughed and sighed and made tea on a bunsen burner and music in a room with many windows, two wee children with jammy faces playing with broken toys in the front garden and a solid woman with a pudding-basin haircut and brown brogues calling to them in an English accent out of her kitchen window. Every now and then we would both be hit by conscience, I plodding through correct fugues with wooden heart, wooden fingers; he dancing through them in a vain attempt to uncover in me some untapped seam of self-discipline. But I went on languishing over my piano after I got home, coaxing the last ounce of romance out of it — however much my granny told me the Hard Work it Takes to Become a Musician and what happens to little girls who Don't Practise Their Scales. Sometimes I opened our kitchen window in case some impresario might be passing and come dashing in to promise me a great musical future. Oh aye — in his helicopter, no doubt, on the way to Benbecula? Very good, Anne. At night I went on playing tunes in the bed — twitching my way round my body from left wee toe up left leg left hand left arm across face and down the other side. You can get four octaves if you can find enough muscles.

Saturday afternoons I gave up the cream horns with Granny and Mother in the Lorne Tea-room and went instead on the bus for dancing lessons — to Taynuilt. Fay and Una came on at Dunstaffnage; Hetty came on at Fearnan; Esme and her sister last on, and Dolina walked over from home. White socks in spider's web of black laces. We were good all right. We curved and stretched our crinkly leather feet like ballerinas, calf muscles bunching, backs straight and supple as withies, eye-line unswerving; into the centre quarter turn up and down quarter turn set to your partner half turn round fall back fall back. Petronella and Jenny's Bawbee and Jessie's Hornpipe and Hamilton House and Scottish Reform. Dougie's brother putting the snarl of bagpipes on his fiddle tunes and us gracing flabby Lowland figures with snappy Highland footwork. We did it so well Mrs Anderson gave up telling us not to. On the bus home we sat on our crisps to make them tiny and greasy; sometimes there was an extra blue salt sachet. We counted up the numbers on our bus tickets to see if we would get good luck. Hetty disappeared into the darkness, past the forestry sign, the bus waiting to light her round the corner and us squeezed into the back seat laughing and licking our fingers. After Dunstaffnage I was on my own again, but on good days I could get the lucky seat over the wheel, knees up to my chin, dancing pumps dangling between my legs, drawing pictures in the breath on the window. Rolling my bus-ticket between my fingers till it became furry and illegible. Hearing fiddle-tunes in the engine's noise. If I hurried I could make it home in time for *Scottish Dance Music* on the wireless, pumps on again, doing the dances with an imaginary Fay up and down the byre floor. Must she keep doing that, Mother? Can't she sit down and give us all peace? Soon we would begin performing in public. WRI socials, choir *cèilidhs*, hospital wards, Masonic dinners (wait outside the door till called, no peeping now girls). We were Much in Demand. Till Dougie's brother stopped playing and I had to thump out the tunes on the piano to keep the class going. But that was much later and Hetty and Una were away by then.

Saturday nights, when there was Something Good On, e.g. Danny Kaye, my mother would take us to the pictures. Not that there was Anything Good On very often:

Geordie, or *St Trinians,* or *King Solomon's Mines.* If it was something Really Good my father would come too. Like *The Barretts of Wimpole Street.* Or Charlie Chaplin. I couldn't see what was So Good about Charlie Chaplin — I mean we enjoyed him all right, but I wouldn't have thought he was Really Good enough to make my father put off his working clothes on a Saturday night. But there you are. And *The Barretts of Wimpole Street* wasn't that good either as it turned out. The poet Browning was played by the same actor that played Geordie, and every time he came on everybody roared with laughter and shouted, 'Take your porridge, Geordie laddie!' On the way home we would have a terrible job persuading my father to stop for chips. Engine oil. They cook them in. But he was always laughing and joking with Mr Faccenda or some town councillor that was in for chips. 'For the wife of course, Mr Gillies. The wife likes a wee chip sometimes before she turns in.' It made me happy to see him laughing and joking even if it was embarrassing. And then he wouldn't let us eat the chips till we got home. He would stride along, chest fully expanded, talking about the meaning behind the film. Charlie Chaplin as Everyman. The Underdog. Working-class symbol. The counter-attack against Capitalist Corruption. McCarthyism and rank Imperialist Propaganda. 'Pah! Iain's always got to be agin the government,' my granny says. Personally I like the way Charlie Chaplin can make you laugh and then cry. My father cried too in *Limelight*.

Once a year on a Saturday night we all go to my mother's Strathspey and Reel Society Concert. Even my father, if the cow's not calving or slates are off the roof. I look forward to this all year, jumping in my seat, slapping my thighs. People grin. Wee Anne always enjoys the concert. My brother sinks lower into his coat collar.

I know each face on the platform. Dougie, red and ginger and puffy; his brother, dark grey; the procurator fiscal, hollow eyes like a skull in the bright lights; Doctor Atholl in his kilt, wee round head bobbing and brown with hill-walking; Margaret at the piano, pretty nutbrown maiden in a low flowery dress like Doris Day; the scout-master, handsome and fair-haired and English upper-class looking; the butcher, red-veined and perky as a sparrow; Cally MacInnes, skinny black farmer with squint bushy eye-brows and gnarled hands flying; Duncan, curly-haired and snub-nosed and double-chinned with concentration — tall as the double bass he twirls round to make the lassies look at him; my mother, plucking her cello like a guitar and making faces in time with the music as usual; Charlie the conductor, radio officer on the boat that goes to Barra.

Taking their lead from him they are all strangely dignified — arms fiddling away, feet tapping in their shiny best black shoes, on their faces only the slightest hint of a self-conscious smile as if to say, 'Yes, we know you're all there and that you're enjoying yourselves. But modesty forbids, and anyway we've got to keep our eyes on the music.' When they go into jig-time and a huge hooch goes up all round the hall, they allow their smiles to widen momentarily. But Charlie's so gentle and serious in his black dinner suit, his baton whipping up and down so precisely, his manner of introducing each set so modest, that you can hardly believe the wild music that's coming out of them. And then in the last set he does what we've all been waiting for. What he always does. Turns round to face the audience and does this silly wee shuffly *pas de bas* which is so much at odds with himself, still so dignified, still so shy, that everyone loves him and goes wild and claps and roars and hoochs and my face feels as if it's going to burst across the middle.

I love the soloists too. Doctor Atholl always dances of course, though they say he's well over seventy; tanned knees wizened with age, leaping high off the platform and landing like a feather, holding his arms in a perfect curve, cradling his head towards one arm or the other, looking down his nose with eyebrows raised haughtily above his precise mouth. If you're near the platform you can hear the whisper of his pumps and the flop of his sporran and the snuffle of the breath coming down his nose. He never smiles even when everyone is clapping. He's a very superior person. He climbs Ben Cruachan every Sunday. My outrageous granny is dying to know what he wears under his kilt.

Then the elocutionist: stories and poems with droll accents and funny actions. The elocutionist wears a long dress and has a chiffon stole and long satin gloves, but can be a wee girl sticking out her tummy and hopping from foot to foot as if she needs the toilet; or a wee Hieland-man who went to an o-ra-to-ri-o by mistake; or another one called MacAllister who met the Queen. For her encore she recites a poem by Angus MacIntyre about people going to the *Mòd*. Kenny MacIntyre's in my class at school, granny. Oh yes dear, very nice.

Then the guest artistes. One year it's a vast Gaelic singer, legs like oak stobs, magnificent in maroon velvet and lace, with an enormous black leather belt with a silver buckle. Voice wide and maroon as his belly singing love-songs. Everyone joins in all the choruses. I make up the words, showing off to my granny. *Puirt a beul* — words crackling and spitting, voice cracking and yodelling, face humorous and sparkly. We go wild. Encore. Encore. He sings more and more, faster and faster. Has to sing another love-song, just to get off.

Another time two posh sisters in great long dresses with swishing skirts. They are very popular. One sits at the piano and the other stands up, one high and trillsome, one low and treacly. They say words like laddie and lassie in a very refined way, not with the sort of rolling l's we do. You can tell these ladies aren't from Oban all right. They're proper singers. Real ladies. The concert makes up for my mother going out to her practice every Thursday night. Just about.

Then one year my mother's Strathspey and Reel Society go away to take part in a play out in the open. We go to watch it, eaten by midges. A wee rowing boat coming in off the loch, Bonnie Prince Charlie I think it was, and then a trial on a wooden platform in the middle of a reedy field and they hanged James of the Glen. You can't hear all that well, and you don't like to ask too much because you ought to know it all already. I see a lady on a white horse up on the horizon. Is that part of it, Daddy? But no it seems that it's a person called Wendy Wood. My father knows her. She's a Scottish Nationalist. I can't work out whether he approves of her or not. Poor Wendy, he says, sighing. Whatever that means. I wish she would come down till I get a look at her, but I take my eye off her for a moment and when I look again she has disappeared. Anyway I don't like horses. Or midges. I'll be glad when this play finishes and we can get away home.

We have started going to church on Sundays.

One day I came round the edge of the stable and saw my granny standing in the yard with her hair all hanging down, holding onto the broomstick like a witch. I started laughing, but then I realised she was holding onto the broomstick to keep herself from falling over. When she tried to move, her legs staggered all ways as if they didn't belong to her. It gave me some fright. I had to run and catch her before she went down and broke her arm, and then I had to put my arms under her oxters from behind to push her back into the house. I hadn't realised how funny she smells till then and her flesh is all floppy. We can't assume that Granny will live forever. We have to think about where (how? whether?) she will be buried. We have started going to church on Sundays.

Not my father, of course. Not with his Ideas. God who made thee mighty make thee mightier yet. God grant that Marshall Wade may by Thy something-or-other aid victory bring; may He sedition hush and like a torrent rush rebellious Scots to crush, God save the king. You couldn't expect my father to sit in the same church as a God like that.

Not my granny. She's too wobbly on her pins now. Remember the time the bus screeched to a halt just as it was coming into Argyll Square and we all lurched forward and nearly fell out through the front windows? That was because my granny was wobbling across the road without looking, on her way to the Playhouse. The bus had to stand there in the middle of the road for about five minutes while she crawled across at a snail's pace and my mother had to get out and hold her arm. I didn't know where to put myself. My father says it's because she will wear her fur coat even in the warmest weather, but my mother says my granny has almost certainly had a slight stroke.

We can't go to the Parish Church. That would be far too embarrassing. Prodigal sons returning to the fold after all these years in the wilderness. Everybody knowing you, and sniggering if you went into the wrong pew or something. And all those *cèilidhs* and socials and whist-drives and things you'd have to take part in. And the minister coming to visit you without any warning. And the elders coming in with the Church Magazine. And us maybe having to go to Sunday School. Oh help my bob.

But there's a nice old minister who lives in Soroba Road, that my father knows from somewhere. He's a very interesting old man, with a great interest in history and Gaelic literature and all that. They say he puts stuff like that into his sermons instead of hell-fire and damnation. That would be better. He preaches in the wee church out in Kilmore. It's a lovely wee church. It would only take about half an hour to ride there on the bikes, and it's downhill all the way home. My mother and my brother and me become members of the church. We have to sit in the vestry with the elders and answer questions, and they shake our hands and then we can take Holy Communion.

It's not very long before they start asking me to play the organ on days when the organist can't come, and as soon as I've done it once the organist asks me to do it more and more. I think she's winching in the town. Mind you, I quite like playing the organ. It makes me feel important. And it means I don't have to stand beside my horrible brother during the service, trying not to laugh when he puts on all his funny voices in the hymns. There's one woman who has a voice like a fog-horn, and when she's there it sets my brother off. He sings very high and very loud and people look round, trying to work out whether it's me or my mother making that noise while the fog-horn lady takes it as a challenge and sings louder still. By the way, I hope you aren't imagining a big huge organ with hundreds of stops and pearly pipes up the wall and your feet darting about on a row of wooden slats while your hands dart about on the keys? If so you are going to be very disappointed. The organ is smaller than a piano and you have to keep pumping away with your feet all the time or the sound stops completely. Left right, left right, you pump, rather like riding your bike up a very steep hill. If you forget it's an organ and use the pedals like piano pedals it gives a horrible groan and grinds to a halt and the congregation stops singing and looks all worried.

It wasn't until the summer, when I had to go down to the primary school for extra practice for the *Mòd*, that I discovered that people actually go out and about in the evenings during the week. Not just older folk out for chips, the fag machine or the milk machine, but kids out playing peever and ball. Older ones out winching. Folk out on bikes and standing around the street corners doing nothing. I was most surprised. When on earth do they do their homework?

Normally the Gaelic choir meets in school from four-ten till half-past five. Then you go home. The *Mòd* is somewhere different every year. We can't afford to go every year, so we alternate with the primary school choir. We hold concerts now and again to raise money for the bus-fares and the hotel. The BBC came to record us at one of our concerts. It was rather embarrassing. The producer was being really stupid. First of all he had to be helped up on to the platform. And then he started telling the audience over and over again how proud he was of us because he had been at Oban High himself — and then he fell into the flower arrangement. I didn't think Oban High would be very proud of him that night, but nobody else seemed to mind.

I enjoy Gaelic choir. It gives you a chance to get to know girls from Fifth and Sixth years — you can have a good laugh with them. One of them tells me a story that reminds me of myself. One day when she was in Primary Six her pinky finger got stuck up in a peculiar position over the knuckle bone. She was sitting there in her desk pulling away at it but it wouldn't come down. She got really worried and put her hand up but Miss Hope was busy with the poor readers and never saw her. So she got up and started walking forward and her finger clicked down as she got right out in front of the teacher's desk. 'And what are you doing out of your seat, pray?' Please miss my finger was stuck up but now it's come down again. Thank you. Die of embarrassment. I laugh and laugh but my gut clenches sympathetically.

The Gaelic teacher wears a kilt all the time. They say that one day he went to an education meeting wearing a suit and this wifie came up to him in front of all the other teachers and said, 'Why, Mr Thomson, this is the first time I've seen you with your trousers on.' He's good fun at choir. He pops his eyes out like a frog if we get our Gaelic sounds wrong — like when the Tiree ones are singing in their own accents. The Music teacher agrees. Glottal stops ruin the vocal line. I think we should sing it the Argyll way, but I suppose they know best, so the Tiree ones have to pretend to be from Lewis and fall about laughing at themselves. Mr Thomson knows we call him Dòmhnall Beag but he doesn't mind. When we had to sing *Dòmhnall Beag an t-Siùcair* he kept making us go over and over it for devilment, pretending he didn't know why we were giggling. He's not like this in class.

They built a new music room with the walls completely covered in white panels like cribbage boards. Sound proofing so that the Domestic Science teachers next door can concentrate on their scones. It plays havoc with our voices. We sing until we run out of puff but nothing comes out. So workmen come and remove every second panel. Is that better? We think so. A bit. But when we sing at the *Mòd* our voices fly all round the hall and the judge says he's never heard a choir with such a wonderful tone. Thanks to the sound-proofing, the Music teacher laughs, cradling the trophy in her skinny oxter. We buy Irn Bru and Vimto and fill up the trophy and pass it round and round. *Slàinte mhath. Slàinte mhath.* We wish the Music teacher hadn't worn that stupid outfit for the concert: a long black skirt and her black V-neck cardie buttoned on backwards. You can see all her vertebrae at the back. All the other conductors wear tartan skirts and white blouses. That's what they're supposed to wear. I bet it's in the rules somewhere. Trust her to be different. My father knew her father. He was a famous Scottish writer. So my father says. It doesn't seem very likely. Still, she wrote 'Burns was not only a great poet but also contributed greatly to the preservation of native Scottish music' on her blackboard the first week she arrived, so maybe it's true right enough.

The Music teacher gave us an awful fright the day of our competition. The chairman announced 'Oban High School Gaelic Choir' but there was no sign of the skinny Music teacher. Where on earth could she be? The judges were getting fed-up. They'd already finished their tea and biscuits. 'We'll have to close this competition in five minutes' time,' the chairman said — in English of course: the only person you really hear talking Gaelic at the *Mòd* is the winner of the story competition. The audience all laugh at the *sgeulachd*, so they must understand Gaelic. Maybe if I heard more Gaelic I'd start to follow it better. Anyway, here we are about to be disqualified for lack of a conductor — after all that practice — when somebody says, 'Anne Gillies can conduct us. She can do it fine.' Oh mammy daddy. It is a far far better thing I do.

I go across and get the note from the piano. My stomach's turning, but imagine the headlines in the *Daily Record*. WEE ANNE'S A LIGHTNING CONDUCTOR. Or the *Express*: TEENAGER WINS THE DAY IN MOD MUDDLE COMPETITION. I'm just getting them to hum the note when the skinny Music teacher comes steaming in at the back of the hall. 'Oh dear, sorry I'm late.' I bet you were relieved, eh? Oh aye. Definitely. No I was not. I had to go back into my place and sing as if nothing had happened, with all the Govan ones sniggering and thinking I was a big show-off and all for nothing.

At the Glasgow *Mòd*, when I'm in Third Year, I become a Native Speaker. That's a bit funny if you think about it. You have to pass a test and then you're a Native Speaker for life. Even if you still don't get the jokes in the *sgeulachd* competition. Even if you stop learning and never speak another word — which of course I'm not going to do because I want my children to be Gaelic speakers from birth. They'll be Native Speakers all right. I'll need to try and find a Gaelic-speaking husband.

Now that I'm a Native Speaker I can enter for the Silver Medal. I have to sing in this St Andrews Hall at nine o'clock in the morning. From the stage it looks big enough to hold thousands of people, but there's nobody here that I can see except the competitors and the judges, the BBC folk and my mother, who has taken the day off work specially. I wonder how she got here so early. She must have sat up all night on the milk train, poor soul. She's sitting away back in the darkness where she thinks I won't notice her. She would die if she had to stand up here on this huge platform, that's for sure — but I don't mind. I'm actually looking forward to singing the prescribed song. It's about this girl whose boyfriend has gone away to fight for King George of England. That would be after the Battle of Culloden. Here she is left with nothing at all in the world, no cows or sheep or money, but she's not going to let anyone see she's upset.

The judges ring their wee bell and so I can start. I can see my mother taking huge great gulps every time I breathe in. But I don't let her put me off. I just think about the girl and how the people felt after the Battle of Culloden and I smile as if to say we won't let these Glasgow folk see we're down in the dumps. When the judges read out the marks it turns out I've won the Silver Medal. I know I shouldn't say it but I'm not really all that surprised — though of course I pretend to be suitably humble. Some days I couldn't win a button never mind a silver medal. That's when I start thinking about the people in the hall, or what I'm wearing, or whether I'll forget my words. But other times I just think about the people who made up the songs and what they must have been feeling. It's just something I can do now and again — and you can tell it makes the audience feel the same things too. Sometimes I can recreate this feeling when I'm not even singing. Just thinking about it. I remember one day I was walking across the school playground on the way back from my dinner and I suddenly got filled with the feeling of singing to an audience and them all smiling back at me. It was quite incongruous really, with the boys playing football all around me.

Anyway, winning this medal is one of the most satisfying things that's ever happened to me. Everyone feeling proud of me, and me knowing I'd done it as well as I could. Lots of other people in our group win prizes too. When the bus driver drives into Oban, it wouldn't surprise me if the pipe band had turned out to welcome us — which of course they haven't. But the best bit is still to come: seeing how proud my father is of me. He doesn't say much but you can tell he's fizzing inside. I bet he's thinking that my grandfather would have been over the moon if he'd been alive. Maybe next year they'll let me start wearing nylons like the big ones.

Probably the worst thing about the *Mòd* is having to sing duets with girls who can't hold the tune. The first one I get given has been competing for years. Her mother used to wind her hair up in rags the night before the *Mòd* and it came out like big fat sausages. We go up on the platform and she wanders about through all the different keys, smiling round at the audience, quite unaware that anything's wrong — while I follow her with my harmony: up and down, in and out and all round the houses. It's so funny that eventually I burst out laughing right in front of all the people. She stomps off the stage in a terrible rage. It was all your fault, she says afterwards, and I'm still laughing so much I don't even bother to argue.

Then they try me with someone who's got great Gaelic and a big bust, but she's just as bad as the first one as far as singing is concerned. She comes to our house to practise and flirts with my father. Not that he notices. My mother and I try for hours to get her to keep the tune, but finally I say I'm really sorry but it's no use. Once bitten. It's simply not going to work. She is really insulted. Then I get a girl in my brother's class who's got a terrific voice, only it's not much fun singing with her.

She's as prickly as gorse and she doesn't want anyone to think she cares about anything at all, which makes it hard to get inside the song. The music adjudicator gives us first prize and then says she would like to shake us both. I know exactly what she means. But then she doesn't know about this girl's mother dying of cancer.

Finally Sheena asks me if she can try a duet with me. I've never noticed her much before. I don't even know if she can sing. But we have a go, sitting on the wall in the playground. Everybody stops to listen. Oooh, that's really good. We're the same height, the same colouring, and our voices mix in to one another so that nobody ever knows who's singing which part. It's an awful shame you can't really get to know people like that who live away out of the town. Her brother plays the piano, her cousin has digs in Dalintart Drive, and that's just about all I know about her. I wish she had digs in Dalintart Drive.

FOURTEEN

We are very muted people — muted voices, muted clothes, muted lives, surrounded by muted landscape. A hundred and one different shades of mute. It would be nice to paint like Gauguin or Kandinsky. Perhaps in another life I could paint like that. But you can't go against your legacy, can you? '*Thèid dualchas an aghaidh nan creag*' as we say in Gaelic. Of course there are exceptions — sunset, and the Northern Lights, but they don't stay still long enough. Our most dramatic effects are monochrome: a row of dark cows strung out against the sky, with crows eating the warble-flies off their backs; the single tree on the horizon above our house, with the buzzard directly above it; the forestry like jagged teeth where the wind blew it apart last year; autumn — swallows on telephone wires and geese making a V-line far off; winter — jackdaws' nests in bare tree-tops.

Mind you, some pretty colourful things happen to us. Like the day my father was digging in the garden and I was standing in the yard and I heard him shouting. The cock had got through the hedge and was digging up the seedlings. You could hear him chasing the cock round the rhubarb and it squawking when he caught it. Next thing you know the cock comes sailing up into the air and right over the hedge — ten feet high at least. Down he comes into the yard, flapping and birling, feet pedalling, lands right on top of a hen and goes straight into action as if absolutely nothing had happened. The poor hen nearly died of the shock. She must have thought it was the Angel Gabriel.

The day starts at eight o'clock. I wake up first. I have my own internal clock. I have to set it the night before, saying 'eleven, twelve, one, two, three, four, five, six, seven, eight' — starting at whatever time it is and finishing with the time I want to waken, counting with my fingers all the time, and then I wake up no bother. The formula never fails. I can even set it for five in the morning if we're going somewhere on the train. And as soon as I waken I'm ready to get up. Not so my mother. She's always so late at night, her and my father waiting for my granny to go to bed so's they can talk and so on. Now that she doesn't have milking to do before going to her work she simply can't get out the bed before half-past eight in the morning.

My granny used to come to the bottom of the stair about eightish and say 'uppy uppy ducky ducky' to all and sundry. It used to annoy me so much that I'd not get up for at least another ten minutes on principle. Now it's me shouting through to try and get my mother on the go — in vain, let me tell you. She has alarm clocks all over the bedroom — ones that wind, battery ones, travel ones; ones that buzz, ones that ring, ones that ping, ones that whirr, ones that go on alarming you at intervals till the Judgment Day — or till you get up and stop them. My mother sets them all for slightly different times, and stands them on tin lids away across the room where she can't reach them. I lie there and listen to them all ringing and pinging and buzzing and whirring, and shout, 'Och for goodness sake, Mummy, wake up.' Sometimes my father throws shoes at them, but even that doesn't wake my mother for very long. Eventually I just get up and go downstairs to get away from the cacophony.

I always make my toast the night before, as you can't guarantee there will be any heat left in the fire by morning. It's just as well I like cold toast. But only if it's buttered when hot. I always take toast to school for my play-piece. By the way I use 'buttered' figuratively. In fact I don't like butter. Isn't that incongruous, surrounded by cows? Or cheese, if it comes to that. I like Summer County on my toast, or, better still, dripping — if there's any — with lots of salt. I usually meet my mother on her way downstairs in her brushed nylon goonie just as I'm leaving for school. She looks like Lady Macbeth till she's got her teeth in and her hair done.

We all come home for our dinner. That's our main meal. Mashed potatoes and something. Mince or grated cheese or corned beef or fish, with tinned peas on the side and bread to fill up with. Sometimes the potatoes are put through the strainer and made into soup with tinned tomatoes or leeks, and grated cheese on top. My father can eat four plates of that. I like it too, but it's disastrous if we have gym in the afternoon. It disappears and leaves you gibbering with hunger. I keep telling my mother, but she can never remember which days we have gym. Most of all I hate it when my mother makes rehash. That's her word for anything made out of yesterday's dinner with something added — a tin of mixed vegetables or spaghetti or beans, or Sunday's meat put through the mincer. For pudding they eat something milky (custard or rice or semolina) with stewed apples or rhubarb or tinned mandarins or guavas. I only like the mandarins but my granny loves her pudding. She used to make fiendish things like bread-and-butter pudding or treacle tart, but nowadays she can hardly even manage custard — sometimes it's all watery with lumps. Not that I care anyway. She can't understand why I won't eat milk puddings. Whatever's the matter with Mary Jane, she isn't sick and she hasn't a pain and there's lovely rice pudding for dinner again, whatever's the matter with Mary Jane. If she says that once more I'll murder her.

For tea it's usually whatever's in the cupboard. Eggs, spaghetti on toast, sardines, tomato fritters, mock crab, toasted cheese. I'm sure Real People don't have things like that. They have lamb chops and black pudding and tattie scones and dumpling. And plain bread. Personally I could live on tomatoes boiled in marge but There's Absolutely No Nutritional Value in That, Mary. Sometimes on a Sunday afternoon my mother makes pancakes on the girdle. I love that. It makes me feel like she's a Proper Mother. I always make wee totty pancakes round the edges, and we usually have them all eaten up before they can reach the table. You can use up the preserved egg in pancakes. You can't risk boiling them. My mother also makes jam — bramble and apple, strawberry, plum, goose-gog, marmalade, lemon curd. But I don't like jam very much. Or lemon curd. I'd rather eat the fruit. In the summer holidays I make the puddings. I use Mrs Kirk, or Mrs Beeton, but I usually have to adapt them to what's in the house, and/or cut the quantities by about half. By golly, they must have had good appetites in the olden days. The first time I made rhubarb pie I put a plastic egg-cup in the middle instead of china, and it melted. My brother nearly killed himself laughing. I was terribly upset. But then I remembered about this girl in the B-class who brought home her first soda scone from Domestic Science. She was really chuffed with it. Her mother was out when she got home, so she left it on the table and went out to play. When she got back in again her big brother had nailed it up on the kitchen wall.

On birthdays my mother bakes a cake and puts silver ballies on it. I don't like cake either, but you have to eat a bit to be polite. We have a family tradition of always getting a melon for our birthday, as he's September and I'm October and you can get them fairly cheaply. Of course you have to share them with the whole family, but the birthday person gets the thickest slice. It's not fair him having his birthday a month before me. It means that for a whole month he's three years older than me.

We have a new Tilly lamp on the table. I hate it. It hisses like a goose and it's terribly complicated to light — stinky meths in a wee pan that you clip onto the stalk to warm it up, and then you have to pump and pump to make the mantle light. It starts with a horrible whoomph that nearly takes your eyebrows off. My father loves the Tilly lamp. You'd think he had invented it. Like the fire. He makes this huge fuss about the fire. He being the only person that understands about draughts and flues and what not. On Saturday evenings he smoors it all over with dross and very carefully digs holes in it, straight down with the poker. Then you freeze for about half an hour before it begins to glow. I must admit it's really good once it gets going — particularly good for toast, or for heating the irons, and it lasts for hours and saves coal. If it was left to my granny she'd be poking and poking and stoking and stoking, and she would have the coal all done by about Tuesday and we'd have to starve of the cold till Friday. When she was staying with Uncle Ian she let the Aga go out and they never let her hear the end of it. We have to split the sticks for kindling when we come in from school. My brother can do it no bother, but I'm hopeless at it. I mostly keep my eyes shut because of the skelfs and the racket, often crashing the chopper down on the concrete or on my foot, and I cut them all squint, getting some so thick they won't light, others so thin they burn away in seconds.

People come to visit us. Their Scottish relations. One lady writes to say she's going to be up in Edinburgh and can Granny pop across for afternoon tea. She's the same one who is always writing to sympathise about how bitterly cold we must find it away up there in Scotland. She ends up taking a train from Edinburgh to Glasgow and a bus from Glasgow to Oban, and Granny has to take a taxi down the town in time to meet her in a tea-room in time to have a pot of tea and two cream horns in time to get the afternoon train back down south again. The bus is late in and they miss each other and she phones up to the house and we have to phone around to tell everyone we can think of to look out for my granny somewhere in the vicinity of George Street and my mother has to go back to her work all worried with no dinner. My father takes a very dim view of it all. But I suppose you'll learn the hard way all you people.

The summer after First Year my father's sister and her husband come up with their two children. They hire a caravan out at Ganavan Sands. It's called 'Bambi' and it has more things in it than in our whole house put together — a fridge and a cooker and beds that fold into a table where you can sit and play cribbage or pontoon. It's really great. We go out there almost every day and have terrific times with my cousins, swimming and exploring and being daft in the sand and rowing and fishing and playing deck tennis. The boy is a wee bit younger than me and the girl is a wee bit older than my brother. It all works out very well.

My wee cousin plays the descant recorder and can keep a burp going for fifteen seconds; my brother plays the treble recorder and can manage eighteen. They can both make farting noises with their oxters. My big cousin is a terrific violinist and when she smiles one side of her nose wrinkles. She is not the least bit stuck up. Also my uncle and aunt laugh most of the time and so we all laugh as well. Even my father. We all go out in the car to Ballachulish to look at the cottage where my father used to stay. Then we sit out in the car while they go into the King's House. They keep coming out with crisps and lemonade which they hand in through the window. They keep saying they won't be long, and they're sorry, but (a) we know they'll be ages yet because they're *bona fide* travellers and can stay all night if they want and (b) we don't mind anyway because we're having such a good laugh out here. On the way home we have to stop the car and my auntie stings her bottie on a nettle. We spend the rest of the time doing tongue twisters. My auntie is very serious about it all. Blue blood bad blood blue blig blag blob. And then she roars with laughter.

It was all such a success that the next year my father's other sister comes up with her husband and children. My uncle and aunt are really nice. They stay in the same caravan beside the same sands. The same everything, only this time the children are all younger than us. Which might have been all right only my wee cousin Laura doesn't look younger than me. She looks about four years older, and she teases my father and tosses her blonde hair. 'What a little madam,' he says, but I do believe he likes it. The snake. Laura wants to go about with my brother all the time. On their own I mean. She takes him away exploring and leaves me behind with the little ones. I don't know what you're so cross about Anne, everybody says. Laura's nearer his age after all. No she's not. You work it out. She's younger than me. Oh. Yes. I suppose she must be right enough. Och well, seeing they get on so well together . . .

Then there are all my mother's cousins. She has lots of cousins. Having had only brothers she is very fond of her lady cousins. Girls, she calls them. Ha ha. I like Bonnie and Nora. They don't argue with my father and they talk to me like a grown-up. By the way, have you ever noticed how many single women there are about that age? Sometimes I reckon my mother was quite lucky. I don't mean to be nasty. It was the War: all those men being killed at the one time.

Then there's Diarmid. He's an actor. Or is he a writer? Well, he's a bit of both really, dear. 'Never did an honest day's work in his life,' my granny says. 'Wrote a book and half the family never spoke to him again.' You can get the book in the library. My father and Diarmid talk and talk.

Diarmid talks such a lot of nonsense. Yes dear. But my father seems to enjoy it. One night the three of them went down the town together for a dram in a pub, and on the way back my father was talking and arguing and Putting Diarmid Straight on a Few Facts and Uncle Diarmid suddenly stopped stock still in the middle of the pavement in Combie Street and started bashing his fists against the corrugated iron fence and shouting, 'Help, help, let me out, let me out!' At the top of his voice at ten o'clock at night. I feel a bit like that with my father too sometimes. My mother thought it was very funny.

Then there's Granny's birthday. The whole Cathie clan wants to come up for her Eightieth. Uncle Ian the Harley Street specialist and Lord of the Manor and Local Magistrate and Master of Hounds and Underwriter at Lloyds' and corner-stone of the Good Food and Wine Society; with Auntie Joey and their four public school children and Uncle Donald the General Manager of the Midland Bank who knows Diana Dors and Margot Fonteyn. I mean, you might boast about things like that sometimes if you wanted to impress Ann Taylor, but you don't expect them to come up to Oban do you. It could be most embarrassing. You know how people in Oban talk. My Uncle Ian uses the Rolls to go up to town and keeps the Daimler for collecting eggs from the outlying farms. My Daddy was absolutely furious when he found he was in *Burke's Peerage* as the husband of the sister of. Oh mammy daddy. What if Uncle Ian brings the Rolls up here? We'll never live it down. I wonder if these people know my granny's had a Slight Stroke. It's not as easy as they think looking after somebody who's had a Slight Stroke. They don't have to live with her do they.

Well of course they can't stay here. That's quite obvious. It's all right, Iain, they don't expect to. They're going to stay in the Great Western Hotel. I've already booked them in. It was either that or the Esplanade. I wasn't sure which, but I think the Great Western's got the edge. I hope it'll be all right for them. We'll go down there and have a birthday dinner and then they can come up here and have afternoon tea and stay for a bit. It'll be very nice. Granny's eightieth birthday after all.

What a scouring of pans and catalogues, and a painting of doors, and a brushing of yards, and a killing of weeds and blue-bottles, and a mending of gates, and a mucking out of byres, and a trimming of wicks and hedges, and a clearing away of creosote and mole-wrenches and putty and weed-killer, and a washing of china and a polishing of lamps and coffee-spoons, and a scalding of tea-pots, and an airing of rooms, and a scratching up of dog-hairs, and a dusting of books and sherry glasses and cake-stands, and a disinfecting of pos, and a decanting of newspapers and spiders and milk-strainers, and a hiding of cigarette-burns and an emptying of Elsans, and a burning of rubbish, and a darning of pullovers, and an ironing of shirts, and a washing of hair and tray-cloths, and a de-hairing of upper lips, and a shaking of rugs and cushions, and an oiling of tea-trolleys, and a testing of hearing-aids, and a polishing of grates, and a buying of tinned asparagus and sugar-lumps and incontinence pads, and a soaking of dentures, and a hunting for primroses and flower-vases, and a baking of fruit-cake and cheese straws and girdle scones, and a cutting off of bread-crusts and ingrowing toe-nails then ensues. We leave everything ready under muslin cloths in the byre — I mean the kitchen — and embark for the Great Western. Us in a taxi. My father and brother walking. We can do with the fresh air.

We have never been in the Great Western before. Oh golly I hope nobody we know works here. They were on the phone last night to let us know they'd arrived safely. They had an accident with the Rolls on the way up — some bloody fool going too fast round a bend of course — and when they got there the water was barely hot enough for a decent bath. Food not wonderful but don't you worry. Uncle Ian will see to it that they pull the stops out for granny's birthday lunch. Oh mammy daddy.

Hullo Granny. Happy birthday darling. Aren't you looking smart then, old girl. Life begins at eighty, what? Hullo Mary. Where's Iain? He would walk, wouldn't he. And wee Wally? Do you remember your cousins, Anne? No, dear, I wouldn't order sherry if I were you: Ian's asked them to put some nice champagne on ice — if they've remembered — and then he seems to have found what looks like a reasonable claret.

We know all the waitresses. I nearly die. They're all flustered. Uncle Ian has them running round in circles. Granny is being just as bad. Put my stick down there young man where I can reach it. Yes I can hear perfectly well thank you. They think I'm hard of hearing you know, Joey. It's just because they will mumble all the time. Everyone in Scotland mumbles and I can't make out a word of it. No I don't want to go to the Ladies thank you. Don't fuss Mary. Thank goodness mummy told us the rule about the knives and forks. But what are you supposed to use for melon? She never thought of that. Uncle Donald is grinning across at me, pointing surreptitiously to the right things to use, winking now and again. He doesn't need to tell me. You start on the outside and work in. Does he think we don't know anything up in Oban? You're just being horrible. You know you love Uncle Donald. I bet he likes me better than that Janet. I wish I hadn't put that ginger on my melon. It tastes horrible. Oh golly I can't swallow this meat. I keep chewing and chewing and it won't go away. My father's face is flushed. Uncle Ian is making jokes about the Scottish economy. He turns everything into a joke. My father doesn't get angry but you can see he's dying for a cigarette. My two big cousins have very loud voices that come down their noses. They can make all that noise without hardly moving their lips. My two wee cousins are quite quiet in comparison. They're wearing very neat wee skirts and lacey blouses. I bet they're not out of J. D. Williams catalogue. I see them looking across at me now and again to see what I'm thinking of it all. I hope they didn't notice when I couldn't swallow my meat.

Then we go out on to the esplanade to get a family photograph. Oh God, please don't let anybody I know come by. Auntie Joey is like a sergeant-major ordering everybody into place. It takes ages. Janet climbs up on the esplanade wall and puts her arms around Uncle Donald's neck to keep herself upright. She would. Don't they know my granny can't stand up for long? But she's not complaining. She's waving her stick around and making silly remarks. Well I suppose she's enjoying herself — that's the main thing. She'll not be like this after they're all away. What's Auntie Joey doing now? Oh no. She's stopping a man and asking him to take the picture. So's she can be in it too. Do I know him? I don't think so. Maybe he's a tourist. Thank goodness for that. Smile. Everybody say cheese. No no not cheese up in Scotland. We should say haggis. Haggis. No, that's not much good. Try porridge. No. What about whisky? Yes that'll do nicely. Whisky. Come along everybody say whisky.

My father is going to walk home with wee Wally again. There's really no need. Plenty of room in all the cars. Nonsense Joey. Oh well, if he insists. I want to walk too, but I'd better not. I need to help Mummy with the tea things. You should see them all in our kitchen. I mean sitting room. You could hardly swing a cat. Not that the cat's anywhere to be seen. She's got more sense. Granny is making all the conversation as usual. I wish she wouldn't talk about me as if I'm not here. Anne this and Anne that. At least they won't ask me to play. Hamish is sitting on the piano stool. Uncle Donald is sitting on the sofa. His tummy is like a wee football in his fine grey trousers. Kyle suddenly gets up and goes across and pokes it. How dare she. That's my Uncle Donald. You're just being horrible again. He's her uncle too. Anyway, you know fine you wanted to poke it too. Well but I wouldn't. I'm too polite. Huh.

'Well, what about a nice cup of tea and a wee sandwich?' my mother says.

'Now don't go to any trouble Mary. We know it's not easy for you.'

'No trouble at all. I'll just pop out and put the kettle on and then Anne can come and give me a hand with the trolley.'

I sit hugging myself, thinking what a surprise they're going to get. Wait till they see the cheese straws and the asparagus tips rolled up in brown bread. They probably think we've never even heard of asparagus tips in Oban. Wait till they see my Mummy's fruit-cake. I hope it's set in the middle. You can't always rely on that wee tin oven. Wait till they see the sugar lumps and the tongs to get them up with. I didn't even know we had sugar tongs till my mother found them in the back of the drawer. But we'll just pretend we always use them at tea-time, eh.

I hear a strange noise from the byre. I mean the kitchen. I rush through.

My mother is standing against the sink, kettle held weakly in her hand, holding onto the draining board for support. What's wrong? What's wrong? Are you not well? She can't speak. She waves the kettle distractedly in the direction of the tea-trolley. The muslin cloths are on the floor. There is nothing left on the trolley. What has happened? Where is the fruit-cake? Where are the asparagus tips rolled up in brown bread? Where are the scones and the pancakes with raspberry jam and the milk and the sugar lumps? Oh Mummy! Poor Mummy! What has happened? She waves wordlessly towards the kitchen table. I peer under it. The dog is lying flat out on the lino, peching weakly. Our wonderful collie who never steals, who can wait half an hour to get a chocolate drop off my father's knee, nose lying right up against it, drooling all over his trouser leg. Oh no! My poor Mummy. No wonder she's crying. The dog has eaten it all. Jam, sultanas, asparagus, sugar lumps. The lot. Appalled, I look round again, but Mummy's not crying. She is laughing and laughing and laughing and laughing. I start too. Laughing and laughing, hanging on to each other to keep ourselves up till my brother comes through to see what on earth's going on and he joins in. Imagine what a job she must have had getting the milk out of that stupid wee jug. Can you not just see her crunching those sugar lumps. I didn't know dogs liked asparagus tips. Or raisins. A whole fruit-cake! We explode into more gales of laughter. The dog twitches one ear, but otherwise is quite incapable of movement.

'Don't give poor Sine a row, mother,' my brother says. 'I bet she thought it was her dinner left out for her.'

'Yes, she must have. I should really have left her a bone to keep her going while we were out.'

'Maybe she knew it was Granny's birthday. A special treat for Granny's birthday.' We are all off again.

My relations think it's funny too. Well we'd never have wanted all that anyway, after all that lunch. Just a nice cup of tea. That's all we need.

'Don't bother with the rosey cups, Mummy,' I say, an older, wiser

Anne. 'Why not just give them what we use ourselves. Oh golly, I hope there's enough milk left to go round.'

'Oh Mary, what lovely cups,' my auntie says. 'Willow pattern. Just like we had when I was a girl. And such a good size. We just can't lay hands on them in London.'

I take my wee cousins out to look at our hill. Alison rolls all the way down the *dùn* just like I do. She doesn't seem to care about her smart skirt getting all grassy. She tells me they were really scared to meet us. Their parents have told them how clever me and my brother are. They're always telling them they should try and work a bit harder to be as clever as their cousins up in Scotland. Well now, there's a turn-up for the book.

FIFTEEN

'He's taken a great shine to you, dear,' my mother smiles after he's gone.

'Funny old thing. Well that was a lovely day, don't you think?'

'Yes Ma.'

Well. What are you supposed to say? Eh? Such a nice man. So kind. A real friend. After all, how many other people are there that we could just call in on casually like that, uninvited, on the way back from a rare Sunday jaunt in a Visitor's car? Such a nice man, and living all by himself in that big house.

'We'll have to send Anne along to keep house for you,' they'd said, all smiling away over the tea-cups. 'You'd like that, wouldn't you dear?'

Wee Anne. It was all part of the rare Sunday jaunt. Rare Sunday mood. Rare Sunday jokes. Anne will help you bring in the tea things. Anne's a real wee helper around the house. He was in on the joke too, of course.

'House-keeper indeed!' he'd said. 'You send her along in a year or two's time and I'll do better than that. She can be the lady of the house. I'll make an honest woman of her and keep her in the manner to which she's accustomed all right!'

Oh you'd like that wouldn't you dear. To live in this lovely house. Yes Ma.

'I do hope he didn't take us seriously. You never know with men that age.'

'Och don't talk such nonsense, Mary.'

No don't be daft. Wee Anne with her tight-buttoned cardigan, her missing front tooth and her lace-up shoes. Wee Anne smiling desperately so's not to spoil the rare Sunday. I mean, how many times did we ever get a chance to go out together as a family? Father hearty, mother giggly. We'd have happily stayed all night at his lovely big house — if it hadn't been for Granny waiting at home.

Poor Granny. Poor old soul. We mustn't neglect the old ones.

'Never mind. We can still make an evening of it,' he said. 'Why don't you all go on ahead and put the kettle on. I'll just wash up these few things and let the dog out, and then I'll follow you along and we'll make a right *cèilidh* of it. Granny and all. Poor old soul. Maybe we'll get a tune later on.'

Oh yes. Now that's more like it. And to H with tea. We'll get out the whisky glasses. That's more like it now eh.

Father has had a wee dram already obviously. Rare Sunday dram. Rare anyday dram.

'Why doesn't Anne wait behind and help me tidy up,' the man said, 'since you say she's such a rare wee house-keeper? I'll wash and she can wipe. And then we'll come down together. She can get a lift in the new van. How's that now? In fact I don't know how you all ever squeezed into that car in the first place — all the way to Easdale and back.'

Now that's a good idea. Anne would like that wouldn't you.

No she would not. She would rather die. But what are you supposed to say? Try everything. I wasn't the least bit squashed thank you. Anyway William's bigger than me. He takes up more room in the car.

'Ah, but William's no good in the kitchen. If you're going to be the lady of the house one day you'd better be getting in some practice, eh?'

That's right. Now no more nonsense Anne.

Mummy I want to go with you. They're not hearing me. Did I say it out loud anyway? I thought I had. But maybe it was just in my head. They're away, in the Visitor's car, red tail lights disappearing into the darkness leaving me alone with the man. Keep smiling. Keep up the joke.

The man lets the dog out and we are in the kitchen washing the dishes. He is a nice man right enough for an old guy. Good for a laugh. I suppose he must be about forty or fifty but you can talk to him quite easily. About school and other sorts of nonsense. What class am I in. How old am I. Who are my pals. Where do they all live. Have I got a boy-friend. Ha ha. No fear. Have my pals got boy-friends. Oh aye. Loads of them. How's the piano coming on. What are my hobbies. All the usual stuff. You don't really feel awkward with him at all once the rest are away. We get the dishes done quickly and he shakes my hand and pats me on the shoulder and says he can't wait to get me to himself. Hurry up and grow up and come and be the lady of the house. He'll bring me tea in bed every morning he promises. Ha ha. You're just saying that. All the men say that before they're married. Then after they're married it's a different story. He laughs and laughs at that. What an old-fashioned wee thing I am right enough.

So we're outside in the rain getting into his new van. It's a really nice van I suppose, if you like that kind of thing. As far as I can see in the darkness. He lets me switch on the ignition and then he shows me how you move the gears. He puts his hand over mine to move the gear-stick. Then he keeps his hand there on top of mine as we bump into reverse and then jump forward and out onto the road. I feel my face going very hot though I'm sure he just forgot. I pretend to cough to get my hand back without making him think I'm angry or embarrassed or anything. Though I am really. Inside. Men shouldn't do that kind of thing. He just smiles at me though. Thank goodness he's not cross. I coorie away into my corner as we drive along. It's not far to home anyway.

Then we're coming up our road. I'll get the gate. I get out to open it, rain lashing at my hair, cooling my cheeks, and he waves like I'm the queen as he drives through. I wave back, like I'm the queen, pulling bits of wet hair out of my mouth. I get back into the van. But he doesn't start driving. He leans across towards me. I've got my coat buttoned right up to the top. He undoes the top button and tickles round under my chin and into my neck. I am trying not to shiver. What on earth's he up to now.

'Well we're nearly home now,' I say brightly like an eejit, making stupid conversation the way Granny does. Hoping it'll remind him to get going again. He goes on tickling. Then he leans across closer. I'm trying to coorie away as far as I can without making it look as if I'm doing it.

'Yes, we're nearly home,' he says. 'And I've really enjoyed our wee drive together haven't you? You're my wee sweetheart now. Eh?'

It's all part of the game isn't it.

I think he realises I'm scared.

'Right you are then, we'll need to get you home, eh? But first you'll need to give your new sweetheart a wee kiss, eh?'

He is leaning right across me and kissing me now. It's not too bad really. You can put up with it OK. At least his lips aren't too wet. It doesn't last too long anyway. It's just pretty embarrassing. He's squashing my whole body. I feel sick.

'Now you're not going to tell are you? Sweethearts eh? No other boyfriends eh? I'll be waiting for you.'

Oh no, I mean yes, I mean anything to get him off me and on up the road. Mustn't spoil things for the *cèilidh* eh. He holds my hand again till we're nearly at the house and then pulls it quickly into his lap, sort of affectionate like, and gives it a squeeze against his trousers and then lets it go. I am wanting to cry though I don't really know why. Smile away as usual. What a lovely new van. Yes it goes like a bomb. We've come down that road at the speed of light haven't we Anne. Yes yes yes.

Oh yes, it was a grand day all right, and a lovely evening. A real *cèilidh*. Father whistling as he went in and out the byre with the drams.

'I don't like that man,' our Visitor says suddenly, after the man has gone. 'I wouldn't trust him further than I could throw him.'

My mother thinks that's a very strange thing to say. She says afterwards she thinks our Visitor's jealous. Likes to be the centre of attention. Doesn't like to play second fiddle to anybody else. But I wonder if our Visitor guesses more than my mother about the man. I'm not going to say anything anyway. After all, it was just a game, and I was playing too wasn't I? If I'm so stupid that I can't say what I think then I have to put up with the consequences don't I?

But I think it's quite funny about the Visitor too, because actually he's the worst one for kissing me. He's far worse than the man for that. Whenever he's had a dram he sticks his tongue right into my mouth. I don't like it, but nobody seems to notice and we're all so fond of him I suppose it must be all right. At least the man didn't stick his tongue right into my mouth. Thank goodness. It was more the way he was talking that scared me really. Sticks and stones after all. I'd have died all right if he'd stuck his tongue into my mouth in that dark van. But he didn't so that's OK isn't it?

After that I make sure I'm not in the van with that man. It's quite easy to avoid really. Everybody's busy getting on with their own lives. But I talk to him often whenever he's passing. He stops the van and we blether for ages on the street. I enjoy talking to him. He treats you like a grown-up. We have loads of laughs together. As I get older I forget that I was ever scared of him.

But then a very funny thing happens. Just after I get my first boy-friend he passes us when we're sitting on a gate together out Glencruitten Road. We aren't even kissing at the time, though I suppose we are holding hands. I wave to the man, expecting him to stop for a blether as usual. But he takes one look at us and then screeches by in his van without stopping or even waving. And after that he doesn't stop in the street any more. And he stops speaking to my parents altogether. Suddenly, without giving them any reason. They are completely mystified. They can't understand it at all. He's going most peculiar poor soul. Cutting himself off completely. Too long on his own, perhaps. I tell my mother I think I know the reason, though I feel a right nit saying it myself. It sounds so daft, when you think what a poor soul I was at the time. All that time ago. I couldn't have been more than thirteen, could I?

'Oh there must be some mistake,' my mother says. 'It can't be true. There must be some other explanation. He couldn't have taken all that nonsense about you going to keep house for him seriously, could he?'

That's when I tell my mother about the night in the van. About him kissing me and holding my hand. Not that I give her all the gory details of course. She is horrified. She feels so guilty. Oh my poor darling. I didn't know. I didn't understand. How could we have been so stupid. My poor wee lovely. You must have been so upset. Why on earth didn't you tell me.

Then she thinks back, and remembers what our Visitor said.

'Seems he was right all along,' she muses. 'You see – he's a better judge of character than all the rest of us put together. All those years that silly man was thinking of you like that.'

She shudders.

Poor Ma. I'd better not tell her about the Visitor and his French kisses. They're still friends with him after all. Nor did I tell her about the time my brother and I stayed the night in the Visitor's house, either. When he took a dram and came up to tuck me into bed and lay down and squirmed about on top of me in my bed. On top of the eiderdown, of course, but it still wasn't very nice at the time. When you're wee, you know, and don't know what the hell's going on, and you're staying in his house, away from your parents and all, and his wife's down the stairs and you wouldn't want to upset her. Better leave my poor mother with some faith in human nature. She'd die if I told her about all that. I mean, I'm nearly sixteen now, and I know what's what. But my mother's always been that innocent. I don't know how she ever had us in the first place actually.

But maybe I'm not that smart myself either. I mean, I know you're not supposed to speak to strangers. Of course you don't get into cars with strange men. Everybody knows that. In principle. What they don't tell you in practice is, who actually is a stranger in Oban? You know everybody really, sort of. It makes things much more difficult, even when you're fifteen.

I mean, where would the world be if we all stopped trusting each other? Eh? Highland hospitality? Huh. You wouldn't open your door to anyone if you were scared it might be Jack the Ripper, would you. That's what you get in Glasgow, not Oban. Think of Manuel, for example. He'd have had a field day in Oban. He could have been in and out all the houses no bother, murdering half the population. The Paki-man, the man from the Pru, the rates assessor, the gas-meter man, the Ministry vet — in Oban they all get asked in for a cup of tea and a scone. Some people bake specially for them coming. And where would we have been the day my granny set her newspaper on fire and a man we hardly knew came running all the way up the road and put it out before the whole house went up? If my granny had had the door locked she'd have been kippered. But you wouldn't think of locking your door would you? Any more than you'd think twice about offering somebody a lift if it was raining and you were lucky enough to have a car. People are always giving other people a lift in Oban, specially when it's raining or if it's an old buddy with messages or some guy who's had one over the score and is having a job getting up the road. That's the good old Highland way isn't it?

So here I am, one wet day in the summer holidays, on my way to the dentist, being blown along Soroba Road, minding my own business. Three big fillings needed at the back and an extraction, and Mr Hill's not as young as he was. He gave Mrs Lawrie such a fright she went running right out the surgery and fell flat on a newly dug flower-bed in his front garden. You should have seen the hole she made. 'Look at that now, Mr Hill, yous are after murdering me and now yous are trying to bury me.' My father won't go to the dentist at all. He's going to take his own teeth out himself and then go for a set of falsies. He works away at them every night. He's got most of them out now. Cowardy custard. 'What nonsense! You hear that Mary? I don't believe in all these dentists and doctors. Mind over matter that's what I say. Look at the time I cured my wart when I was only a wee boy. Spittle every morning. Acid. A natural source. Just as good as any of their medicines. I won't let them get their hands on me.'

My teeth are a source of interest and agony. My brother says I'm a throw-back. A rhinoceros. The missing link. All those years with a baby tooth at the front, stupid wee thing lodged in between the grown-up teeth like Uncle Paddy sitting there in his miner's cottage after the council knocked down the whole row on either side of him and he refused to be re-housed. Very embarrassing. My front tooth I mean. All I want for Xmas is my two front teeth. Very funny. Anyway — Mr Hill takes the baby tooth out this day and then there's a gap. Nothing happens. Nothing at all. 'You'll need to work away at it with your pencil, a spoon, anything you can lay your hands on,' the dentist says. 'The ones on either side are so big the gum's not getting any stimulation.' Well I stimulated it all right. Mind over matter. I chewed and chewed and poked and probed until right enough one glorious day down shot the new big tooth, shouldering and jostling its way past the others. Complete at last. No more teasing. Until, about two days later, there's a funny feeling in my mouth and out pops a tooth, a big long jaggy stalactite, in the middle of my hard palate just where you make your Gaelic L's. 'That's not a tooth. It's a tusk,' my brother says. 'That explains everything,' he says. 'Overcrowding. That explains everything,' says Mr Hill. Oh. Well. 'Well, we'll have to extract it. You don't want that in the middle of your mouth, catching on your tongue now, do you?' No, but I don't want your oil of cloves and your nose-freezing jag and your shaking hands and your pincers and your spit out the blood in my wee sink either. And who knows how long it is. My brother says it's probably connected by a huge long root right up through my nasal cavities and up into my skull. 'If Mr Hill takes it out, your brain'll probably leak out into your mouth.' Oh very funny.

A car is driving slowly along the side of the pavement. I didn't notice it till now. A man is trying to attract my attention, leaning across, winding down his side window.

'Hullo there, you're Anne Gillies, aren't you?' he calls across.

That's me. Large as life. Anne Gillies, heavily disguised rhinoceros, soon to be brainless.

'Maybe you don't recognise me,' he says. 'I've been away for a bit.'

I recognise him right enough. His mother's one of my mother's favourite patients. A lovely lady, well-known around Oban. Lives in a beautiful big house in its own grounds on the edge of the town. County set — just about.

'Where are you off to then?' he asks.

'To Hill the dentist,' I reply, still walking on with the car trickling along beside me.

'Well now, that's a coincidence. I'm on my way out that road myself. Come on. Hop in and I'll have you there in no time.'

'Ehm it's OK thanks. I'm not in any hurry. I'm fine walking.'

'Och don't be daft. That's a terrible brae. You'll be soaked by the time you get there. Come on. Your mum's been good to my mother. I reckon I owe you a lift at the very least.'

Oh hell. What are you supposed to say? How can I refuse without being rude? The door swings open and I slide in and sit hard against the door staring straight ahead.

'Well, well, you've fairly grown up since I was away,' he says and similar inane embarrassing things. I feel like saying well well, you've fairly grown up and got stupid since you were away. But of course I don't. Wonder where he's been this last while. Don't like to ask. It might seem rude. That doesn't stop him asking me a whole lot of personal questions. All the usual. What age am I. What class am I in. Have I got a boyfriend. You know the sort of stuff. Never mind, it shouldn't take long getting to the dentist.

But this is not the way to the dentist, is it? I don't like to say anything at first. Maybe he knows another way. A quicker way. I don't want to seem stupid. Don't want him to think I'm scared or anything. He's driving away up the back of the Hydro.

'This isn't the way to Mr Hill's house, is it?' I venture at last.

'Don't you worry,' he says. 'When's your appointment?'

'Half past two,' I say.

'There you are then. Loads of time eh?'

He's driving away off the road, over the grass. I am really scared now. Go on, tell him you idiot. Say what you think for once in your life.

'I don't want to go up here,' I say. 'Take me to Mr Hill's please, if you don't mind.'

'Och don't be daft. A wee run. That's all. No harm in that, eh?'

I really don't like this guy at all. But he wouldn't try anything on, would he? He's about twenty-two or three, I think. He was away out the High School before I came there. Where's he been this last while? University? What an idiot you are. He could have been in Barlinnie for all you know. No — not him. Not with that nice mother. We'd have heard surely. Well maybe, and maybe not. Maybe my mother wouldn't tell me. The shame and all that. And they're funny about not telling me things that might scare me. When Manuel was in the paper my father stopped Granny's *Bulletin* for months. I won't have that trash in the house. Preying on everyone's minds. Vicarious rubbish.

He's stopping the car. Switching off the engine. I am really shaking now. He's smiling in a funny sort of way.

'What's the matter then, little girl? You're not scared, surely?'

Go on, say it.

'Yes I am. You've no right to take me away out here. You said you were going to take me to the dentist. I want to go there now. Right away please.'

'Och come now. What's your hurry? Look at the lovely view. What's there to be scared of?'

'If you don't take me straight to the dentist I'll get out the car and go for the police.'

'Ah, but I won't let you.' He leans across quick as a rattle-snake and locks my door. 'Now don't you touch that lock or I could get really angry. You wouldn't like that would you?'

'I know your mother. I'll tell on you. I'll tell the police on you.'

'Oh no you won't. You won't get out of here to tell them. Stupid girl. What do you go and take lifts from people for if you're going to get scared when they want to have a bit of fun?'

He's just sitting there grinning at me, arms folded. He doesn't do anything. Just goes on and on teasing me like a fish on the end of a line. Till I try to open the door. Then he snakes across and holds my arms very tight. He's going to kill me. He holds on and on. He's very angry.

'I told you not to touch that door, didn't I? I told you.'

He holds on to my arms for ages. He's hurting me. Then suddenly, without warning, he seems to get fed up with it.

'Och well have it your own way you stupid wee bitch. Go on. Out of here. Scram. Vamoose.'

The door is open and he is shoving me out of the car. I run and run over the grass towards the road. He passes me with a screech of his tyres, throwing up mud on to my raincoat. My legs are shaking. I'm not sure of the way from here but I run and run till I reach houses. Then I slow down and take big breaths. I'm very wheezy and still shaking.

When I reach the dentist he gives me a row for being late. We'll have to leave those fillings today. Just do the extraction. When he gives me my jag it makes tears come rolling down my face. What, not scared of a wee scratch are we, a big girl like you. I thought you were one of my prize patients.

I don't tell anyone about the man in the car. What could they do anyway? They might even tell the police. And I feel so guilty about getting into a car with a strange man and I don't think I could take a row on top of everything else.

Anyway, the police are just as bad. Look at the time the plain clothes cops chased me in the dark on my road home from painting murals for the school dance: caught me in a half-nelson from behind, shone a torch right into my face, and then said, 'You seem scared. Why are you acting so scared if you've done nothing to be ashamed of?' Ha ha, very funny. I reckon you just have to learn to look after yourself in this life.

SIXTEEN

Is it only me, or does everybody feel like about ten different people all rolled into one? Deciding which one to be according to the particular circumstances, the company you're in at the time, your mood and so on? I watch myself disapprovingly while I'm with other people. Even my accent changes. I don't mean to do it. It can be very embarrassing. Like when I was on the bus after country dancing and I heard myself saying 'Oh look, Hetty's greeting.' I would normally say 'crying', but I was trying to make myself blend in with my surroundings. Only of course nobody says 'greeting'. It sounded most incongruous. If you're going to use words like that you have to get it right: 'He''y's gree'n.' I stared out of the bus window to hide my red face, but I could feel them all looking at me as if I was a Martian. I wish I could just discover one me that I liked and stick to it, come hell or high water. Then maybe other people would change themselves to fit in with me. But I suppose that would be asking too much.

No wonder people get me wrong. Even my own mother. One day when I was in her waiting-room she went and told her assistant that 'Anne loves babies. Anne will baby-sit for you any time you like, won't you, Anne?' I was horrified. To hear her you would think I'd been baby-sitting for years, whereas in actual fact I've never been near a baby in my entire life. I should have said no on the spot, instead of smiling obligingly and ending up tipping the poor wee soul out of his push-chair in the middle of Combie Street. I was embarrassed the whole afternoon: making inane conversation with the back of the baby's head all the way down Polvinister Road, clinging onto the push-chair at a ninety degree angle while simultaneously trying to find something gossipy to say to the folk that stopped to chat to him on the brae. Then trying to apologise to him after I tipped him out on the ground while trying to think of something smart to say to the boys that shouted obscenities at us from across the road. I couldn't wait to get home. I never want to see another baby as long as I live. But if my mother asks me to do it again I don't suppose I'll dare say no. After all, you don't want people to know your weaknesses, do you?

I've started thinking about all this a lot. Supposing we're not really who we think we are at all. Like in the Gaelic stories. Changelings. With our real personalities desperately trying to reassert themselves through all the learned behaviour: nature v nurture, as my da would say. Supposing your mother isn't really your mother at all. Someone else pretending to be her. Like the wolf in *Red Riding Hood*. Eeek. After all, my mother goes away to the hospital every day and behaves like someone completely different. In charge of her physiotherapy department. Making decisions all the time. Not like at home where my father is in charge and my mother witters about trying to keep the peace. We used to go to the hospital for ultra-violet light after we had the pneumonia, and my mother treated us differently. It made us all into different people. We weren't us, we were patients in gym-shorts and goggles. She wasn't her, she was Mrs Gillies, efficient, confident.

My mother gets really involved with her patients, who are people we don't even know. We just hear snippets. A beautiful old lady from Mull, a roguish sea-captain from Lismore . . . I'm quite used to that. But when Olly Proctor got the polio that was another story. My mother getting involved with someone you knew, someone of your own age, someone who was so pretty and so brave it made tears come into your mother's eyes just thinking about her. And you couldn't complain when she took time to go to Olly's actual house to visit her. You couldn't possibly be jealous of poor Olly, could you? My mother is campaigning for better conditions for physiotherapists. She can get really fierce on the subject. My father rolls his eyes whimsically — a bit nonplussed — but he can hardly disagree with what she says. But the folk who read her letters in the *Journal* would probably be surprised if they could see her smoking nervously and picking at her hands. Of course she always gets my father to read over what she has written. He's so good at putting things in a way that will be sure to get published. He can put issues in a nut-shell.

I used to tell my mother everything. As soon as I had bought her birthday present (usually about June, for her birthday in August) I used to start saying, 'I'll bet you can't guess what I've got you for your birthday,' and I couldn't leave her alone till she'd guessed. What a daft wee thing I used to be. I can get quite sentimental thinking about myself when I was wee. But now I keep most of my thoughts to myself. I mean, apart from your mother, who else is there to confide in? I have the most wonderful dreams nowadays. I can fly. I fly along just above the hedge, all around the yard and halfway down the road. I suppose I could go much further away, and I might be able to go much higher, but I don't bother. I just like moseying about all the places I know, having a look at them from another angle. It's like swimming in the air.

The television is coming to Oban. Not that that will affect us, as you need the electricity first. But it was really interesting the day they came to try out the picture up our hill. They are looking for the best place to site the aerial thingie — the Battleship Hill, or Pulpit Hill, or our hill, depending on where they get the best picture. Men came and sat in a tent all day with their equipment crackling and spitting. Needles and dials and knobs — not unlike the radar in the *Claymore*. It was pouring with rain outside and everything looked grey and smelt of oilskin — the sky, the rain, the hill, the tent, the men, the machines, the picture. You couldn't hear a thing for the rain on the tent and the men's legs scraping together.

The men made lots of jokes about the weather. If this is an Oban summer I don't want to be here in winter — all that kind of thing. I told them the one about how if you can see Mull it's going to rain and if you can't see Mull it's raining. I felt a bit disloyal telling it. You know how everyone always goes on about the weather here — like when the Queen came off the Royal Yacht to attend the Games and all the people were singing 'Will ye no come back again' and my uncle Alasdair the Councillor heard the Duke of Edinburgh saying 'not bloody likely'. Anyway, the men thought it was very funny. Well, they thought it was quite funny. What with the weather and the terrible picture and everything they weren't disposed to think anything was terribly funny. They wanted to get back to their B and B and get a good bath and a dram. They let us into the tent because it is our hill. The wee boys from the Houses had to hang around outside, trying to get a peek in when anyone lifted the flap. They were furious. The men decided against our hill eventually, but it was interesting while it lasted.

Fourth Year. I am not quite the smallest in the class. Section One in Gym: the wee *troichs*. We get showers now. I hate that. Everybody seeing you. I avoid Gym by every means at my disposal, forget my towel to avoid the showers. One day I'm in the changing-rooms stripping off for Gym, thinking away as usual, and I forget where I am and what I'm doing. Blazer off, jumper off, tie off, shoes off, socks off, skirt off, knickers — oh golly. What am I doing? Did anybody see? Knickers off right over my backside. I thought I was going to my bed.

A lot of new people have come into my class now. People from Islay and Tiree and Ardrishaig. I like them very much. Quite a lot of them take Gaelic. In fact I like school much more now. I've dropped Science and

Geography, thank goodness. Now I can get on with all the important subjects. I wish I could have done Music, but you can't do Music in Oban. I'd have had to go away and board in Dunoon, which was obviously out of the question. I am doing Higher English, Latin, Gaelic and Art. Lower History — but I may take my Higher in Sixth Year. Haven't thought yet what I want to be after I finish University. Anything but a teacher.

I'm even in the Higher Maths class, but I hate it. Old Troup is one of the few teachers who has been in the school for years without getting a nickname. That shows you how people feel about him. I sit praying he won't choose me to answer. Usually I don't even attempt to think out the question, my brain being so taken up with working out the best way of avoiding having to answer. All stand, those who don't understand this elementary question. You have to judge it carefully: vary your tactics. Sometimes you can stand up and not be noticed in behind someone else. Sometimes, if it's a really hard question, or he's in a reasonable mood, he may let you off lightly if you stand. The worst is to be caught sitting down when in fact you don't know the answer. Your deceit reflects on him too — makes people snigger. He's waxing fulsome about the poor intelligent people sitting patiently waiting — being held back by the fools, the time-wasters and the congenitally ignorant. Come along, then, Anne, be so kind as to enlighten us in the vain hope that we may be able to complete this straightforward piece of work before the end of the period. God help you if you can't answer him then; if you answer and get it wrong; if you aren't even sure what the question was.

One day a boy from Connel got two per cent in a test. Two per cent! A record! And if that wasn't bad enough he sniggered. Old Troup's face goes red, then purple.

'Ah. I see. You think it's funny do you? Funny to get two per cent, less than a year before you sit your Highers. If I had ever got two per cent — nay if I had got fifty-two per cent — nay eighty-two per cent, I would have been hanging my head with shame. Apologising to my parents, to my teacher. Resolving to redouble my efforts. But not the wonder-boy from Connel! Does he hang his head in shame? Does he resolve to work harder? Does he apologise? Ah no. The wonder-boy sniggers.'

We watch, paralysed. Old Troup sweeps back his academic gown and hangs his thumbs in the sleeves of his waistcoat, puffing out his chest to illustrate the foolish bravado which epitomises the wonder-boys of the world. I am using all the muscular strength of my throat to hold in the spasm of nervous laughter welling up from below.

'Ah no,' old Troup continues. 'I am above shame, above correction, says the wonder-boy. I have no need to work. No need to worry. No need to consider the distress my wilful ignorance is bringing to my parents, to my teachers. The shame my ignorance — my laziness — my arrogance is bringing upon my school. The effect my presence has on the more able — the more hard-working — the more self-disciplined of my class-mates. No need to listen to the warnings of my teacher who at my age never took a mark lower than ninety-two per cent home to his proud parents. Ah no. I am a big shot, says the wonder-boy. I am a clever fellow, says the wonder-boy. I am — sniggering!'

During the histrionic pause before the last word, old Troup puffs mightily like a pouter pigeon and pulls his arm-holes up by the thumbs to enhance the effect. Pulling his waistcoat six inches up. Revealing above his trousers a striped shirt tucked into high-waisted white locknit drawers with two large creamy buttons marking the top of the speever. A loud and prolonged snort emits down my nose, unbidden, uncheckable.

Well that's done it. I've had it now. I sit digging sweaty hands into my lap, head down, waiting for Nemesis.

But nothing happens. I hear a unison of indrawn breath, then a terrible silence broken only by the slight rustle of bum-swivelling. Part sympathetic, no doubt, part gleeful. By the time I dare to raise my head and peer through the blessed cover of my hair's overhang, old Troup has subsided, exhausted, behind his usual sarcasm and the class has relaxed.

'What on earth happened! Did he not hear me snorting? I thought my end had come,' I say afterwards to Flora, on the way to Gaelic.

'Oh he heard it all right. They'd have heard it in Connel. I never heard anything so funny in my life. I had a job not giggling myself. If he hadn't been quite so beside himself I mean.'

'Well why didn't he get me? Did he look across at me?'

'Oh he looked across all right. But don't forget you're sitting beside Katy Troup, aren't you? That was what saved you I reckon. When you snorted Katy Troup went red as a beetroot. He must have thought it was her.'

Poor Katy Troup. She's always going bright red in the maths class. Especially when her father makes jokes. 2P or not 2P that is the question. And she got the giggles one day herself, snuffling away beside me when an angle came out BTM. I wonder if he did it on purpose? It didn't make anyone else laugh. Most of us call it bum or bahoochie. BTM's a bit posh for most folk. It must be a Troup family expression. I just happened to know it from my granny. It's as well for her that Katy Troup is so good at maths.

I don't stay sitting beside her for long. End up near the front in a desk with Maggie Rogers. Twice running we both get twenty-three per cent in our exams. Isn't that a coincidence? We each get a different twenty-three per cent mind you. Not much point in copying off Maggie Rogers. Or her copying off me if it comes to that.

I must be really dumb. When we get on to calculus he gives us a talk about cars going at a certain speed and passing a point in the road — something to do with radar. That might be OK if you understood what radar was. Then without warning we have to do it. Calculus I mean. At this point I still haven't discovered what calculus is, let alone how to do it. My brother tries to explain it but it's no use. My brains are addled. One day I go completely green in the maths class and have to be sent home and put to bed for the whole of the afternoon.

By the end of Fourth Year I am one of the tallest in the class. In Section Eight in Gym. One of the giants.

Old Troup says would I mind very much if he put me down into the Lower Maths class next year. Why is he being so polite to me? Why doesn't he tell me I'm one of the congenitally ignorant? No I wouldn't mind, I say, it seems like a good idea — trying to keep the joyful grin off my lips. In Lower Maths Fanny smiles and murmurs and falls asleep gently at her desk after lunch-time. I get ninety-eight per cent in my exam. Mr Troup says that perhaps I would like to come back into his class and sit my Higher in Sixth Year. Is he kidding? Not if you paid me. Thank you very much, that's very kind, sir, I'll have to see how my time-table works out.

The Boy Captain and Girl Captain gave back their badges rather than agree to stop holding hands when they walked down the street together.

There's a lot of it about it. She was only sixteen; a teenager in love; a wiggle in her walk and a giggle in her talk; stupid Cupid stop picking on me; lipstick on your collar. It's hard for me to keep up with it all. My father won't let us listen to Radio Luxembourg. We have to keep the wireless turned down very low and whistle loudly if he comes in unexpectedly — a bit like himself, singing hymns to fool the *cailleach* in the kitchen in Ballachulish when they were playing cards on the Sabbath day. And of course we can't get a record-player because we haven't got the electricity. I got really caught out when everyone went wild about Adam Faith and I hadn't even heard of him. That dreadful yowling, my granny calls it. Anglo-American commercial claptrap, my father calls it, preying on people's emotions. One day even my mother got fed up with him. She got up from the tea-table without any warning and went dancing round the kitchen like a dervish singing shoot that tiger, pom pom shoot that tiger!

My piano teacher doesn't like the Hit Parade either. I got really excited when the Theme from *Exodus* got into the Hit Parade: surely that proves that pop music isn't all rubbish. But my piano teacher didn't like the Theme from *Exodus* either though he was really apologetic about it. I think it's very narrow-minded of him. After all, I put up with his Bach and Hindemith and stuff. Who was it who had to play a March, Strathspey and Reel and a Brahms duet and a set of Renaissance dances all in the one school concert? That's all I'm saying.

We have a dance every month in the school now, to keep us from going to those aaawful dances in the town. We're not allowed to go to them. It's a school rule. We provide dances. If you want to go to town dances you will forfeit the privilege of school dances. What an old sweetie-wife the Rector is. He sits on the edge of the dance floor fussing away.

'Is Mary MacInnes wearing lipstick, Miss Maclaine? I'm sure Mary is wearing lipstick. I'm surprised at her. Would you mind asking her to wipe it off please?'

And Big Mae says, 'No no I'm sure you're mistaken, Mr MacLean,' and then on Monday morning tells Mary MacInnes to stop upsetting the Rector. Surely a more subdued shade would be quite acceptable. She's all right, Big Mae. It's just as well pale lipstick's in. He doesn't seem to notice foundation, even when Maureen Ferguson comes with a bright orange face and white lips.

Mary and Flora and that lot all stay in the hostel. They can swop dresses and try on make-up when Foosty's out the road and they all come to the dance in a big group together and can go home together if they don't get a lumber. I have to go down to the doctor's house to have a bath and then rush home to dump my sponge bag and get changed into the dress I made out of an offer in the *Woman's Own* and have a sandwich in time for seven o'clock. For me it becomes imperative to have a steady boyfriend. That makes you Somebody. I got one after the first dance of the term. It wasn't the one I wanted, but he was all right to be going on with. His nickname was Dracula, but if you shut your eyes it doesn't make much difference who you're kissing. I was so relieved my mother had let me get high heeled shoes, even if the heels were quite stumpy compared to most of the other girls'. I wore my new shoes on our first date. I met him at the Corran Halls and we walked out to Ganavan. He didn't look all that great in daylight. But kissing is fantastic. You have to make sure you breathe through your nose all the time, but after a bit of practice you can keep going for half an hour. It fairly saves you having to think up something to say. In school I can make the feeling come in my stomach again. It helps to make Religious Instruction pass quickly.

We go to the pictures every Saturday night now and sit in the back row. You don't pay much attention to the film. Some people smoke in the pictures, but I think they're really stupid. I only see Dracula at weekends and I still have to walk home myself after the pictures because he's in the boys' hostel. If I meet him by accident after school in the George Café we just ignore each other. It's just something quite nice that happens at weekends. Sometimes you hear about girls having trouble with their boyfriends. They put pressure on them to do things they don't want. But I don't have any of that kind of trouble, thank goodness. I don't know where those girls go anyway. You couldn't get up to much on the road to Ganavan.

I don't go to the George Café every day. Giggling and gaggling, my father calls it. I must admit the conversation is a bit limited but I enjoy listening to it even though I don't have much to contribute. Most of them have been down to their cousins' in Glasgow where all the interesting things happen. They're always cracking jokes: hullawrerr china and yabadabadoo. I don't know where they get them all. Mary showed us how to back-comb our hair after she'd been down in Glasgow one time. We were all hiding in the cloakroom back-combing away all through the interval and it was such good fun I forgot to eat my play-piece and nearly starved during maths. I'm ravenous most of the time now but I never put on any weight. I'm like a bean-pole. It's getting worse now that I'm getting so tall.

One day I saw an advert for something called Wate-on. It was really expensive: nineteen and six for a bottle, but they said that would last you till you became curvaceous and attractive like all your friends so I thought it would be worth it. I saved like mad until I had enough for a postal order. I was really excited when it came but I had to watch my brother didn't catch me eating the stuff. My piano teacher had lent me a book called *The Lord of the Rings* — I thought it was a bit strange him reading a kids' book like that, but I started it just to please him. Sitting there on my bed, swallowing this disgusting thick yellow stuff drop by drop and trying to read my piano teacher's book. By the time I'd finished the whole bottle I still wasn't past chapter two. I was also still as thin as a rake. It's not often I find a book I can't get into.

Next I saw an advert for a Bust Enhancer, so I saved up and sent away for that. It was even more expensive than the Wate-on. It was ages before it came — in a plain wrapper as promised. Wow! Somebody must have made a mint out of that. It was just a wee pink bakelite thing, shaped like a mussel shell, with a spring in the middle. You had to squeeze and squeeze at it and success was guaranteed. I was too ashamed to ask for my money back. Mind you, I wasn't the only one with trouble in that department. There was a rumour that one girl had got so upset she persuaded her mother to let her have an operation and then her real bust grew and she became as big as a house. Certainly to see her you could believe it. My mother says I shouldn't worry. My auntie had a big huge bust and she would have done anything to get rid of it. It's either a feast or a famine, eh?

The school is going to put on HMS *Pinafore* at the end of the year. We all want to be in it. The music teacher decided who's going to sing what. She tells me I'm to be Little Buttercup. I can't wait to get the score to see what Little Buttercup is like. I hope she's the heroine. She turns out to be a great big fat woman who's meant to be funny. The music teacher must have had a brain-storm. The heroine is to be played by a girl in my brother's class who can't sing in tune; she goes to elocution lessons and the Rector is always telling us we should try to speak like her — it's aaawfully important in life to be able to speak well, he says. He's always putting himself down. Him and his Gaelic accent. He sits in my brother's Greek class practising pibroch on his ruler.

I hate the songs I have to sing. Little Buttercup is meant to be a contralto and I don't feel comfortable singing out loud away down there, let alone trying to be funny at the same time. I don't think I'm very good at being funny. I don't want to be funny. When it comes to costume fitting, the others all have lovely silky romantic dresses in pastel colours — even the chorus. But I am to be in canary yellow cotton with bits of black and white gingham sewn on. It hangs off me, drooping down all round on to the floor of the Domestic Science room. Ah but it won't be like this once we've finished with you Anne Gillies. They start stuffing sheets of newspaper up the dress. Everyone else is getting bits of lace sewn on and flowers tucked into their bonnets, and I'm standing there in front of everybody with the Domestic Science teacher sticking the *Oban Times* up my skirt and into my knickers and down my bodice. I rustle when I move and every time I sit down on my barrel my backside slips up my back and I have to push it back down again when I stand up. I'm not looking forward to it at all, though I feel better about Katy Troup getting a pretty dress when I discover she has to make love to Gilleasbuig MacMillan. He can't sing either, by the way.

We are to perform for the whole town — three nights in the Argyllshire Gathering Hall. On the Opening Night we all go down on one knee and sing 'Hail Ralph Rackstraw!' But Ralph Rackstraw does not appear at the top of the stage as required. We hold our position as long as we can, beginning to totter. The music teacher is furious. She bashes her baton on the desk and hisses 'Again!' through her teeth. So we all wobble back upright, and I pull my backside down, and she gets the orchestra to play the chord again. 'Hail!' we all sing, wobbling back down again. But still no Ralph Rackstraw. She makes us do it one last time. As we hang there, arms outstretched towards the empty space, we hear a voice backstage shouting, 'Where the hell's Ralph Rackstraw?', and in the silence that follows we hear another voice shouting, 'Oh Christ he's away for chips.'

Every now and then the Rector sends for me to come to his study.

Oooh Anne Gillies you're for it. I ham up extreme terror for their benefit, and then I go along to the study to learn another Gaelic song. They just come back to him without warning when he's in the middle of something else, and he has to pass them on to me quickly before he forgets about them again. He only has to sing a few verses through and I've got them. Then he writes out the words for me, and I jot down the first note or two in sol-fa at the top of the page to remind myself how they start. Once you get started the rest comes back no bother. He has given me some songs nobody outside his family in Raasay knows, in addition to some of the ones from other islands he's heard from his brother Calum the collector. Also he writes Gaelic verse himself — translations from Pindar and *The Aeneid*. He composes them in the morning while he's shaving himself in the mirror and when he gets to school he wants to hear how they will sound to the tunes of waulking songs. He's not much of a singer himself mind you. Sometimes I have to guess what he means. Sometimes I have to be careful not to laugh, but sometimes it's impossible.

'Ah, Anne, isn't it an aaawfully funny thing, Gaelic singing,' he says. 'It strikes straight at the emotions. It was George Campbell Hay that explained it to me. I was a bit put out when he started laughing, until he explained it. Strikes straight at the emotions, he said. Laughing and crying — such a narrow margin between them. Aaawfully funny things the human emotions.'

Yes sir, I croak, tears streaming down my face. I love him so much. He is the most exasperating man I've ever met.

I'm getting quite good at making my own clothes now. Luckily straight skirts and dresses are beginning to come in. You can make a dress which is just a tube of material with a couple of darts at the bust, and put a waspy belt round it and call it a sack dress.

I get a skirt length from the Tweed Mill and sew the back seam and the zip, then put the material round, wrong side out, and pin the side seams and the darts on me. It makes it fit very well and shows off my backside which is the only part of me with any shape at all. Then I get a thick ribbed V-neck sweater from the Scotch Wool Shop which makes me look as if I've got a bust and comes down far enough to hide the fact that I've got no hips without entirely hiding my neat wee bum. It's a lovely fawn colour. With nylons and my high-ish shoes I feel really good for the first time. At the Christmas dance a boy in Sixth Year asks to get me home. I feel a bit guilty about Dracula, but you couldn't turn down a Prefect could you? Anyway they're both in the hostel, and he says he'll explain to Dracula. I feel really grown up and proud of myself. We start going steady.

Not that he's much better looking than the last one, mind you. His name is Cod. He's not very tall, and his face is red, and he's got funny wee eyes, but he's a great runner and I'm not exactly Connie Francis myself, am I. I expect I'm all he could get.

It's good fun going with a Prefect. I sometimes go out to the boys' hostel, and we all sit around and have coffee with the matron. She's really nice. Prefects are allowed out longer than the younger boys, so Cod can get me up the road, all the way home, which is a real luxury. And on the school picnics you really feel Somebody, being in with that crowd — all the ones in the athletics team and their glamorous girlfriends. Otherwise nothing much changes. He doesn't put any pressure on me either. We just kiss and hold hands in the pictures at weekends and have nice long smooches on the way up our road, but that's about it. I'm really glad I've got my straight skirt and my fawn sweater to wear under my reversible cotton swagger coat, which was one of J. D. Williams' better lines.

Then one day a letter arrives through the post. I'm very surprised. Nobody ever writes to me. I don't recognise the writing.

I open it up. It's printed in peculiar writing. Don't tell me it's one of these awful chain letter things.

> *Don't think we haven't seen you and what you get up to Anne Gillies. Don't think we haven't taken note of you in your tight skirt and your tight sweater and the way you go with all the boys. We see what you get up to in the darkness with all your boyfriends. We know what happens to girls like you. We are the Oban point watchers. We will be watching you and waiting. Don't say we didn't warn you.*

My mother and I burn the letter ceremonially in my wash-hand basin. But that doesn't take away the feeling. I am sick to my stomach. I feel guilty and dirty and bad. It's not true what they're saying, is it? Of course not, dear. They're just jealous, whoever they are. But who can it be? Who would write such a thing? Please don't tell Daddy. I'll die if you tell Daddy. He'll say that's what comes of all this giggling and gaggling.

I am too sick to go down the town. I walk down the road to school with my head hanging, my shoulders hunched, afraid to look up in case I see people watching me from their windows. From behind their lace curtains.

My mother starts going on again about a perm, to keep my hair back out of my eyes. You've got such a pretty little face, she says. Why not show it? But I need my hair to hide behind. And anyway there's the monkey ears. Och what nonsense. They don't stick out at all. Yes they do — well, one of them does anyway. Look at it. It's hideous. Well if you really care all that much about it maybe we should get it operated on, she says. The surgeon in the hospital fancies himself as a plastic surgeon. Maybe he would do it as a favour on the National Health.

The surgeon agrees, but I'll have to go to the doctor first. He'll need to say it's causing me distress. Is it really worth it? But I go to the doctor. I hate having to show him my ears. Well, Anne, it's really not that bad is it? No but . . . All right, if you really want it done . . . You girls, you're all the same. Nothing but vanity.

So in the holidays I go into the hospital. Just for one night. They give me a room to myself, so I won't be embarrassed by Oban people in the ward asking a lot of nosey questions. When I come round from the anaesthetic my head is extremely sore and swathed in bandages.

When I feel a bit better the nurse comes in and says why don't I pop along to the lounge for a bit of company. You don't want to be away down here by yourself surely. I don't like to say no. In the lounge are a whole lot of women I half know, sitting in slippers blethering.

Ah, Anne Gillies. We heard you were in right enough. A wee private operation was it? Aye aye. A wee tummy operation that would be, would it, they say, looking meaningfully at one another. A wee touch of appendicitis, eh? They must be crackers. I look like the invisible man. Can't they see my bandages? No, I reply, very embarrassed. A wee operation to my ear. Oh aye, dearie, that'll be right. I can see they don't believe me. I know what they think. I don't stay very long in the lounge. Thinking about it afterwards it's quite funny. I mean, my periods haven't even started yet.

When I get home I can't wait to see my lovely new ears. But they're just the same. Afterwards the surgeon tells my mother we should have kept the bandages on for at least a fortnight. Well, why didn't he tell us before?

My granny is doing the ironing, with the oil-lamp standing on the end of the ironing board. It's raining outside and my mother has rigged up a piece of string across the byre to dry the rest of the washing on. When I go to take down my fawn jumper, the front of it has got all scorched with the lamp.

SEVENTEEN

Dear Mary Grant

I wonder if you can help me. I am a teenager who has multiple problems. Firstly I experience great difficulty in standing up straight. I have grown so tall that I feel very far from the ground and quite unsafe most of the time but especially when descending stairs, when I seem to lose contact with my feet altogether. I think I may be suffering from chronic mild vertigo. Or perhaps short-sightedness. I try to combat this by holding onto bannisters, walking with my shoulders rounded and my eyes towards the ground, and standing on one leg with my hip stuck out to the side. I have found this latter particularly effective when talking to short boys. However I feel it may be detrimental to my spinal column in the future (I am already very round shouldered) and it is of no help whatsoever when dancing.

Secondly my face is too fat and my cheek-bones are not prominent enough. This I have been attempting to combat by sucking in my cheeks on each side and clamping the flesh between my back teeth. I have grown quite expert at maintaining this position for long periods, achieving a look which is reasonably reminiscent of Audrey Hepburn, and after months of practice I have evolved a method of talking fairly naturally without letting my cheeks go and with minimum loss of clarity as regards diction. However this is obviously far from ideal, and renders smiling a physical impossibility.

Thirdly I have difficulty swallowing. I used to have no problems in this area until one day I started making a very strange rasping sound in my throat each time I swallowed food or drink. A sort of highly-localised burp. Although it was not very loud it was extremely embarrassing. It has got so bad that now I chew and chew my food but am afraid to swallow it in case the sound is audible to other people. This has the effect — A-anne! Time you finished your homework and off to bed or you'll never wake up in the morning. OK Ma.

At the end of Fifth Year we have to sit our Highers and Lowers. It makes the teachers very jumpy. Our shortcomings reflecting on them. On average my year is not quite the calibre of my brother's. The English teacher asks questions round the class, beginning whimsically then working himself up into a nervous lather. Amplifying his Lewis accent with its histrionic preaspirations.

'What was the motivation behind Hamlet's action at this particular juncture? Sam . . . ? Charles . . . ? William . . . ? Christine . . . ? Margaret . . . ? Maureen . . . ? Sandra . . . ? Mary . . . ? Katharine . . . ? Ann . . . ? Leahping hohpelessly from brain to brain like a mountain goaht meandering across the arid pinnacles of a desehrted hillside. God! You peohhple mahke me sihhhhck!'

Then he goes to lean his arms against the window-sill, staring out of his condemned cell and hurling chalk at the glass. He keeps on retiring to concentrate on his writing, but so far he has always reappeared at the beginning of the next session. I wonder if they make him give back the retiral presents? I sit right under his nose in the class, waiting like a wicket-keeper to catch the jokes he bats. Sometimes batting them back. Heeh heeh heeh, he goes like an aspirated hyena. Shuht uhp Anne Gillies. It wasn't thaht funny. I don't think half the folk in my class even notice when he cracks his jokes. They all like *The Goon Show*. Nothing so subtle as the English teacher and his word-wit.

I absolutely love English. Especially Shakespeare, though I've never seen any of his plays on the stage. T. S. Eliot has changed my life, though the English teacher prefers Auden. But I like my poems a bit discursive. A discovery on every line. Classical references. Wit. Mysterious, challenging, but not too convoluted. Like the Border Ballads. I try to write poems, but secretly of course. You couldn't show them to the English Teacher, what with him being a real poet. I am also completely besotted by John Donne, though I suspect my reactions are a trifle more carnal than he intended. But then again perhaps not.

The English teacher chews liquorice. Dribbles boiled egg on his tie. Wears a canary yellow sleeveless jumper from one year's end to the next, wearing it right way out first term, reversing it wrong way out after Christmas.

Then a new girl comes into our class and takes him in hand.

Well, that's an understatement. She didn't come. She burst. Exploded. Bounced. Irrupted. Catapulted. Arrived. Hair black as her Red Indian grandmother. Voice cocksure as her aristocratic father. She didn't take the English teacher in hand. She took him over completely.

People like that don't come to Oban High School. They are all at private schools in Cheltenham or Roedean or Henley-upon-Thames. They come up to grace the family estate during the Easter hols, or just before the Twelfth, or in time for the Highland Games. Cluttering up the Oban train with their straight fair hair and their fairisle jumpers. Green mackintoshes waiting at the ticket barrier to hoist their trunks and fishing rods and binoculars into Land Rovers or onto ferries. (Swimming upstream to spawn, as the man in the *Stornoway Gazette* put it. 'Knowing the hardy characteristics of this Bulldog breed we prophesy success,' he said. Or words to that effect. Good for him. That gave us all a laugh.)

Oban people congregate along the pavement to watch folk like that punting themselves with their cromags up Soroba Road and into the Games Ground. Oban people gather outside the Argyllshire Gathering Hall to applaud folk like that going into the Ball in their white silk mufflers and satin evening gloves. Next morning Oban people meekly rescue the park benches and litter bins folk like that's sons have cowped down into the bay: boys will be boys. Luckily folk like that don't get the same summer holidays as Scottish children so you can avoid them almost completely. My brother and I met two of them one day when we were up by the lochan in Glencruitten. 'Who the hell are you? How dare you come up heah? Don't you know you're bloody well trespassing?' My brother and I know there's no law of trespass in Scotland, but we turn on our heels sullenly and slink off like tinkers.

You wish you could hate the new girl, but it's quite impossible. She spreads anarchy like laughing gas.

The English lesson is underway. Dull Monday morning calm before the delightful storm. As yet she is nowhere to be seen.

Clatter of well-heeled calfskin footsteps across the wooden hall, thud of fashionable oilskin shoulder against the door, she falls into the classroom, staggering under battered real leather school-bag, parcels, umbrella — guitar getting caught between her legs, ham roll clamped between her lips like a duck's beak, chin held high to keep flour off navy-blue cashmere sweater. Offloads burdens at door. Shifts ham roll from mouth to front desk, leaving butter-trails on Kenny MacIntyre's uncomplaining English jotter.

'Look here, Sir, I've brought you a present. It was time someone cleaned you up.'

She tears off brown paper, leaving a trail of tissue paper and cellophane across the floor. A shirt, a paisley-pattern tie. A jumper too, memory? 'Now you've got no excuse. I should really insist that you go off and get changed right away.'

Heeh heeh heeh. The English teacher is twittering and blushing like a bald-headed girl. Nonplussed. Delighted.

You wish you could hate her. Search your heart for jealousy, resentment. Find only scandalised, delicious laughter. She and I form a folk-group and she persuades two of the boys to join us and sing *La Mer* and *Puirt a beul* at the Ossian *cèilidh*. She can persuade anybody to do anything. Turns up in Argyll Square at the Oban Day Parade wearing a strident trident-motifed bin-bag with a placard saying O-BAN THE BOMB long before any of us had even heard of CND. It's hellish quiet when she's not in school. Which is often. Which is a hellish pity.

The Gaelic class has been great since Mary and Flora came. There's tons of hard stuff to learn — eighteenth-century nature poetry and semi-religious prose, and next year we're going to start on ancient Irish — but Mary and Flora are such terrific Gaelic speakers, so full of fun and Tiree air, that it puts Dòmhnall Beag in a good mood most of the time. He lets us talk quietly as long as he can see we're getting on with our translations. Mary is a great giggler — especially when Dòmhnall Beag and his furry sporran are right up beside you doing corrections. Or when the word *cèir* appears in *bàrdachd* (the word *cèir* is always appearing in *bàrdachd*) and you have to work out in mid-sentence whether it means wax or rumps. It can make quite a difference you know. Sometimes the Rector wanders across from his study to find out which piece of *bàrdachd* we're on and to let us hear the tune to it. Did you know that all Gaelic poems were composed to be sung? That's the oral tradition. I suppose I'm carrying on the oral tradition every time I go to learn another song from the Rector. That's a nice thought isn't it?

But Dòmhnall Beag is really hard on his son in the class. It must be hellish having a member of staff for a father. At the beginning of this session every single person in Sixth Year was made a prefect except Dòmhnall Beag's son and the Art teacher's daughter. All the others went to the study — including my big brother — and threatened to hand their badges in if the other two weren't added to the list. I thought it was really admirable. And they got their way. The Art teacher's daughter is really nice if you know her, but she has an awful habit of speaking her mind. I sometimes wish I had the nerve to be like that.

I find it really interesting to discover that you can sometimes change teachers' minds if you act together. United we stand and all that. You feel really nervous at first, but when you begin to see them wavering you get a real buzz and you feel really close to the other people in the class. Like when we put the kybosh on Dòmhnall Beag over his son's entry for the School Magazine. He was pleased with my entry, and with Mary's and Flora's — reading out all our correct wee anecdotes from local tradition. The *Muileach's* first visit to Glasgow. The *cailleach* who sent the kippers through the post. Get the picture? But then he came to his son's.

'I don't know if this is supposed to be a joke,' he says. 'Perhaps it is I who am at fault in that I can find nothing amusing about a Higher Gaelic candidate who thinks it is clever to revert to ill-written nursery tales in his Sixth and final year at school.'

And then he begins to read, face puckering, like someone holding up a really revolting exhibit for inspection.

But his son has written the story of how the bears lost their tails. It is irresistibly funny. Him deciding to write that in the first place. The deadpan way it is told. The whole situation is pure *Goon Show*. We begin to laugh, quietly at first, then louder and insistently, making a political as well as a critical point. Dòmhnall Beag falters, glances up at us to make sure we are not laughing at his son's grammar. Or at him. By the time he has finished reading the story the class is in uproar, and Dòmhnall Beag is saying, 'Well, perhaps there's something that can be salvaged from all this, with a little help as regards the appalling spelling, the disgraceful grammatical errors . . .' He seems quite pleased with himself. Perhaps there's hope for his son yet.

I don't like Latin, but you just have to get on and slog through it. From what I know of Greek literature it seems to be much more interesting than Latin literature. All these damn military exercises — though I like Catullus of course. I thought about taking Greek in Fourth Year: usually the most brainy people in each year take Greek. But I'd have had to drop Art and obviously that is out of the question. Anyway, I don't want to trail along behind my big brother, doing all the same things as him only not quite so well, though I must say I like the sound of Greek lessons with the Rector. Just you and him. Apparently the other day he started heaving with laughter and saying 'Ah Willie, Willie, wait till you read Plaaautus. Plaaautus is terribly funny. But we don't read Plaaautus in school.' When the Rector was in Cambridge he had to go into the Gents to practise his bagpipes. Can't you just imagine him at Cambridge with all these aaawfully clever fellows, pretending to have heather growing out of his ears and then beating them all hollow in the exams. I'm beginning to think I'd like to go to Art College instead of University.

I've gone off the idea of doing Higher History next year. The new History teacher isn't the least bit like Mr Murray. It's just another long slog. You could really panic about History if you let yourself go: how could anybody possibly memorise everything that's happened over the centuries? Who could possibly be interested in Henry the Seventh's domestic policies? And where the hell's Scotland in all this anyway? Feudalism and the barons and the Tudors: wasn't anything happening up here all that time? Oh yes sorry, I forgot. We were busy being lawless savages, fighting among ourselves and spawning dreadful people like Mary Queen of Scots and Bonnie Prince Charlie to annoy the poor English. The Rector says I can take up French in Sixth Year. He'll organise it that I get the Mademoiselle all to myself five periods a week for the whole year. That sounds much more interesting.

When the results of the Highers come the Rector calls me into the study. It seems I have got the highest mark in English in the whole of Scotland. Golly, that doesn't say very much for all the others, eh sir. I just hope my Art mark was high enough to get me into Art College, though there's plenty of time to get my folio up to scratch. They say that's what really counts. Oh Anne, Anne, there can be no question of a girl of your intelligence going to Art College.

The Rector's brother Calum has died. I am so sad. I had hoped to get to know him if I went to Edinburgh — help him in collecting his Gaelic songs. The Rector has composed an elegy, wants me to sing it to the tune of a pibroch. It's a lovely poem, but he can't trust himself to teach it to me. So instead he takes me down to Combie Street to meet a beautiful little old man from Uist. We sit enthralled while the man sings to me — hard to decide at first whether he is a piper singing Gaelic songs or a Gaelic singer playing the pipes on his voice. But the long vowels are longer than any singer's vowels; the short vowels are more clipped than any singer would risk: *rubato* at once more subtle and more daring. Only a piper, proud, expressive, extolling his glorious instrument, fearless of accusations of vocal showmanship, cheap personal aggrandisement, would have the cheek to sing like this. I listen minutely, try to pick up his inflections, learn his graces. I have never heard anything like it before. In the Drill Hall, at the piping competitions, I do my best to follow the pibrochs, to winnow the chaff of tuning, marching, turning, echoing, doubling out of my ear and be left with the pure grain of the melody and its variations. But it is so long, and the mind is so inclined to wander, the ear to grow dull. And once you have lost the thread you fall back on day-dreaming and watching moustached old men scratching at their fishing-flies, or thin bearded devotees taking bound scores out of haversacks. Years later, singing the songs the old man taught me then, I still feel possessed by him, singing in unison with his ghost. Hearing his voice as clearly as when seventeen, I still wait anxiously in case anyone else hears it and accuses me of *buideachas* (witchcraft).

Towards the end of Fifth Year I am sent on a pre-University study course to Newbattle Abbey, along with Morton MacLeod from my brother's class. Everyone else on the course is in Sixth Year, but the Rector is sure I'll cope. I am impressed by the ivy and the huge trees and shining wooden floors. Most of all I am impressed by the people.

I have never met people like this before. They are so articulate; have opinions about everything under the sun — including some things I haven't given a thought to. I'm quite good at writing things down if I've got time to think them out, but I'd never be able to spout profundities like that. What do you think about euthanasia or capital punishment or behaviourism, you might ask my father a day or two before a school debate. But you wouldn't get a straight answer. Oh boy, no. It's a very complex issue, he'd say, and give you a whole lot of books with scraps of paper to mark the most salient references. By the time you'd read half of it you'd realise that there's so much to learn before you can even begin to grasp the underlying principles that you'd file the whole subject away for future reference and end up with no firm opinion of your own meantime. Though of course school debates are dead easy after reading all my father's references. After all, you only have to represent one side of the argument in a debate, and nobody ever knows whether you actually believe it or not. To tell the truth, I'm not sure if I believe in anything.

Who am I to have an opinion anyway if it comes to that? Surely you have to learn what the great men's opinions are. Just sounding off a whole lot of half-baked ideas of your own won't get you very far at our age. Well, I suppose it might if you were a genius. Which I am definitely not. I mean, for example, I might have a few interesting insights about literature now and again: the English teacher seems to think I do. But you can tell he's even more impressed when I quote what Daiches has said about Burns, or the latest Leavis pronouncement on Shakespeare. I'm lucky in that my father's always buying me books or pointing out articles on what the great men are saying about this and that, especially literature — since he knows that's my best subject. Also over the years he's chosen very useful books for the school to present to me as class prizes: he reads all the book reviews in *The Listener*, then makes a list and the school orders them in time for the prize-giving. I used to get a bit cheesed off about it — I mean you can't get much of a read out of *The Humanist Frame* on the first day of the summer holidays, can you? But believe you me I was glad by the time the Highers came. A wee off-beat quote here, a wee untraceable plagiarism there, maybe a cunning inarguable cross-reference to something I know from Gaelic tradition — they all like that.

But underneath, the more I read the less I think I know. Or rather, the more I realise I don't know. Not like these people, who seem to have made up their minds on everything. How do they do it? It shakes me rigid. I'd better just sit here and listen. I notice Morton MacLeod's not saying much either.

Their clothes are something else too; denim and leather and crinkly cotton, as if they have slept in them. Hair long and faces pale. Black sweaters. Straight out of Sartre. And here's me in my coral pink lipstick and Scotch Wool Shop paper nylon waist slip. Thank God I didn't listen to the Rector and brought something else to wear besides my school uniform. There's another girl from Argyll here. They put us in a room together. She's really boring. Like me, I suppose. She wears a twin-set and tweed skirt, and she brushed her hair a hundred times before retiring last night. She believes in God too. You wouldn't get many folk here admitting to that, but she's too naïve to keep quiet about it.

There's one girl from Fife that I really hate. She is particularly intellectual, and yet all the boys seem to jalouse that if they got her on her own she would become feminine and yielding and passionate before you could say existentialism. What a combination. Boys I know don't like you to be intellectual. You have to keep quiet about it or it puts them right off. Last night the girl from Fife got so drunk that she slid slowly down the radiator, still spouting away at some theory or other, and was out cold by the time her backside reached the floor. The boys were falling over themselves to carry her up to bed. No puking on her jumper, mind, or getting maudlin about her granny in Skye. And today not even the trace of a Calvinistic hangover. Nods and becks and passionate *conversazione* over the coffee. I'd have died of shame if it had been me.

One of the boys is handicapped. A lame revolutionary! Imagine it. You can't get much more cosmopolitan than that, eh! The girls are wild about him. They rush to help him through doorways, hang upon his every word. He holds court from his wheelchair in a hard English accent, delivering hard cynicisms. I mean, you couldn't argue with that, could you. Not after what he's been through, you know. Personally I can't help wondering what withered things lurk beneath his trouser-legs, but that just shows you what a small-minded parochial creature I am. It's really awful. I'd never realised how parochial I was.

The seminars are the worst. I was too ashamed to ask the Rector what a seminar was. Found out soon enough. An hour and a half of feeling exposed and inadequate at close quarters with all this erudition, praying vainly for something mature and cogent to say, stomach churning. By the time I have wound myself up to speak someone else has already said it, only better, and I am left to agree lamely. 'I agree with Marc.' To my horror they are all listening, waiting for more. Yes — please develop, elucidate, exemplify, qualify . . . Some hope. My mind a million miles from my stupid big mouth. After that I develop a sort of camouflage, looking exaggeratedly interested in every pronouncement, nodding sagely but non-committally. It all takes so much effort it stops me from taking in all their arguments properly so that I can use them for myself when I get home.

But another few weeks of this and I might just begin to communicate. The tutors are really encouraging. If only school was more like this. Mostly we have to work silently. Our English teacher would like us to express ourselves, right enough, but most of the folk in my class just sit there like puddings. I suppose I must be as bad as all the rest. I can see that now. No wonder he throws chalk at the windows. I can't wait to get to University. How could I ever have considered Art College?

On the last day we have a lecture on international affairs by a man who used to be the British ambassador in Persia. I'm not so keen on this. Hide-bound right-wing English imperialist attitudes. I'm surprised none of the revolutionaries notice; take him to task. They're all sitting there like mice, listening reverently to this so-called VIP. But I'm no better if it comes to that. I don't argue either. I'm not sure enough of my ground. I wish my father was here. He'd make them all sit up. Afterwards I creep up to the dais, surprised at my own daring.

'My cousin taught me a Persian song, sir — I wonder if you could translate it for me please.'

This turns out to have been a mistake. The diplomat goes alarmingly purple. He thinks I am having a go at him. Then he realises I'm not: 'My dear young lady, whoever taught you that has a very warped sense of humour. If I were you I should put it straight out of my mind.'

Still it earns me a certain belated notoriety. Quite accidentally. Everyone wants a copy of my snooty cousin's song.

And now it's time to go. How will I ever be able to re-enter my homely paradise having eaten of the fruit of this tree of knowledge? I am aflame with the need to speak up for myself, to express an opinion or two of my very own, even if they do turn out to be dull and derivative. You've got to start somewhere. There must be something I can have a personal view on with impunity. Something to be going on with.

I try to convey this at the tea-table. But they shoot through my faint hopes like a cannon, even when I muster my new-found gurus to my aid. 'After all I've told you, Anne, you should know better than to be taken in by half-baked bunkum like that' and 'Oh for heaven's sake, Anne, where's your Willie James?' and 'The poor lame boy. No wonder he had such a chip on his shoulder' and 'You're looking completely exhausted dear — hop off to bed now and Daddy'll give you Whitehead to read in the morning.'

So much for Buckingham, as my father would say. Whoever the hell Buckingham was.

EIGHTEEN

Today is the last day of the session. Just the prize-giving tomorrow and then the holidays. My brother is going to University at the end of the summer. So are Jim and Donald. Classics, science and medicine in that order.

The school will seem very insipid without my brother's class. I don't think we're nearly as interesting as they were. Only this afternoon, as I was walking up Dalintart Drive with my brother, I got a foretaste of how boring it will be next year. Coming towards us in the distance a little scuttling figure, bending from the waist: Iain Islay Davidson. He came into my class last year. Star of Bowmore Junior Secondary, out to show the Obanaich a thing or two. Small and worried-looking and obsessively neat and white with lack of oxygen. Has digs with Mrs Lawrie. Swots all the time. Sent by the Lord to try me, in case I should find Sixth Year too cushy. Next year's Dux, if I'm not careful? And here, my brother — this year's Dux, expected to get a First in Classics at Edinburgh before going on to Oxford, walking slowly, calmly, towards Iain Islay Davidson, face unreadable, half-smiling, broad forehead tanned and shining, top shirt-button undone, tie slightly loosened, blazer thrown back casually from chest thickened by farm-work, strong hands hidden in grey flannel pockets, knees loose, hips and shoulders swaying in relaxed counter-motion. Whistling softly through the gap in his teeth. He could flatten Iain Islay with one finger.

A cloudless June afternoon, the Dalintart womenfolk all away down the town doing their messages, the menfolk still at their work. A radio playing a love-song through some open window. Sunshine shimmering along the high metal fence and eddying the pollen from our hay-field in its shaft. A dragonfly suspended in time. Cows lazily chewing the cud, watch without curiosity from the hill above. My brother transfixes Iain Islay with inscrutable eyes.

'Good afternoon, Iain Islay my dear,' he smiles with consummate courtesy, and flies into a wild arpeggio of hand-springs, cartwheels and backward somersaults — past Iain Islay, down the middle of Dalintart Drive, vaulting without interruption over the gate to land, cat-like, in our field; brushing hot tarry gravel off his hands, resuming his whistle, his nonchalant stride, walks out of sight down the far side of the fence, leaving Iain Islay goggling dumbly. 'Have a good holiday then, Iain Islay,' I say, forcing myself not to grin smugly, and leave him open-mouthed.

At the beginning of the summer holidays I solemnly shook hands with Jim.

'Thank you very much for a lovely year. You know how much I like you and I hope we'll always be friends. But you're going away to University after the holidays and there's no point just now pretending we want to get married or saying we'll wait for each other till we meet up again in four or five years' time or anything like that. That would just be daft, wouldn't it, at our age? We'd best stop going steady now while we're still fond of each other.'

What an eejit. How sensible can you get?

Jim lives in the nearest house to us on Dalintart Drive. I've known him since I was five. Not all that well, mind you, till that dance near the beginning of Fifth Year. He's in the same year as my brother, but the B-class. Technical. Science. All that kind of thing. I'd never really looked at him before. I only noticed him that night because suddenly he gave me quite a few dances, which he'd never done before. But then that blinking Charles MacDonnell went and took me up for the Last Waltz, just before Jim could get to me. Normally I'd have been far too proud to do anything more than be really rude to Charles all through the Last Waltz and then go off home all miserable by myself. But for once in my life I took the initiative and gave Jim a very meaningful 'What a bore this person is, I wish you'd got there first' look over Charles's shoulder, and after the dance was finished he caught up with me in the corridor and asked could he get me home. I look at Jim very slowly and carefully to make sure he means it. No plukes, no buck teeth, no wee eyes, no red face, a reasonable height, nice hair, a Prefect, and he's asking to get me up the road. Do I dare believe this? Then I start grinning like an ape and dancing away off to the cloakroom like a twelve-year-old, leaving him standing there wondering what sort of a nut-case he's seeing home.

He was a perfect boy to go steady with. Whatever I wanted to do he was willing to go along with it. He understood about me having to work extra hard for the Highers: 'I went to the pictures by myself last night and did you know you look exactly like Shirley MacLaine — I couldn't stop thinking about you all through the big picture.' He understood about not going too far when we were smooching — however much both of us wanted to. He understood how awful I felt the night I threw a lemonade bottle high into the darkness out of sheer happiness when we were sitting by ourselves up the Hydro, miles away from all the others, and it came down and hit Helen Cameron on the forehead — I'd have died that night if it hadn't been for Jim. He was protective and deferential and good-humoured and intelligent and kind.

He made me laugh, especially when he told me about how it was his week to say grace in the canteen and he got as far as 'For what we are about to receive may the Lord make us truly thankful' and then one of the cooks dropped all the tin plates with a huge clatter and after all the noise died down he had to say 'for Christ's sake, amen'. Or when he told me about how he called in to his auntie's at the other end of Dalintart Drive, just to make sure she was all right, and he went into her kitchen and then her living room and then her bedroom but there was no sign of her though he was sure he could hear her calling his name very faintly, and then he went back into the kitchen and noticed two wee fat legs sticking down through the plaster in the ceiling: she'd gone up into the loft and fallen down between two rafters and had been stuck up there all afternoon. Or when he tried to write 'Put that in your pipe and smoke it' in his awful pidgin Gaelic: *'bitheadh sin 'nad pìob agus smogadh e'*. He was nice to my parents, even Granny — especially Granny! He had always got on well with my brother and he could give us a hand now and then around the place if we needed it. But he never pushed himself in if it wasn't appropriate. We went everywhere together and talked about everything under the sun. He was a real pal for the whole year and when we were lying together in the grass up our hill on a sunny afternoon you could have easily started thinking you were in love with him.

But I knew that wasn't really love. Everything you read and sang — in Gaelic and in English, everything you imagined and dreamed — pure and illicit, everything you heard on the wireless and saw at the pictures, told you that real love was something infinitely more strange and special and sharp and poignant and frightening and exciting and sweet and bitter and heroic and passionate and tragic and poetic and unfamiliar and painful and uncontrollable and tortuous and unattainable and euphoric and adult than that sweet friendship. That sweet, unassuming boy who lived next door in a council house with two cheeky wee brothers and an adenoidal mother and a father who kept his garden neat and tidy. What I want is an Intellectual. Like my da. Like my big brother. I suppose.

So I said goodbye to Jim on a slender pretext and without regret, and went off down the road to fall in love with Donald. Donald, my brother's friend, who was also going away to University, but who was unhappy and tortured and vulnerable and unreachable and deep and dark. Whose parents came from Lewis. Who turned to me for a little disbelieving comfort. Who spoke in short self-obsessive riddles, laughed frequently but without humour. Who, despising himself, resented me, avoided me and sought me out by bitter, unpredictable turns. Who fought my virginity with dogged but pessimistic ingenuity, keeping a sardonic tally of his failed campaigns. Who turned away from me to spew a black stream of misery and alcohol across the *Oban Times* pier. The catcher in the rye. The outsider. Tragic hero to his classmates, fair game to lounge-bar predators.

For him I wrote poems, haunted streets, consorted with succubi. After he had gone I laid my head on the wireless and cried in tune with Elvis Presley. Waited hopelessly up our hill to scour the lighted windows of incoming Friday night trains. Wrote unashamed unanswered letters. Grew pale and listless and Worried my Poor Mother.

Bathed in the reflected light of his distant star, I find myself in Sixth Year playing unexpected dramatic heroine to several desirable Lotharios. Sympathy and veneration combining to temper their usual ardour, they dance with me respectfully, confide in me shyly — their troubles, their exploits — see me safely home, kiss me with gentle chivalry, take me out at weekends in case I feel lonely, and then go off to sow their notorious wild oats elsewhere. I don't suppose any of them would have looked twice at me otherwise. All in all it's a smashing arrangement.

That summer before my brother's class went away to University was also the summer when the hurricane struck.

My brother was out working at the caravan site in Ganavan and all the caravans blew over, some of them right out into the sea.

I had been out in Tiree for a wee holiday at Flora's house. Flat flowery island; solid farm-houses with yapping collie dogs and tea on the stove; squat stone black-houses, moss growing on their thatch; white sands on the shore and in the furrows at the Cattle Show; grey lowering skies and a warm wind blowing constantly across the *machair*. Flora's granny refusing to speak English to us, using her mirror to see out across the whole island from the chair to which she is bound. *Thig air ais dh'ar faicinn a-rithist an ath bhliadhna, a cheist.* (Come back and see us next year, dear.) *O thig. Thig gu dearbh, tapadh leibh.* (Oh I will. I will indeed, thank you.)

Things were not well at home.

Granny becoming more and more forgetful, crouches at the piano intently conjuring up strange ghostly sounds, gets scissors and cuts up the edge of the jumper sleeve she has just knitted because it was not straight enough, tears up her library book into little pieces and throws it into the fire because the last page was missing, stands playing her violin absent-mindedly with a dark stain appearing down the inside of her well-turned ribbed stocking-leg.

My brother is the best at humouring Granny, now she's getting a bit dotty. One morning she called me into her room.

'What were the fire engines doing in the yard last night?' she asks me.

'Och don't be daft, Granny,' I reply cheerfully. 'There were no fire engines here. You've just had a wee dream.'

But Granny is furious, unappeased. She calls my mother in.

'Anne won't tell me, Mary dear, but I know you will. What were the fire engines doing here last night? They were in the yard half the night.'

'Now now, you silly, there were no fire engines here,' my mother coos. 'You've had a nightmare, that's all.'

Granny calls Willie into her room.

'Nobody tells me anything in this house. Anne won't tell me, your mother won't tell me. I know they're only trying to keep me from worrying. But I want you to tell me, Liam. What were the fire-engines doing in the yard last night?'

'Of course, Granny, I'll tell you. It was absolutely nothing to worry about. It was the leopard.'

'The what?'

'The leopard. A leopard escaped from Edinburgh Zoo and got all the way to Oban and up our hill. They sent the fire-brigade to catch it. It was really exciting. They turned their hoses on it to calm it down and then caught it in their nets. They didn't put it on the news because it's all had to be hushed up to avoid panic.'

'There you are. I knew there was something.'

Years later we are still getting Christmas cards from Granny's buddies in England remarking on how frightened we must have been when the wild animal was up our hill.

'Anne wouldn't tell me, your mother wouldn't tell me, but I can always rely on you, Liam.'

That's a laugh. At Christmas time I spend a fortune on a lovely fluffy bed-jacket for her. My brother gets a plastic plant out of Woolworths for half-a-crown and tells Granny to be sure and not water it as it's a Desert Daisy and isn't used to rain. She's desperate to water it, so he says, 'Salt and pepper. Put salt and pepper on it to simulate the conditions in the Sahara. It can't get enough salt and pepper, a Desert Daisy.'

My mother has to snaffle it away at night when Granny is asleep, to wash all the seasoning off its plastic leaves. Granny is as pleased as Punch.

'See the lovely plant my grandson got me specially. It's very exotic. A Desert Daisy.'

To be perfectly honest I don't know how we'll manage without my big brother. It drives me mad how puny I am physically compared to him. I go to do jobs we used to do together and can't manage them. And my parents are not keeping very well at all. Mother walking to work, face yellow, leaving wee mouthfuls of her dinner behind her on the road as she goes. One day she fell asleep by the fire and woke up sick. Couldn't make it to the sink. Green-pea soup it was. On the stove. I hate grown-ups being sick. It makes me really scared. Personally I am hardly ever sick. Even when I had the pneumonia I would do anything rather than puke. I think puking is quite revolting. I remember when I was wee, one of my mother's patients took me and my brother to the Schoolboys' Exhibition in the Kelvin Hall, and I was car-sick going round Loch Lomond, but I never even let on. I just held my nose shut with one hand and my mouth shut with the other hand and swallowed it back down every time it came up. And if you really do have to be sick I think the least you can do is do it quietly — not like my mother. She howls and screeches like a gibbon. It's enough to turn your stomach.

My father's stomach is none too healthy either. He has water-brash if he eats anything fatty, and he gets a sore back if he attempts anything too strenuous — fence-posts, sack-lifting and so on. It's surprising to realise how many of those things my brother has been doing for him lately. Of course I help my brother — for example I kneel on the ground trimming the slates and then run up and down the ladder with great armfuls of them, while he sits on the roof hammering them on. We have a good laugh at times like that. It's such mindless work you can let your head roam away on any subject you like while your hands are otherwise engaged. One day we made up an epic which I'm sorry to say was rather blasphemous but which seemed so funny at the time that my brother nearly fell off the roof and nipped his promising career untimely in the bud! It would have been a Judgment if he had, I'm telling you!

But there's just no way on earth I could do his part of the work. I don't have any head for heights and I can't hammer a nail in straight, never mind a stob or a staple to hold the barbed-wire down and keep the cows in.

Then Father off work with shingles. They say that always has a nervous component. He has always had trouble at his work. Once a rumour went all the way round Oban that Mr Gillies had got the sack for embezzle-ment. Can you imagine that? My father, who is the most scrupulous person in the whole world — too scrupulous for his own good some would say. Having to prove himself innocent of something like that! My father who paid all the nurses out of his own pocket one week because their wages got held up by an office mix-up down in Lochgilphead. But there seems no doubt at all that some people on the Hospital Board would like rid of my father, for whatever reason. They say they want to concentrate on their offices on Lochgilphead and Dunoon, and do away with the Oban office, which is hilarious, if you think that all the hospitals are in Oban — three hours from Lochgilphead and half a day from Dunoon. But I think my parents suspect there's more to it than that. Something personal someone has against my father. I can't judge whether this is just them being paranoid. I somehow think not. If you saw a Mason's funeral, with all the men out in their aprons, you'd realise how peculiar people can be. Not that I think that's the sort of conspiracy we're talking about here. More a class thing, or a political thing maybe. You can't imagine my father toadying to the Honourable This-and-that, can you?

Of course I have to piece all this together for myself. They don't tell me much about it. I know my father must have won one of his battles when my mother buys him a kilted warrior in Douglas's and, with shaky Indian ink, prints *Latha Inbhir Lòchaidh* on the grey stone upon which he stands waving his triumphant claymore. (*Latha Inbhir Lòchaidh* is my father's favourite Gaelic song. J. C. M. Campbell, one of my father's old cronies from the London Gaelic Choir, is the best singing it — which is ironic, as it celebrates the great victory of the MacDonalds over the Campbells at Inverlochy!) I'm glad my father has won some sort of victory, but there always seems to be another battle. Not just at work, either. He borrowed a camera and took photographs of our ground all round the edges where the Council should be maintaining their side. The broken down fence, the bedsteads filling gaps, the reeds and mud where they should have dug drains. One night I lay awake sweating, listening to my father in the next room, weeping uncontrollably all night long. What was all that about? I don't suppose I'll ever know.

Anyway. When I got back from Tiree we had to hurry to finish putting up the hay-stacks before the rain came. During the day I'm on my own with the hay-rake, turning and re-turning the bits they haven't had time to stack in their fortnight off. I don't think too much about Himself, swanning away down in his wee wooden hut at Ganavan, trying to get off with all the nubile English holiday-makers, and getting paid for it! I take an apple out to the field, a drink of orange, some biscuits, and place them at the ends of random rows to give myself something to work towards. My parents hurry home early, work through tea-time, and by the fourth evening it is finished. We stand momentarily at the gate, looking at the neat field jaunty with hay-stacks, walk back to fuss over a rope, comb down a tangle, pad out a brick, then rush into the house to bathe eyes in cold water and midgie bites in bicarb, put washing soda on cleg bites and stretch our aching backs.

My mother sits by the fire later that night and makes a wee dolly out of hay and ribbons. Even the dog is flat out. This is about the one time in life you really miss being able to say a prayer of thanksgiving.

Next day at dinner time my father is upstairs in the bedroom, looking out the skylight window to admire our handiwork again. Suddenly shouting out in loud, uncontrollable rage. Blundering down the stairs banging himself against the narrow walls.

'Boys! Boys! There are boys in the hay-field knocking down all our haystacks!'

Oh God no. We leap up from the dinner-table, hurry outside after him.

At first as we run, panting, we hardly hear the strange sound beyond the garden, more sustained, more ominous than thunder.

But as we emerge from behind the shelter of the high hedge the wind catches us, tearing off my mother's hair-net, whipping my father's cigarette ash away in an orange stream, plastering our clothes against us and making puppets of our arms and legs. We cling together watching it topple the remaining stacks. Try stupidly to catch clumps of precious hay as they pass us, bouncing, flying up onto the *dùn* and away into the sky. Next day the frightened cows come out from the byre and eat their prodigal way along the feast hung out for them along the barbed wire fence: all that is left of our labour — of their winter feed.

Maggie Rogers asks me down to stay at her place in Balvicar. Just for the night. I go in the bus. The driver chucks out newspapers and packages as he passes people's road-ends. He's a terrific aim.

Balvicar is pretty in its own way once you get past the new, modern, concrete-and-glass houses all the English have been building up near the road, and the low, dark, ramshackle shop with its ramshackle, eccentric, ill-tempered, incomprehensible, weather-beaten owner. Down in the village proper, rows of wee, old, white-washed cottages strung together around the shallow bay. Like a Dutch landscape only greyer. Flat grey slate rocks, flat grey slate skies. You can hardly tell whether you're still on the mainland or on Seil Island.

The tiny bridge over the Atlantic is unique and truly picturesque, as they say — a terrific tourist attraction. But Tigh-an-Triubhais is more interesting historically, 'The House of Trews' — the inn where the

Easdale folk stopped to doff their kilts and don their trousers on the way to the mainland. The English tourists probably think that was very quaint, but people got arrested and deported to Botany Bay if they were caught wearing tartan after Culloden. They had to make trousers out of meal-pokes, sails, anything they could find, because there wasn't time to weave all that plain material. But of course they got to wear the full regalia if they joined the British Army. Oh yes. A sporran and a feather in your cap and one of the smart new regimental tartans. Straight into battle at Waterloo, or the Heights of Abraham, or the Somme. And play your pipes while all your countrymen are being slaughtered in the front line. Oh yes. Ladies from Hell. Jolly frightening sight, a battalion of hairy, kilted Scotchmen, dontcha know. Ladies from Hell ha ha. Keeps them out of mischief. Helps with the depopulation of the Highlands. Relieves the economy.

But we don't get taught about things like that in the History class. Only the Gaelic class gets told about things like that, and most of us know it already from our fathers. By the way, everybody in the country places like Balvicar and Easdale spoke Gaelic until quite recently, but nowadays you hardly ever hear it. And nobody seems to care either. I find that incredible. Even Christine MacAskill takes French in school and the level of historical understanding of most folk in my class is kilts up pants down cocks up fire.

The Rogers haven't got a bathroom either. Or a toilet. It's really interesting. I can recognise all the signs in Maggie, long before anything is actually said — hoping against hope I won't need the toilet after dark (what does she think I am? a hen?) her mum being dead casual about it all and that making Maggie even more embarrassed though she must know it's got to come out at some stage in the evening. Where does she think I live? Buckingham Palace? But you can't help someone else, can you? They just have to go through their own personal agonies. I wished I could have the nerve to say, 'Thank you, Maggie, for not having a toilet. For being a wee bit like ourselves.' But I didn't. I just tried very hard to make it obvious I didn't care where I peed as long as it wasn't in my breeks. She's nice, Maggie.

I'm getting asked to do quite a bit of singing now, walking down to perform in hotel lounges and church halls and hospital wards. Sailing away to sing in Salen and Bowmore and the Tobermory Games, staying with little old school-teachers and their cats. By bus to *cèilidh*-dances in Easdale — getting asked up between songs to do the Military Two-step with likely lads from Luing called Farouk and Hughie. Transported by

Dòmhnall Beag to *cèilidhs* in Taynuilt and Duror and Kinlochleven and Aberfeldy — getting stuck in snow and sniggering with uncontrollable terror while he reverses the car back down a steep and narrow two-mile tunnel of sheer ice and out on to the main road at the bottom past the Road Impassable sign which I had been meant to be keeping a look-out for. Going by train and taxi to Glasgow halls — sitting up on the platform beside the two-guinea *Mòd* Gold Medallists till your turn to sing, listening to the minutes of last month's meeting.

'Item five: small balls. Small balls! *Small balls?* Miss MacIver, may I most respectfully enquire why, in your capacity as our ever-diligent Assistant Secretary and with your usual admirable legibility, you have seen fit to write "small balls" here among your customarily efficient list of items for discussion at the outset of this month's brief business committee meeting? Ah yes, of course — now I recall. The entertainment sub-committee voted at their extraordinary general meeting of sixth ult. for a month's consultation and private deliberation before putting to the general vote Mrs MacLeod's typically thought-provoking motion to the effect that, in order to grace our annual syllabus of social functions with a little more formal dignity, we should stop calling them dances. Please show, all eligible to vote, in favour of small balls. Thank you. Against? Thank you *a chàirdean*. Motion passed. And now we pass on to the Treasurer's Report before addressing the important matter of floral arrangements for this year's Gathering.'

Afterwards the Treasurer advances with a pencil and note-pad while you are standing making conversation with the minister and two members of the congregation:

'You'll not have many expenses then, Anne? Just your train fare? Very good, very good. I enjoyed your singing at the *Mòd* in Stirling. Mr Thomson's making a grand job of her wouldn't you say, Mr MacConochie? You'll be trying for the Gold Medal soon, no doubt. I was at Oban High myself you know.'

At the *Mòd* in Stirling Dòmhnall Beag had tried me out among the senior competitors. Sixteen-year-old adult among the broad-hipped old war-horses. The Provost welcomes us to the town: 'It's great to see yous Gaels coming here. I havny the Gaylick myself but *slàinte mhath* one and all.' Press cameras flash. Now just one more, girls. Running towards the camera please. Sit there on the wall now. Closer together. Put your arms round the girls, boys — they won't bite. Can you show a bit more leg there ladies. One more for me. A high kick this time. All together. Whee. Two of you together under the umbrella. That's nice.

That's really nice. Singing in the rain. Gael force. Gaels blow in. All Mod cons.

In the morning I sing in praise of Ballachulish, painting the sunlight on its sloping mountainsides, tasting in my throat the excruciating *cianalas* of its sad exiles. I come second, one uncomplaining mark behind the other young upstart with his relaxed pop-eyed, round-chested, precise-voweled, expressive-handed, honey-gold, operatic tenor voice.

In the afternoon I sing in praise of the Misty Corrie, roaming fearlessly, sure-footedly, observantly, joyfully across Ben Doran's familiar slopes — black-green, fertile, flowery, fresh, calm, fair-morninged, blue-grey with dew and rich with mavises, sprightly murmuring moorhens, showy heather-cocks, clear glittering springs, watercress, bog cotton, fecund white-rumped hinds and most plenteous proud-antlered baying stags. At the first-prize-winners' concert I recreate the rich Argyllshire scene, draw out its assonances, caress its consonants, in a Victorian concert-hall stretching back high as Ben Doran, showy with tartans, glittering silver trophies, fecund white-breasted sopranos and most plenteous proud-antlered baying baritones. Am presented with a small golden medal but never get round to having it engraved.

On the bus home I sit low down in the velvet seat, close-smiling and conspiratorial and teasing and hand-touching and hair-brushing and thigh-pressing with a handsome, fresh, dewy, soft-cheeked, downy-kneed, dark-haired, brown-eyed, precocious, Gaelic-speaking boy newly-come from Jura; his light, sweet, inquisitive, barely-broken, still-drowsy early-morning voice mingling intimately with my worldy-wise extempore harmonies. What a baby-snatcher, Anne Gillies. But they're all jealous as hell.

At the Christmas Dance last year's Sixth Years are allowed to come back to the school for the evening. I am in an agony of nervous anxiety. Will Donald come? Will he be seen with me publicly, justify my claims, my dreams, my pain, my bitter-sweet tragic reputation over the last term? The alternative is too sore, too shameful to contemplate, tempts me to plead sick and stay at home. But instead I take extra care over my clothes, my make-up. The best thing would probably be if he doesn't turn up at all — after all, that would be par for the course. The Outsider. The Dharma Bum.

He is there, but does not dance with me. I glitter with brittle vivacity and, smiling ostentatiously at everyone but him, avoid his eyes to watch his every move. At half time he lets Charles MacDonnell — him again — take me up for the Supper Dance. I am sitting in the canteen picking at a sandwich and being unconscionably rude to poor MacDonnell; feeling sick at my own meanness, but quite unable to control myself; homicidally resentful of a system which gives me no say in all this, leaves me victim to these outrageous slings and whims; tautened to hysteria by my physical awareness of Donald sitting behind me, back to back almost, among an insouciant crowd of his own contemporaries.

Did he hear me? Catch my miserable undertones? Feel sorry for a silly unrequited school-girl? Suddenly recall with seasonal kindness some past affinity which has obsessed me while becoming a vague, unimportant memory to him far away in Aberdeen in a new life, among new friends, new problems? I feel a hand against my side, groping to find my elbow, pulling down my hand to hold his between the two wooden benches. Without warning Charles is subjected to a manic change of mood. For the rest of the meal I sit holding Donald's secret hand convulsively behind my back, hot-faced and sweaty and sparkling unaccountably at the dull fellows all around me. Later snuggle into Donald's white raincoat in the Games Ground grandstand, suspending all judgment, happy in this moment alone.

On New Year's morning my brother is going to take me out first-footing for the first time. With the usual faint Hogmanay embarrassment, the usual forced Hogmanay gaiety, we all stand around, glasses in hands, hardly daring to breathe; shake hands, kiss each other, sing *A Guid New Year*, open the door to let in the bells, the ships' hooters, the brave New Year, my dark, male brother pocketing a lump of coal and father's whisky bottle to masquerade as a stranger. Then, as soon as politely possible, he and I are off down Dalintart Drive, sitting on fluffy hearth-rugs round drink-slopped coffee tables in all these houses we've never been in before, among all these so near and yet so far people — drinking in their once-a-year *bonhomie* and looking round at their empty patterned walls, their well-stoked little fires, their rubicund relatives.

In the houses where kids live we are received as the younger generation, valued friends of sons and daughters, and I am given sweet sherry and biscuits by fathers, aunts and uncles. In the houses where no kids live we are received as newly-blooded equals, given whisky, dumpling and — for him — a can of heavy by strangely conspiratorial adults. I leave Dalintart Drive feeling like a giant, a man among men, a native among my ain folk. In Mossfield, down Miller Road, along Soroba Road, the feeling is maintained, fuelled by the indiscriminate laughter, cracks, kisses, cuddles, blessings, lip-smacking swigs of the population sliding past us along the slippery street. The breath-taking frost keeps us sober and our wits about us until we reach Donald's house. His parents themselves gone a-visiting, the usually warm house is untidy, unwelcoming, the fire gone out, the cushions scattered, the little sister spying in her night-gown from the landing. After I have been sick, it is Jim, appearing like my guardian angel from I know not where, who wipes my mouth and my eyes, rubs my freezing hands, puts his coat around me and supports me home across the swirling icy town, opens my door softly, helps me up the stairs and leaves me to my misery. Next day I wander up the hill, cursing the trains which do not run on Ne'erday, will not come when I most need them to end my heart's pain, my spiritual emptiness, my physical malaise, in one last sweet thunderous swoop.

NINETEEN

I have become a Hostel stowaway, hiding in Mary's wardrobe till Foosty's footfalls die away, flattening the herbaceous border underneath Rona's bedroom window. 'You're really weird, Anne Gillies. You're always sneaking in here while all the rest of us are trying to escape.' I don an arthritic Tiree accent in the phone-box at the foot of the brae to ask permission for my niece Flora and her friends Mary and Mary and Rona to meet me down in the square for tea and the pictures before I go off to sleep in my cabin on board the *Claymore*. On the night of the Annual Bean-feast (out-of-bounds to Hostel girls after last year's excesses) I persuade my gullible, obliging mother to perjure herself by phoning Foosty to invite the entire Sixth Year out to a Gillies family picnic.

I have become a two-faced Prefect, straightening lines and quietening blethers and confiscating cats-cradles to play with over the coffee in the Prefects' Study above the First Year cloakroom. Hiding a fag in the palm of my hand to shout last warnings at Third Years smoking in the Games Ground grandstand. Locked hastily by Mr Gordon into the Art Room cupboard and the key pocketed until the Rector has gone out of the Art Room again — standing horror-struck in semi-darkness fanning the smoky fug out of the side window with swathes of sugar-paper and suppressing giggles with my fist.

I started smoking the morning after my mother went into hospital. Found myself possessively irritated with my father: come on for heaven's sake you'll need to get up and eat something before you go to work — I've made us both some nice toast. Found myself patiently condescending with my granny: here's a nice cuppa now you just lie there like a good girl and I'll get you up when I get home at dinner-time. Found myself in Joe Boni's at dinner-time hurriedly scouring the cardboard adverts for the name of a cigarette brand: any brand — parents both roll their own. Bristol. That'll do. Ten Bristol please. Can't stop, got to hurry, got to make my father's dinner, no — no news from the hospital yet, yes I'll pass it on, cheerio then. Found myself just past the first gate, bouncing the cigarette up and down against the back of my other hand like she does, lighting up, dragging a huge mouthful of smoke deep into my lungs, tamping down the cork spat compulsively with the tip of my thumb, picking imaginary tobacco threads from my tongue and spitting imaginary tobacco threads from my lips as I staggered from side to side up the road, head reeling, eyes squinting back over my shoulder trying to focus and check my father is not behind me on his way home from work.

After father fed, granny watered, had another fag out the skylight window, blowing smoke high into the air, trying to catch sight of the Cottage Hospital away up there among the trees. Mother's gall-bladder operation relatively routine for a woman in her forties if it wasn't for her chest. For the danger of lung congestion. Pneumonia. Death. I put on her blue tweed coat to go back to school in the afternoon. It fits pretty well over my blazer. I wish my granny would just stay in her bed instead of getting up guddling around trying to help. It would be much easier all round. She didn't need to put the tatties on. I'd have had plenty of time to do it. She might scald herself and then where would we all be? I've got enough to do with all her draw-sheets and everything. Why don't she and my father play the game? I'm doing my best. What more do they want?

Most of the other girls have given up smoking now, after a few months of giggling and passing fags along the second-back row trying to inhale. I stagger to and from school, an addict from the first drag. Pumping away at my puffer to persuade my bronchial tubes to stay wide long enough to enjoy their smoky libation right down to the tip. Coughing through English. Topping up in Art. Bunching up my fists to hide the nicotine stains from Dòmhnall Beag. Keeping my head turned away from the Rector. Exhaling hastily up the chimney, pretending to be warming my hands at the fire, feeling the concealed fag burning away into my fingers while father talks on and on. After mother is a little better, she looks out of her ward and sees smoke rising from the skylight window — persuades nurse to phone home to make sure all is well; solves the riddle months later, plunging her hands into her blue tweed pocket, finding forty thousand clothes pegs plus three cigarettes in a crumpled packet.

They let me stay at home as much as I need to. No reason to drag yourself into school and sit there worrying about your granny, the dog, the cows, the hens, your father's dinner. This year I'm only doing a few subjects at advanced level for the Bursary Competition; painting a mural outside the Latin room and filling up my portfolio in case I decide to do Art after all; laughing and drinking coffee with the Mademoiselle; organising the Debating Society and doing art-work for the School Magazine; being Vice-captain of the school and Chieftain of Ossian.

While mother is ill I stay at home till I've got everything organised, then make pancakes and take them in warm, wrapped in a tea-cloth for the rest of the prefects to eat with their coffee at the interval. Nobly nobly Cape St Vincent.

That was about the time when the stirk fell into the ditch and drowned. Neither me nor my father could get it out. It's more shaming for men to have to admit physical defeat.

That was also about the time when Mr Gordon the Art teacher shot Skite by accident. He only meant to frighten him. Fired out his bedroom window into the pitch darkness. Found him flat out next morning underneath the washing line. He was very apologetic.

'Och don't be daft, sir. Good riddance. Stupid cat.'

'Well he certainly did have a very horrible miaow.'

'Dead right he did. He was a complete pervert. Hey, what do you think about this — is it good enough for my folio?'

Throughout the year I swither about my career. Perhaps I'm just being daft even contemplating Art College. Trying to be a rebel. Agin the government.

On the other hand, wouldn't it be wonderful to spend your whole life doing what you enjoy best? I'm only really happy when I'm endlessly doodling, as my father calls it. (Or playing the piano, but I'm certainly not good enough to make a career of that.) Being me, of course, I avoid self-discipline even in my drawing: observation, draughtmanship etc — the scales and arpeggios of art. I am pretty bored now with the endless high-lit wine-bottles, the carefully-posed gym-shorts, the rules of composition and scale and perspective, the flying buttresses and Corinthian columns, other folks' allegories. From within myself I can feel the expressive set of shoulders, the muscle-flow of fingers, thrust of thighs. The ache and leap and gush of emotions and, above it all, the beckoning will o' wisp of intellect if you had time and talent and encouragement to think through to what you are actually trying to express. Taking raw, malleable materials and kneading them into shape like a sculptor. Checking them against lips, tongue, cheek, like a monkey. And then holding them up to the light of mind and spirit.

Heaven help us, what kind of basis is that for a career decision of this magnitude? Where's the self-discipline in that? What are the prospects? You'd be best to keep your art for your own amusement. Like Grampop advised you about Music: never become a professional musician otherwise all the pleasure will go out of it. Well he should know. Hells bells, what a miserable life, eh? My grampop, my father, each of whom has, in his own way, led me into magical gardens most kids never see. Each of whom now turns round and tells me I've got to close the garden door firmly when I grow up. Go and do something sensible. 'Life is made of pain and woe', Willie Blake. To his eternal credit my father never once says anything about the opportunities he never had. But they're hanging in the air all around us.

The Rector discovers a course which combines Art and English. You move between the Art College and the University. Now that sounds like a good idea — the best of both worlds? Keep everybody happy? I am over the moon. But the Art teachers are furious. That is a perfectly ridiculous idea. Compromise. Falling between two stools. Perhaps you could become proficient in English Literature in a half-time course, but you certainly could not become an artist. Come on Anne, show a little faith in yourself. Make up your mind. Don't fall into their stereotype.

How could they be so cruel? I thought they were my friends. Why do they not understand my dilemma? Can't they try to put themselves in my shoes, just for a moment? Feeling betrayed, I decide to go to University to spite them. Well, I suppose it's one way of making your mind up.

But which University? It is generally assumed that I am going to Edinburgh. My brother is at Edinburgh; the Rector went there too, before Cambridge. But they are Classics scholars. It is generally assumed that I am going to do Eng. Lit., though goodness knows what I'll do with it. Throw chalk at windows? But in any case, is Edinburgh any good for Eng. Lit? Nobody seems to know. My mother would like Willie to be on hand to look after me, though I wonder if she'd think that if I let her read the letters he writes to me.

But nobody else I know is thinking of Edinburgh this year. They're either going to Glasgow or Aberdeen. I quite fancy Aberdeen, but it doesn't have such a good academic name as Edinburgh or Glasgow — even if the English teacher did go there. Also I don't want anyone thinking I want to go to Aberdeen just because Donald's there — even if that has crossed my mind. I especially wouldn't want Donald thinking any such thing. I certainly don't want to be a mill-stone round his neck, or an embarrassment, do I? And I don't fancy Glasgow at all, even if Flora is going there.

Then I hear about a Tiree girl who left school a year or two ago: she's doing a combined course of English and Celtic. You can only do that in Aberdeen. In Edinburgh you have to choose: English *or* Celtic, and the Celtic degree is meant to be very academic: comparative philology and ancient Irish and Welsh etc; very little Scottish Gaelic at all. The Professor is an Englishman. The Aberdeen course is based much more on literature and the guy in charge is a modern Gaelic poet from Lewis. Now that sounds pretty interesting. That has a certain ring to it. I could maybe persuade them that there was some sense in that idea.

The Rector arranges for me to go up to Aberdeen to meet the Celtic guy up there. Donald's mum phones Donald and tells him he's to jolly well come down and meet me at the station and take care of me for the day or she'll give him what for. She's really nice, Donald's mum.

Donald meets me at the station, and takes me up to the Celtic man's house, and he and his wife are very pleasant to me. I more or less promise them I'll come to their university, take the course. Well, what else could you say?

But on the way home I think about it again. It was all so unfamiliar: the Lewis boys in Donald's pictures — taken in the station after a pint or two by the looks of it — with their strange nicknames; the pleasant woman who has obviously been mothering Donald since he's been up there; the hard white granite streets — I felt completely shut out from it all. And they don't have a School of Scottish Studies in Aberdeen, do they? If Donald had actually asked me to come . . . but that's just foolish romantic nonsense. You don't make a huge decision like this on the strength of a school-girl crush, do you? I'm daft, but I'm not that daft.

Then again it would be good to have Mary to pal around with — she's definitely going to Aberdeen. But on the other hand everybody has made it quite clear they're hoping I'll go to Edinburgh with Willie. If I don't like Aberdeen, or if I don't do well there, they'll say it was all my own fault. Best do what they all expect of me, and then nobody can blame me if things turn out wrong. As they have a habit of doing in my life.

National Federation of Business and Professional Women's Clubs

Oban Club

12.6.61

Dear Miss Gillies

As programme secretary of the above Club I have been asked to write to you to enquire if you can bring a Youth Team to hold a discussion on 'Working Mothers'. The meeting is to be held in Archibald's Tearoom on December 12th at 8 p.m. I hope you will be able to fit this date in among your other activities.

Yours sincerely

(Mrs) Mae MacLucas

Well, the whole world complains about the behaviour of young people today, but nobody ever takes the trouble to find out what the young people themselves think. The Professional Women want to put that right, it seems.

Before the meeting starts the chairwoman explains to us that they want to explore some pretty personal, pretty controversial areas. Many of them have daughters. They want to find out the truth. They want us to feel free to express ourselves openly. To feel completely confident that no word of what passes in here tonight will go outside these four walls. Sounds OK to me. What could they ask anyway?

We wend our uncontroversial ways through nuclear weapons and corporal punishment and rock and roll and equal opportunities. Then the chair-woman invites a question on sex education in school: you can tell this is what they've been leading up to all along.

'Girls, we have heard that quite a few young people of your age feel dissatisfied with the type of information you are offered in school as regards sex. Is there any truth in this? Or should the onus remain with parents fully to inform their children on such matters?'

Now remember, girls, many of us are mothers. We are looking for honest answers. Anne Gillies?

Oh yes indeed, we are dissatisfied with the type of sex education offered in our school, although we would also expect our parents to answer our questions as openly and honestly as possible. However, it is quite understandable that in some families both parents and children may feel somewhat inhibited as regards deeply personal matters of this kind, and that this may reflect on the quality and depth of the discussion. This is presumably why there is a peripatetic specialist teacher who visits us a couple of times during senior school specifically to inform us and answer our questions on sex.

This could be a very useful exercise, if it were not for the teacher herself. She is fine as long as she sticks to the straightforward biological stuff — where do babies come from and all that. But we could read that in any biology book. I don't think I'm alone in feeling that what we want far more than that, is helpful, practical stuff — the actual mechanics of sex, how to cope with real relationships now and in the future, et cetera.

For example, some boys tell you that you can actually harm them physically by refusing them sex: is that true? I don't know. Nobody's ever explained things like that to us. But when someone asked the Sex Education teacher a question like that she said: 'If I went out walking with a boy and we stood together beside a gate and he did something which I considered demonstrated a lack of respect I would simply walk through the gate and close it in his face. Say goodbye to him then and there and retain my self-respect and my reputation.' (Laughter).

But then, you couldn't expect much more from her. She's not even married, a middle-aged lady, and from the way she goes on you couldn't imagine she had ever had a boyfriend at all. How could someone like that tell us about real sex? What would it do to her precious reputation if we discovered she actually knew the answers to the questions we want to ask? (More laughter).

In fact, to be perfectly truthful, we call her the Uncertificated Teacher. (Eruption of laughter, applause).

When I get home the phone is ringing. I pick up the receiver. 'Oban 2658?'

Ah yes, Anne. Hi. This is Iain from the *Oban Times*. Yeah, hi, fine thanks. But I'm phoning with another hat on today. I don't know if you know that I send off feature articles now and again to the national press. Well I've just heard all about your marvellous meeting with the Prof. Ladies down in Archibalds' and it's given me a terrific idea for a full photo story. I heard about your speech about the Sex Education, and I thought it would be just great if we could get you down the town, as quickly as possible, if you don't mind, to get a really lovely sexy photo — as only you can look — sitting on the esplanade wall, maybe, looking out to sea with your long blonde hair and your long legs in a nice short skirt. Take some time to get a really lovely shot you know. And then we'll get a picture of your middle-aged unmarried Sex Education specialist and run a story on the lines of 'The Uncertificated Teacher' (I like it, I like it): 'This is what's teaching *this* about sex.'

Thank you but no thank you Iain from the *Oban Times*. Yeah you can try one of the other girls if you want. That's up to you. No I'm not telling you who else was on the panel — you can find out for yourself. And whoever gave you all this information, which was given in confidence in a closed meeting, I'd like you to tell her from me where she can go. Good night. Good Lord, was that me? That shows you how angry I am — betrayed by a member of my own sex. But didn't I do well? Shaking after I put the phone down, of course, but what the heck. What was all that about, my father asks. Briefly I retell my story, brimming with righteous indignation, certain of his approval for the efficient way in which I handled the unpleasant corollary.

You hear that, Mary? You hear what she's been up to now? Letting her unruly member run away with her again. In a meeting, of all places! When will she learn? Ah well, go your ways, Ellen Gowan. You'll learn the hard way all right. Aw shurrup. Anne! What a way to speak to your father! Yes — you see — that's what she's coming to.

And now here I am on the train, off to Edinburgh to sit the Bursary Comp. Sitting by myself in a nice cosy compartment, Iain MacCodrum on my knee because I've heard he's the Gaelic examiner's speciality. Plenty of time, plenty of peace to get plenty of Gaelic swotted up before we reach the Smoke. Doing well in the Bursary Comp's an Oban High School speciality. Two years ago Gilleasbuig MacMillan did well; last year my brother did well — well, actually, he did helluva well. Naturally he was first in Classics, and the whole school got a half-holiday to celebrate. No chance of that with me, but it would be really nice to be placed, quite apart from us needing the money. Go on, then, get on with your *bàrdachd* you silly owl, instead of sitting here day-dreaming and getting all nervous. Getting nervous isn't going to butter no parsnips is it?

I am firmly rooted in eighteenth-century North Uist when I feel somebody looking at me. Glance up. Oh God no, a man — standing in the corridor just looking and looking in at me through the window. Crivvens. Eyes down. Please don't let him come in. Please don't let him be a rapist. Or a murderer. Can't I get any peace, just for once, to go and do something important without being raped or murdered on the way? Hell's teeth, here I am — in my school uniform for heaven's sake — we're hardly out of Oban and this man has to come and stand there staring in at me through the window. I can see his trousers still standing there. There's something very funny about him too. He wasn't an ordinary-looking sort of man at all from what I could see of him. He looked sort of — well, sort of American. Oh God oh Montreal. *'Smeòrach mis' air ùrlar Phaibil, crùbadh ann an dùsal cadail, gun deòrachd . . .'* I am a mavis on the ground of Paible, crouching in a dozy sleep, without . . . what the heck's *'deòrachd'* mean?

The door is moving. He's coming in.

Excuse me, is this seat taken? No, I grunt, not lifting my eyes. Do you mind if I sit down? No.

Well what are you supposed to say? 'There's a whole empty mid-week train back there. Why not go and sit somewhere else and give me peace'? Or 'You can sit where you like but I'm swotting for the Bursary Comp so you needn't expect to get a word out of me this side of Waverley Station'? Or 'Sit down if you must, but lay one finger on me, Al Capone, and I'll kick you in the balls and pull the communication cord'?

He's sitting in the window seat across from me now, not saying anything, but I can tell he's looking at me and in any case how can anyone possibly concentrate on eighteenth-century *bàrdachd* with this peculiar man sitting right opposite you, his queer light-coloured trousers clearly visible just the other side of your poetry book?

Are you going far? Edinburgh. Oh. That's where I'm going too. Oh.

Should I light a cigarette? My father told me about the man who was sitting in a train and a woman suddenly pulled the communication cord and accused him of molesting her and he just sat there very calmly, keeping the ash on his cigar intact, so that when the polis came he could prove he'd never even moved out of his seat. Trust my father to know a story about a woman molesting a man. But it wouldn't work if Al Capone molested me, would it? And anyway, cigarette ash doesn't last that long. But maybe I could stop him by sticking my fag in his eye. Actually I'm dying for a fag. To calm my nerves. Not my exam nerves now, this man nerves. I reach for my bag, but then think wait — I'd better not smoke in case it gives him the wrong impression, encourages him to think I'm fast or that. Put back my bag and drop my poetry book on the floor right beside his highly-polished conker-coloured slip-on shoes. Go to pick it up, but he gets there first. Is looking at the cover. What a bloody cheek.

A school book? Not exactly. Gaelic poetry? Are you interested in that? Yes. Well, I've got to do it actually. For school? Not exactly. I'm going to sit an exam. But not a school exam — a University exam. Shut up, unruly member. I'm sorry, but you'll have to excuse me. I really must get on with my work. Of course. I apologise. I didn't mean to disturb you.

But I can't concentrate on a thing. He's staring all the time — you can feel him, looking out of the window for a bit, then looking back at me again.

I'm going to get a cup of coffee from the buffet. Can I bring you something? No thank you. For a blessed few minutes he is away. I can stretch my legs without being scared I'll touch him by accident. But I still can't get back into my work. Willie wouldn't be put off like this. It's not fair. He could concentrate on his work sitting on the dodgems, or in the middle of a thunder-storm, or — well, on a train, if a woman came and sat opposite him and started trying to make conversation. It's not fair.

The door moves back again. I look up. That was stupid. He is just standing there with a paper cup in his hand, looking down at me.

'I'm just wondering if I should go back to where I was sitting before, where I've left all my things, and leave you in peace to get on with your examination work? I don't want to be a nuisance if you want to be on your own . . .'

Well . . .

'It's just that I'm only over here in Scotland for such a short time and when I'm in a foreign country I like to talk to people — it's the only way to get to know an unfamiliar place I find.'

Oh, well . . .

'I hope you haven't misunderstood my intentions. I would hate you to think I was making a nuisance of myself, but I would really be so interested to learn more about Scotland and your Gaelic culture, if you don't mind — if you can spare me a little time. And then of course I must let you get on with your work, so that you will do well in your examination.'

Yes, well . . . Oh what the hell. Book away. In he comes, smiling nut-brown face, polished blond hair.

'You're American, I take it.'

'Oh good heavens no. I'm from Denmark. Here, let me show you. Here is my wife, my children. And this is my office. It's a rather important business in Denmark — electronics. My name is Bang. Jørgen Bang. Funny isn't it? But not in Denmark. And your name?'

MacCodrum is never opened again. By the time we reach Edinburgh he knows everything there is to know about me and most of what there is to know about Gaelic. Well, what I know about it anyway. I know him pretty well too. He takes my name and address and promises to send me some records — a selection of Danish folk-songs. Perhaps I may like to learn some of them to add to my song collection? On the platform at Waverley Station he stops ceremoniously:

'And now I must apologise for all the time I have wasted for you when you should have been working for your examination. But if you will allow I will now make up for it. Please raise your foot.'

Eh?

'Please lift up your foot — no, not like that, like this. I must see the sole of your shoe, but no, please don't take it off. You must keep it on.'

We stagger on the platform, me giggling weakly and trying to keep my balance and hanging on to his shoulder as he grips me round the ankle and turns my foot up to face him. Then he spits — a neat round white Danish gob — landing with practised accuracy right in the middle of my sole.

'Now you will have good luck — better than all the last-minute sweating over poetry books could ever bring you.'

We shake hands, and he is away. Look out for a parcel from Denmark very soon! Not this week, I shall be in London. Next week, perhaps, if I can find the records I want. Good luck. Good-bye.

I had a very interesting time in Edinburgh. Doing something interesting and new every day for the whole of that week.

I stayed in the West End Hotel. My mother had found it on the back page of the *Oban Times* the year before. 'Quiet family hotel close to all amenities' it said. That should suit William fine. It did. He told me all about it afterwards. The *cèilidhs* and the carryings-on. It sounded as if it would suit me fine too. Didn't tell them that though. Mind you, if he hadn't told me I'd have found out for myself. On my way downstairs to my high tea on the first evening, the door of the public bar opened and a piper in a kilt fell out on to the floor right at my feet. I just took my tea and went early to bed, ready for the Gaelic exam next morning.

About five o'clock next afternoon, after I got back from the Latin paper, I wanted fags to sustain me through a read-through of my notes for the all-important English literature papers. Will I get cigarettes anywhere round here? You can get them in the bar dear, Mrs Asher said. Oh. Am I allowed in there? Of course dear. You're a resident aren't you. Oh. Anyway there's somebody in there who's dying to meet you. Oh.

Only one person in the bar. I got the cigarettes and glanced round at him. The most meltingly handsome man I have ever seen off the movie-screen. Tall, dark and handsome. A Gaelic-speaking teacher from the Isles. Wow. You could really go for someone like that if they were ten years younger. Why don't any of our teachers look like that? Very nice to meet you. Thanks for the lager. Well I'd better away and get on with my swotting.

Over the week I met lots of nice people in the hotel: they kept inveigling me away down from my studies to buy me a gin and orange or a lager and lime. The teacher very kindly took it upon himself to take me round the town — to show me a bit of Edinburgh night-life: out to dine in a proper Danish restaurant where we ate raw fish on tough bread, and a quick trawl along the pubs in Rose Street where homosexuals and famous literary men are sometimes to be seen. All very interesting and new. Not that he seemed all that interested in literature himself. But he was very witty and made me laugh the whole time. My brother came down from his hostel to meet us one evening, but it didn't work out very well. The teacher was very tactful and made me feel as if I was at least twenty-three, but my brother looked about fourteen beside him. It was nobody's fault really.

The Rector had arranged for me to meet a really nice woman from Vatersay on my free afternoon. I recognised her immediately as she came towards me across the concrete outside the National Gallery in a raincoat and flat brown slip-on shoes with a striped nylon message-bag over her arm. We went in to see the French Impressionists, and afterwards she took me up to the School of Scottish Studies where she works. I was in seventh heaven there. The men were all really intellectual and they were all really interested in who I was and what I was doing. They wanted to know my *sloinneadh*. Gillieses from Dumfries? Now that's interesting. Yes, I replied — and my great grandfather knew some Gaelic, although his family came from Galloway as far back as we can trace. That was even more interesting. Prof. Watson had things to say about Gaelic in Galloway, didn't he.

They told me about their work — the constraints and disciplines of field-work, the techniques of transcription, the hassles of cataloguing and archivism generally: people complain that we spend all our time gathering traditional material and never release it back into the community, but how can we get the time to do it all? When I let slip that I once recorded a song for Calum MacLean, one of them took me down into the archives to look for it. There were huge metal frames with long wooden shelves containing rows and rows of narrow white boxes from floor to ceiling. All those Gaelic songs. You could hardly believe it. One woman from Vatersay had recorded over eight hundred items. And their work collecting them all only half begun. The tradition bearers dying off fast and all this wealth about to be lost forever. We found a row of tapes marked 'Dalintart Hospital'. And there, in amongst all the wonderful traditional stories and songs, my silly wee song, all gulps and swallows. It was most embarrassing, but nice at the same time. Anne, part of Gaelic tradition. Wow.

On my last evening the teacher took me out to meet a whole lot of his pals. I could tell that one woman was really dis-chuffed. She was not very nice to me at all. She fancies herself as a singer, he whispered to me when she was in the Ladies. Don't let it worry you. Also she doesn't like you being so young and pretty. What me sir? Don't you be fishing for any more compliments now you rascal. Afterwards he took me for a run, parked the car and started kissing me. I must say it was very enjoyable. Like kissing Rock Hudson. Wait till I tell Mary and Flora about this. But I could tell he was not going to stop at that. My usual ploys like water off a duck's back. He wasn't at all bothered when I told him how I'm in love with Donald and he just laughed when I kept moving his hands. Don't tell me you're still a virgin, he said. I most certainly am, I replied huffily. I'm still in school, don't forget. Oh aye, he chuckled, but that doesn't follow. What kind of school did he go to? Ultimately I'm not sure if he was doing it or not. He said he wasn't. All I can say is that if that was it, it was hardly worth waiting for. Anyway, he said he didn't and he's a teacher, so I'm just going to put the whole episode right out of my mind and forget it ever happened. I don't think I'll even bother telling Mary and Flora after all. As far as I'm concerned he was very good to me and a really nice person and I don't suppose I'll see much of him again even if I do come to Edinburgh. After all he must be nearly thirty if he's a day, and not at all intellectual.

The school got their half-holiday. What a brainy lot those Gillieses are. First in the Bursary Comp twice running. I was taken aback mind you. Really surprised — and really pleased. Must have been the Danish gob that did it. And then at the end of term I was Dux of the school, even though the Rector told me that Iain Islay Davidson gave me a run for my money. Poor Iain Islay. It would have meant a lot to him. He didn't have any social life at all. Not like me — though I had an awful sore head the day of the Prize-giving: Nancy had brought a bottle of Martini to the bean-feast. It was horrible stuff. For his speech the Rector was sounding off about the gutter press. A story had appeared in the *Daily Record* that morning about senior boys breaking a window in end-of-term japes: the way they wrote it you'd have thought it was a riot; and a few weeks back they had done a picture of a Third Year girl looking out to sea, longing for the return of her sailor lover. We must root this cancer out from within our community. Yeah, man.

TWENTY

The summer holidays stretched away endlessly at first. A sea of days, colour heightened by impending departure — waves of fear, anticipation, longing, boredom, nostalgia. Islands of laughter and triumph in an ocean of prevarication.

My father's back is still sore, Willie is on a camping holiday in Greece, back here in Oban it never stops raining; Hughie's tractor gets stuck in the mud in the field when the man's trying to get the hay cut; when I finally get the hay dried my father gets a loan of Hughie's baling machine and the whole thing is finished in an afternoon: the dog is bloated with the field-mice shooting straight out the back of the machine into her waiting maw. After that the sun shines for ages. Typical.

I go back to Tiree, dancing in the hall with Calum Mòr and Calum Beag: the boys go out to the cars and come back in wiping their lips; Flora's father says we mustn't go with the RAF boys; Calum Beag's shoes are too small to go on my feet when we reach the final of the Elimination Waltz; a piper from Glasgow up for the Fair offers me a lift back to Flora's house and takes a blanket out of his car-boot to spread on the *machair*: lie down on there? you must be kidding; I don't know why I had to choose you, you silly bitch, I could have got anyone at that dance. My brother's friend from University gets a summer job in the area and we drink whisky from a flask to keep out the damp at the Taynuilt Games: 'A wonderful household of relaxed lunatics' he calls us, but then he doesn't have to live with my father all the time. Nor will I, soon. Oh mammy daddy.

I go for a wee holiday in Epsom, staying with my father's brother, the piper, accompanying him on his daily walk round all the country pubs, handed decorously down from stiles, drinking Babycham under striped umbrellas, shelling peas, playing whist and watching the Donkey Derby over his privet hedge; pop up to London to stay a night in Uncle Donald's flat in Hay Hill, looking for Hayley Mills in the lift, hearing about the party flung by someone who pretended to be a prince, invited half the English Royal Family, got Harrods to do all the catering, including chandeliers, and then ran away without paying for anything;

eating in the Trocadero — oh dear I didn't think it would come with rice, I don't think I like rice; being bought a new straight white broderie anglaise dress and white pearlised stiletto heels. London is exceedingly dusty.

Duncan is arrested for stealing; my father goes down to give him a character reference: we used to think you were a really snobby lot, you Gillieses. I hear Donald is back in town, go to the pictures by myself in the hopes of seeing him before or after; *Singin' in the Rain*. I love it; maybe I should be a singer after all; after I finish my degree of course. I don't see Donald but I don't care: the music carries me home and into my wee bed under the eaves; won't have to look at that wall for much longer. My father pays the last instalment of the mortgage and my parents go down to Edinburgh and buy a wee flat for me and my brother to stay in while we're at University: just a room and kitchen, but it'll give you a base and save money in the long run; you'll need to go down and give the floor a coat of Cuprinol some time before the end of August.

My mother asks this man to give me singing lessons. He comes to the house to hear me sing. To decide if I'm worth his while teaching. Him having been at the Music College and then in some touring opera company, I think. I've never liked proper singers much. Not that I've heard many of them. Now and again at the Music Society concerts. When they sing high I want to go under the seat.

My parents hide upstairs in their bedroom where they can hear what goes on. They needn't have bothered. They could have heard it in Connel. Here's this funny wee man with his wee snub nose and silk cravat and his untidy flop of hair (artistic, I think it's meant to be. Boyish. A-hem) and then he opens his mouth and lets out this noise like the Bull of Bashan. Only higher. Cor. He nearly blew me backwards off the piano stool. Like the time Angus played his pipes in here and the budgie fell down dead. I wonder it didn't bring the plaster down off the walls. I can just see my parents falling about upstairs. Singing doesn't quite count as music in our house. After that I go to his house and do me-me-me, may-may-may's like a diligent wee lamb, but truth to tell I'd rather die than sing like that man. I just don't have the temperament for it. Folk wouldn't know where to put themselves if you sang Gaelic songs at full blast like that. He's got a tape recorder that he sings into to check he's doing it right. I'd have thought your audience would tell you that. They can always tell if you're in good form. You always get an encore. Still, it passes the time, and his wife's really nice, so I keep going anyway. His wife was in *The Gondoliers* with me. We got married together, to a couple of guys from the Oban Gaelic Choir, so I feel a certain affinity. I got the tenor and she got the bass and she made our veils out of net curtain stuff and plastic flowers. Rightdown regular queens.

If I get through to the Finals of the *Mòd* Gold Medal I'm going to sing a traditional song for my 'own choice' — and that man won't be of the least use to me then. Nor any other pesky singing teacher. I've thought it all out. You have to feel traditional songs, but not lay it on with a trowel — sobs and slimey-randos as my da calls them. From inside the song. With proper respect for the tradition. Understanding of the history. Love for the folk who composed them. Mind you there'll probably be some stushie if I do choose a traditional song. In fact I hope there will be. I want to make a point even if they disqualify me. An Comunn Gàidhealach like you to stick to the rules. Traditional songs are supposed to be kept for the Traditional Song Competition. People from the School of Scottish Studies come up specially to adjudicate the Traditional Song Competition and then sit obstinately in the pub when everyone else is at the Prize-winners' Concert. How will they ever change anything like that? The Traditional Song Competition is away in some poky wee hall with six people in the audience. The Medal competitions are in the main hall with all the big guns, adjudicated by people with names like Henry Higginbottom, B Mus LRAM FTCL of that ilk, who don't know the first thing about Gaelic tradition. And the finalists sing chirrupy songs like *Tha Smeòrach 'sa' mhadainn chiùin*. Or fog-horny ones like *M'eudail m'eudail Mac 'ic Ailein*.

I'm going to sing a traditional song anyway even if it does disqualify me. I'll get my mother to write it out as near as dammit, and then put 'this is only an approximation, as the song is sung in the traditional manner' at the top. That'll frighten the hell out of old Higginbottom. Mind you, I doubt if I'll get through to the Finals. I've started learning the songs for the qualifying competitions. They're dreadful. One of them is one I sing at all the *cèilidhs* (*A Fhleasgaich an Fhuilt Chraobhaich Chais*) but it's written out in a completely different tempo, all jerky and convoluted, which is harder to learn than starting from scratch with a song you don't know at all. The audience will think we've all gone mad when they hear us singing it like that, and they won't be able to join in the chorus at the Grand Concert. That'll really confuse them. And the *Oran Mòr* is a queer version of *Griogal Cridhe*, the tune of which you couldn't possibly sing the way it's written without ruining the words. Quite apart from its being an extremely boring tune compared with the other versions I've heard — like a second-rate hymn. Quite apart from its not being an *Oran Mòr* at all — not by anybody's standards: it was composed by the poor MacGregor guy's widow after his father-in-law had cut his head off in front of her eyes and stuck it up on an oak-stob. It's really a lullaby. She's singing it quietly to her wee baby — as the baby's all she's got left to talk to now. Well, that's what I thought anyway. *Oran Mòr* my foot.

Meanwhile we go down to Edinburgh to do up the flat. Stinking of creosote. Sleeping on a narrow folding bed in the middle of the bare stinky floor. It's a ground-floor flat — luckily. I don't think I'd like to be up in the sky. My parents bought the flat from a family with two teenage sons, but I can't work out where they all slept. There are only two rooms in it — the lounge (where I shall also sleep) with a big bay window and red checked wall-paper, and the kitchen (where my brother will also sleep) with the range and a bed recess. Plus the bathroom. Wow! a bathroom of our very own — even if you do have to leave the fire on for about five hours to heat the water, and even if you do set the chimney on fire first go off. I was petrified when the chimney went on fire. I mean, it often happens at home, but there's nobody to think about at home but ourselves and you can carry the hot ashes out into the yard and panic in privacy. Here you share the chimney head with goodness knows how many other people, and you don't have enough salt, and there's nowhere to put the glowing ash except a plastic bin. Ought we to dial 999? Oh help. I suddenly feel very claustrophobic.

But the oddest thing of all is not being able to chuck stuff out to the hens. At first you gravitate naturally towards the window at the end of every meal. It's a terrible waste. All the bits you leave on your plate have to be put into the bin here. Also it's dreadfully difficult to get used to switching the lights on and off. I get used to 'on' first. But I keep trying to blow them out.

The Edinburgh Festival is on while we're down. I put my hair into a pleat over one shoulder to try and look sophisticated but casual, and I do my make-up carefully to look as if I'm not wearing it at all. Which of course I have to — what with my fair eye-lashes and wee piggy eyes. I have a new coat too. Green corduroy. We go to this new theatre and at the bar we meet a man who is supposed to be the Chief of the Clan MacPherson (that means us. Our clan. Should we touch our forelocks?) and someone very flash called Nicholas Fairbairn. They seemed to enjoy chatting with us even though we're only students. Another night we went to see *And the Cock Crew*, staged in a tiny room. It got terribly hot, and I had a job staying awake. Especially after a couple of vodka-and-oranges. Uncle Tom was sitting there scratching his beard in the front row. I think I'd die if I had to act in front of the author. Right under his nose like that. My parents gave us a row afterwards for not going over to talk to him.

But you couldn't. People would think you were showing off. So we just sneaked away.

July, August, September. Gone in a flash.

There were high spots. Like the Tobermory Games and kissing somebody who was years ahead of you in school as the sun rose over the bay. Like biking back from Ganavan with your hair drying in the wind, and going straight to a dance in the town to discover that it wasn't aaawful at all, and there are some really good-looking boys around that you haven't even noticed before, and Helen Cameron's actually quite a decent soul. Like going shooting with Ally and your brother away up our hill, and having to hurry to keep up with Ally in spite of him being bent completely double, and not seeing a single thing you could fire at, and ending up in kinks laughing, aiming to miss at seagulls from behind the ash-heap, and then watching Ally's face get younger and younger as the pain-lines disappear over a brandy or two in our kitchen: as I said to my brother: 'Am I getting drunk, or is Ally getting handsome?' Like finding out you've won £10 in a raffle at a *cèilidh* you never even went to because you had a sore throat and had to save your voice for the *Mòd* next week — that must have made them really sick: you'd have been lucky to get ten bob for turning up to sing. Like singing one of the Rector's traditional songs for the *Mòd* Gold Medal Finals: cursing Prince Charles Edward Stewart, lamenting your big, brave, fearless, peerless, beautiful husband, fair from head to toe, flank like the swan and kisses like honey, dying a hero's death at Culloden and leaving you alone in the world with no means of support, no status, no love, no hope — happiness turned to weeping, like many another woman between Trotternish and Sleat, but how much greater is your pain than theirs, having lost this one man, your fair young love. Like Harry Carter ringing up your father from the phone-box in the Square in a state of high old excitement to tell him about you winning the Ladies' Gold Medal when you were still only seventeen and too young to have started caring one way or the other.

Low spots, like waking up the morning after the night with Ally and discovering you have a horrible big scald all the way down your leg and not knowing how on earth it got there even if you didn't have all that much to drink, well you couldn't have because you washed and dried all the glasses without breaking a single one — it must have been the kettle, thank goodness my parents are away in Edinburgh, I hope Dr Campbell won't say anything to them. Like the night Dòmhnall Beag left you off at the end of the road to walk home in the dark after a *cèilidh* down at Easdale; you see your brother coming towards you fluorescent in his white raincoat: where on earth is he going at this time of night? He comes up to you and gets his hands around your neck and it's not your brother but a boy that you know a bit, except he has a very odd look in his eyes and you know that he's just back from Barlinnie and he wants to have sex with you and if you won't do it, he'll murder you instead. Your new white dress is torn and you spoil your lovely white stiletto heels going in and out the puddles trying to keep him from pushing you down into the field, before you finally manage to get him to calm down and see reason: I'd much rather be raped than murdered, you say, talking to him very quietly as if he is Flora's father's bull, but I know who you are and where you live, and I'll go straight to the police and tell on you and then you'll never get out of Barlinnie, and anyway my father's working late tonight and my brother's at the dance in Kilmore and either of them could come across this field at any moment, and I don't want to get you put back in Barlinnie, but if I screamed now, half Dalintart Drive would come out and get you. You don't wake your parents because it wouldn't do any good to worry them, but your brother gets a few of the lads and goes to hammer him: luckily they don't find him. That would just have made things worse. You stop shaking eventually, and go to bed.

Like the horrible stories the Press printed about you when you won the *Mòd* Gold Medal. The second music adjudicator at the Finals couldn't think of anything much to add, so said he'd noticed some competitors had lit up a cigarette after singing: do you realise what a bad habit this is, and how ruinous to the vocal cords? The Press descend upon you in a swarm: did you have a cigarette? Were you one of the competitors who lit up? You are not going to be caught out that easily by the 'gutter press'. Yes I was, as a matter of fact, you reply; yes, but please don't print anything about it as my father doesn't even know I smoke. Father's phone in the Office instantly overrun by gutter press, the story in the *Daily Record* headlined 'Her Father Knows Her Guilty Secret'. Even the *People's Journal* says what a super singer you are, and how nerve-racking it is to compete when you're only seventeen, and who could blame you if you did light up a wee cigarette in the heat of the moment. Like feeling ashamed instead of proud of yourself as you walk down the town next day to sing at the Grand Concert. Like feeling your voice going as you run between the Playhouse and the Cinema — Oban doesn't have a proper hall, so they have to put on the Concert in two different places, two houses in each place; so I have to sing my three songs four times with hardly time to get my breath back in between, though Dòmhnall Beag helps by giving me lifts when he can. By the time it comes to the second house in the Playhouse I am really croaking and can't swallow, and the adjudicators are all sitting there (replete after a good dinner while I've been tearing about from concert to concert) gritting their teeth and wondering why they ever gave the medal to a pathetic kid like me. At least that's what I assume they were doing. I keep thinking about them sitting there gritting their teeth, all the way through my songs. Nobody says a bloody thing about me singing a traditional song, but everywhere I go people offer me cigarettes ha ha and several folk say I was lucky to get the medal at all after singing *A Fhleasgaich an Fhuilt Chraobhaich Chais* so badly: you had the tune all wrong; we couldn't even join in the chorus. I have to stay up all night, going round all the *cèilidhs* in all the hotels, even if my voice is all to pot and I'm nearly dead of exhaustion. You could really get very drunk if you didn't watch out. Free drinks everywhere you go, even though you're actually famous now for being under-age. Youngest-ever Medallist and all that. Dòmhnall Beag keeps looking at me like a hen that's just laid an egg.

I'm going to University tomorrow. Today, I mean. It's four in the morning. Oh God. I'll be glad to get away from all this. Get on with life. I've already missed the Freshers' Conference. Because of the silly *Mòd*.

Going away, the train says. Leaving it all behind. Trunk in the guard's van. Case on the luggage rack. Sandwiches in the message bag.

Hugging my mother and watching her disappearing, blowing kisses and her nose as the train turns the corner. She'll walk home and tidy up my room. Put my child's life away on top of the wardrobe. I expect she'll cry a bit. Shut up, stupid. Don't play with your emotions.

Waving as we pass the house, my father out on the *dùn* as usual. My father with his 'What has she been doing to herself now Mary?' I wish he would have said something positive about me now and again. Sine leaping about, tail feathering, unconcerned, though only half an hour ago she was whining, head lying mournfully along the top of my case. Inside the house, my granny and her crossed legs (cutting off the circulation — no wonder she falls over) and her hearing-aid (don't mumble, Iain) and the unbelievable things she said if I brought anybody home (and who's this nice young man, then, Anne, another of your little friends to come to play with you?) and her Sennacot and her not wanting to be a burden to anybody.

Ben More. Ben Cruachan. Ben Doran. Ben Lomond. My last farewell to the bens. I know just how Donnchadh Bàn felt. My last farewell to the hens. Ha ha. Donnchadh Bàn went to live in Edinburgh too. Gaelic nature poet turning into a city Guard, with all the wee children running after him and laughing at his funny clothes. His funny accent. But he got on fine, from what we can gather. Canny, cunning, sunny-natured. He'd have got on fine wherever he landed. But how will I get on? I recall one evening shortly after I left school, when I found myself down town in Oban having a surreal Chinese meal with one or two people my own age plus my old English teacher. You don't need to call me sir any more, you know. You can call me Iain. I know. But old habits die hard sir.

We had picked him up in a corner of the Columba Hotel lounge bar. The poet — dirty raincoat, dirty table, liquorice black teeth, empty beer-rimmed glass, thin beer-rimmed lips, small virginal hands obsessively breaking match-sticks. He was especially defensive that night. The way he sat, the way he held his arms, his legs, the set of his neck and jaw all in-drawn — armouring some hairless invertebrate inner creature? He took the drinks we offered him, pouring new into old. He took the fags we offered him, broke off the spats, sucked in a drag or two then nicked them out and stowed the dowps in his top jacket pocket. He must think we're made of money. But we didn't mind. He was doing what we wanted him to do. Giving us something to talk about later. Perhaps we should have let him be. Perhaps all he wanted was to be left alone. We steered him like a dancing bear, across to the Chinese restaurant.

At first the absurd vacuity of the place was enough in itself to fuel our wit. Until at last all our senses flagged. Chewing tasteless food, I rested, letting others take the strain for a while. And now it was his turn to be irritated.

'You're a real bitch, Anne Gillies. You know what you do: you watch people all the time. You're always doing it. Sitting there watching people and judging them. What a bitch.'

He's not joking. I am shocked. Stopped in my complacent tracks. Biting on a hard lump of something distasteful in mid-chew.

But drink has been taken. It is not too difficult to lance the sting with a light neutralising riposte. Soon we will all go home — dull, as if already hungover. Probably he will never think about tonight again. Probably he will never think about me again. I shall be away soon. Out of sight . . . He has more important things to think about. Himself, for example. This internal thing that allows him to write, that he carries about everywhere he goes, defending it with his own shell, feeding it with his own fibre. Is it seed, infinitely renewable, awaiting the exterior stimulus, the mother-context in which to germinate and take shape? Or is it foetal, pre-formed by his Lewis boyhood, awaiting only the creative spasm?

In bed I gingerly bring out his words for inspection. Watch. Judge. Bitch. *In vino veritas?* It may not be fashionable, but I care deeply what other people think about me. Am a fool for chiding. Need his approval in particular. Vainly scouring his poetry for any shade of myself. He has been my muse, but I am not his. I can live with that. Am young yet. One disciple among hundreds. But I wouldn't like to think he disliked me. That he was right to dislike me. Judge not that ye be not judged. Mote in the eye, stone in the hand.

Yes I watch. What are you gaping at? as the big girl asked. I'm not gating, as the wee girl replied. I'm trying to learn. I'm interested. Fascinated. Curious. Amused. Amazed. A calf let loose on spring.

But am I judging? Certainly not when younger — except insofar as sorting, classifying, filing, becomes a form of diminution through time. But who could sustain the indiscriminate sensual bombardment of infancy? Survive without translating the buzzing Babel into some more manageable idiolect? He is a poet. Is observation not the well-spring of his art? But surely he must compare, extrapolate, interpret in his own terms, shine his post-Freudian torch around, in order to refine his inheritance beyond the purple oilscapes, the formulaic portraiture, the naïve reportage, the ponderous satire of earlier Gaelic poetry.

And yet perhaps he is right. Does the Scottish education system from which he has only recently escaped not ordain that he shall be right? Making A, B, C and F of people — first, second, third and nothing. Rewarding the already gifted. Perhaps the jealous Lewis God, by erecting humanly unattainable goals, anoints His followers with His own rich prophylactic humility, uniting them in their common unworthiness whatever their talents and attainments. But my goals are temporal, my yardsticks infuriatingly human. Making me judge myself as harshly — more harshly — than I ever judge other people. Reviewing the household gods hanging in my childhood's gallery I find some people I have loved greatly — for their wit or their humanity, their eccentricity or for what I have found in myself through their good offices. The English teacher has pride of place on all counts. But not one to compete with — to offer me some viable substitute for — that other man, sighing heavily in his sleep next door. Intellect, integrity and sex combining to put him beyond my reach while spoiling me irrevocably for lesser mortals than himself. Myself included.

This would have been the moment to go and wake him. Tell him what I have discovered. Take him this farewell gift. Before I leave home and become another person among other people. But my father dreams on a plane too rarefied to understand. He would make me see this for another sentimental chimera and I, being frail, would wound.

In Edinburgh I expect to find some other hero — if not many — to admire, respond to, flower beneath. Have already had a foretaste when I was down for the Bursary Competition. Recall a fine man, a little younger than my father, kind, intellectual, Gaelic-speaking, meeting my fumbling thoughts with joy and helping them to crystallise, to appear worthwhile. To learn from such as him, sitting at his feet, honing wit and understanding . . . To find other such admirable men of my own age to befriend . . . enjoy . . . marry . . . ?

A telegram was on the mat when I arrived. I stuck it on the mantelpiece before going back to drag in my trunk from the close-mouth:

'MEAL DO NAIDHEACHD GOLDEN GIRL STOP CELEBRATION TONIGHT WEST END HOTEL STOP'

The Edinburgh teacher. Nice big handsome dope. A thing of the past. I don't give him another thought.

Celebration? I am not even tempted. The *Mòd* was yesterday. At home. A complete irrelevance. Today I am a student. At University. At last.

Today I must make friends. People of my own age. Fellow students. I've got to make up for lost time. Have already missed the whole of Freshers' Week. Nothing is going to keep me from the Union — from the Freshers' Dance. I back-comb the long hair which has been my trademark all week and fold it away up out of sight.

First impressions: huge wooden balustrades, bevelled plate glass and polished brass; fatherly wee men in army uniforms comforting maudlin girls and scattering sawdust on sick; green-faced boys leaning heads against arms against walls; lipsticked girls whirling, birling, peering in mirrors; the reek of candle-wax and hair lacquer.

I don't know anyone here. No one at all. This is not like dances I know. No empty floor, surrounded by well-organised chairs; no girls this side, boys the other; no ladies now's your chance — take your partners if you will for a Valeta Waltz, and this time it's strictly ladies' choice. A seething mass of people, indiscriminately mixed; checked paper table-cloths sopping with beer and grimed with ash; I sit down at the first space I see. People look up at me without interest, without curiosity, then return to their conversations. What are you supposed to do now? Can you buy a drink? I've never bought a drink in my life. Anyway, I left my purse upstairs in my hand-bag, wrapped inside my coat like you do at home. There seem to be only men at the bar, brandishing beer-mugs, and singing about Eskimo Nell and looking briefly up and down every girl who comes into the hall. Nudging. Turning away back to their beer-mats. Should I go and get my hand-bag? I sit looking brightly at the snake-pit of twisting bodies on the dance-floor.

'What're you drinking?' someone asks. There is a boy at my elbow. Oh well, that solves the first problem anyway.

'Ehm thank you very much. Can I have a half of lager and lime please.'

Now this very boring boy has bought me two half-pints of lager and we have had a couple of dances. I am now his prisoner it seems. I am with the boy. Just because I chanced to sit at his table and accepted a drink. I can't get up and go somewhere else because I don't know anyone else. Nobody else will ask me to dance because I seem to be with him. I make no effort to be pleasant, but he has made an investment and, it seems, intends to stick around for the returns. My heart is leaden with disappointment. Netted in the first five minutes at University. The evening stretches interminably before me.

'Excuse me, I just have to go to the Ladies.'

I don't, of course, but maybe some miracle will happen. Girls are re-spraying their hair and crying behind closed toilet doors. Much more of this and I might as well go home. On the way downstairs, I look into the other hall. Jazz music and dull red lighting and statuesque couples lost in passion. I let go of the door handle as if electrocuted and hurry back to the light.

Then at the door I see a face I know. What on earth's he doing here? My hero. A fine man, a little younger than my father, kind, intellectual. He places himself between me and the boring boy and puts a gin and orange in my hand.

'*Seo m'eudail. Tha thu feumachdainn air seo, cha chreid mi.*' (Here you are my dear, you're needing this, I reckon.) Sweet oasis of Gaelic in the Lowland desert.

He takes me to sit down at another table. The boring boy comes over.

'I've got you another lager. Are you coming back to sit down?'

In a minute. Not if I can help it.

'I've been watching you from the balcony,' the man says. 'You're miles away. You don't belong here, in this rabble. Won't you come with me?'

'Come — er — where?'

He is telling me about his friends: a professor and his wife, such fine people; sensitive, interesting. They have come to love Gaelic culture through holidaying in the Highlands. He is suggesting we go and *cèilidh* on them for a while, what pleasure it would give them.

What, now? Right now? Well, why not? They just live around the corner. Get a decent dram and a bowl of home-made soup.

Professors impress me. So does food. My stomach suddenly remembers that I have not eaten since sandwiches at Crianlarich.

But the dance? Och you'll be back long before midnight; still plenty of time to find a nice boy!

I am laughing at the daftness of it all. Still, stranger things have happened at the dances at home. People have been known to go poaching in the river and be back in time for the Eightsome. All right; I'll just pop up and get my coat and hand-bag. Och you don't need to bother; get them when we come back. We won't be long.

Together we sail away from the pimply assemblage, waving our private language like a flag, out into the crisp autumn evening. The poisonous boy throws a whey-faced dart as I pass.

The taxi drives on and on through dark, unknown streets. I smoke and smile over exchanges hard to make out above the taxi's noise, through the mists of his fluent idiomatic Gaelic. Alight outside a big leafy house miles away from the Union. Ah well.

I am magnificent. I have sung, played the piano, spun yarns, fielded witticisms. I have been admired from all angles, flattered indulgently, fed hugely. Is she really only seventeen? The whole of life ahead of her. Oh it was so kind of you to remember us, to bring us this refreshing breath of our beloved Highlands. I like all this adult homage. There is more to come.

'I want to tell you something personal. Between ourselves. I want you to know how I felt when you retold what you had written in your Bursary Competition essay. How I responded inwardly. It was extraordinary. So moving. In one so young. To have those insights. To have shared them with me. Things I have felt myself for so long. That has meant a great deal to me.'

Wow! Eh! See me. See insight.

A treasured peat smokes on the fire. A *clàrsach* stands silent in the corner, whisky winks in crystal glasses. I'm not that used to whisky, but I can hold my own. I hope. Anyway, I'm in safe hands. I know the time, but no longer care. They invite me to phone home, trill kind messages which I pass on to my parents. My mother is pleased I am in such august company. Better than that noisy Union dear.

The Professor's wife comes into the room with bitter grainy coffee already cooling in wide-mouthed white china tureens. I pretend to enjoy it. Conspiratorially she mouths to the man. Everything, it seems, is ready.

'Come and see,' he invites me.

I follow, playing along with their little mystery, expecting a caseful of Uist fritillaries or a home-movie of a waulking party. He ushers me next door. Into a bedroom. I can see nothing here of note. Can it be the decor? The pictures on the walls? Am I going to fail this exam?

'See, *m'eudail*. She has made it up for us. Our bed. Come.'

I am completely taken aback — a lamb about to be sacrificed upon the altar of my own vanity. Oh hell's bells. Try to be sophisticated, try not to hurt his feelings, try above all not to giggle. Try to disengage my body from the octopus grasp, my face from the blue sandpaper chin, my lips from the gap-toothed mouth. Try to talk sense into him — like Flora's father's bull. Try to think what arguments might halt, yet still impress, a rampant middle-aged academic. But he is hoarsely describing his prowess in other spheres. The longest in Edinburgh, so it seems. I am not about to put this to the test — if I can help it. Don't giggle, eejit.

Coward, I take the usual escape-route. Don't be long my darling girl. Hurry back to me. I go next door. But the Professor and his wife have vanished. Glance into the empty kitchen. Lock myself in the bathroom for a long time, looming hysterically over my melting whisky-sodden face in the mirror above the sink. When will you learn? What are you going to do now, eh? Daren't go upstairs. Not going back in there. You'd better just leave before he has time to notice you've gone. Apologise on Monday. Plead sickness.

But I have no coat. No hand-bag. No money. No key. Oh God. I don't know where we are. We could be miles from home. To wander the streets of Edinburgh lost, bare-armed, in the October frost?

Oh he must see sense. He must take me back quickly or the Union will be shut and I won't be able to get back into the flat. He will have cooled off by now surely. I open the door quickly and he leaps out upon me in shirt, tie and knee-length white drawers. Half-man, half-goat. Like the Pooka.

In the ancient Irish tale the woman carried the Pooka on her back for hour upon weary hour, across mire and fell, unable to dislodge the creature by fair means or foul, until at last, in the churchyard, the shadow of a cross fell onto it in the moonlight and loosed its devilish hold. Leaving her to limp home to her husband. A marked woman. Scarred for life. A humped back as permanent, public proclamation of her ordeal. The moral is obvious. What was she doing out that late at night? Don't tell me she didn't ask for it. Well she's got what was coming to her.

I have managed to escape from my trial technically unscathed — except for my crumpled dress and the weal on my chin, rapidly turning septic. I have managed to remain physically intact without resorting to foul language, tolerating his probing kisses out of rapidly-waning respect for the venerable tradition he represents. No doubt that proves it was my fault as much as his. Years later he spoilt a proud day for my father by telling him what a lovely daughter he had — I could have fucked her one fine night but I didn't. A wonderful thing, the memory. 'Silly bitch,' he said as I recall it. 'And I having thought you were different from all the other neurotic little girls who come down from the *Gàidhealtachd*. Deeper. Less conformist. More free-thinking. Well you can find your own way home. I've got no money to pay for any taxi.'

My brother is unamused at being wakened at this hour of the morning by an irate cab-driver. A penniless, coatless, dishevelled sister. First night in Edinburgh and just look at the state of you. Stomps crossly back to bed without inviting an explanation, muttering darkly about girls coming to sticky ends. Heavily I drag my disfigured spirit down into the cold slit in the bed-clothes in the front room.

Next day I can barely lift my head. My brother has gone out while I was still asleep. The events of the past week like concrete, entombing me. At tea-time, the day already grown dark, I creep up on the pillow to eat the rest of yesterday's sandwiches, *Sing Something Simple* adding its own wry commentary from the radio in the kitchen. At seven o'clock, longing for my parents, too tired to light the fire, I phone the only person I know in the whole world. He'll know what to do. He'll look after me. Force myself to sound gay. Sophisticated.

'Sorry about last night. Didn't get your telegram till it was too late. Were there many people at the West End? Oh dear — sorry! No — I went to the Union dance. No — pretty awful. A load of pimply youths. Well, you know me. I've always had a penchant for older guys. *Penchant*, I said. It's French, cheeky! Mmmm, chee-ky! Yes, I'd love to come round. Just one problem. I seem to have mislaid my purse. Any chance of a wee lift? Fine. No, of course I'm not crying. Och, I'll tell you when I see you. Half an hour then. Give me time to make myself suitably alluring. *Ceart matà*. See you.'

God almighty. Now what have I gone and done?

CODA: GLASGOW 1990

The City of Culture. My home.

Personally I haven't had much time for Culture lately. Too busy writing a book in between singing, summer schools, festivals, community dramas, Gaelic projects and watching the weans. Lately I've begun including 'currently writing her childhood memoirs' in biogs for theatre and concert programmes — just in case I get up the nerve to send off my book for publication. To blackmail myself into sending it off, perhaps? Have also begun reading my horoscope in the Evening Times. *Definitely cracking up. One day last week Russell Grant said that the time was ripe for all we Librans to start telling our life stories, even if we didn't have any literary pretensions. Then the next day he said we might be feeling like letting it all hang out, telling a few home truths, but how would the world at large feel about hearing them? Whose side are you on, Russell?*

Then, after a Fringe event at the Mòd in Govan, this man from Lewis seeks me out, drink in hand. That's funny. He wouldn't normally do that. Usually men like that stand shoulder to shoulder, facing inwards in unbreakable Celtic knots. Especially at this time in the evening.

'How's your book coming along then?' he asks. 'Mine's due out next year too, you know.' (Aha. That explains it.)

Oh. I didn't know you were writing a book. What's it about?

'Oh, the same as yours: life of . . . You know. Except that I'm not writing it myself, of course. That's one thing I could never do — write about myself.'

Oh. Well. But mine's not at all the sort of thing somebody else could write for you. I'm doing my James Joyce — only in my case it's a Portrait of the Artiste as a Young Worm.

A meaningful pause. Oh God, he thinks I'm serious. He thinks I think I'm James Joyce. No sense of humour some people.

'Oh well,' he says eventually. 'I just hope you've got yourself a good lawyer.'

I gather the kids up and flee.

'Can we get chips, Mum? Please? Can we go to Danny's for fish suppers? Mu-um?'

Oh for goodness sake.

Along Allison Street, on the way to Danny's, we pause to watch a wee shilpit man in his workin' claes: heid down, drunk as a skunk, battling his way through an imaginary hurricane, clinging to the earth with every instinct. Busy moving in a forwardly direction.

Till a sneeze explodes in him, thunderbolting him five yards back along the pavement. Regaining equilibrium, just: swaying, blinking, squinting round for someone to blame, he bunches his fists, ready to sort out the unseen assailant. Finding no one there, he leans into the elements. Begins walking again.

Is relaxing back into his natural rhythm, has made a little unsteady progress, when the second thunderous sneeze wells up in him, blowing him back along the pavement to where he was before. Now he knows they are out to get him.

Others stop to watch the show, indulgent, affectionate. He knows we are not the enemy. Expostulates publicly with God and His Son, sure of our sympathy. Right. This time he must make it. We will him on. Gleefully. Knowing what will happen. No ill-will among the lot of us. But how we laugh when he reaches, for the third time, the exact spot beyond which, it seems, he must not pass.

HARRASHOOOO! Gaun yersel, we cry, as he explodes back to the starting-line again. A lesser being would have played to the gallery, milked its applause. The wee shilpit man has to get hame but. It has taken him all his time to get this far. He has no time for comic cuts. Squares up again. Bruce and the spider Govanhill-style.

'Come on kids. It's not very nice laughing at the poor man.'

Dragging them whining round I head towards the chip-shop.

Turas math, *wee man (Bon voyage). I know exactly how you feel.*

Glossary

a chàirdean	friends
'A fhleasgaich an fhuilt chraobhaich chais'	'Boy of the long wavy hair'
a luaidh	dearie
An Comunn Gàidhealach	The Highland Association (voluntary Gaelic-promotion association)
bàrdachd	poetry
Bidean nam Beann	Pinnacle of the Bens
bodaich	old men
Buachaille Eite Mhòr	Great Etive's Shepherd
buideachas	witch-craft
cailleach	old woman
caman	shinty-stick
Caoineag	Weeping Woman — supernatural apparition said to have appeared in Glencoe at the time of the Massacre
cèilidh	social occasion
cèir	(singular noun) wax; (plural noun) rumps
cianalas	home-sickness
clàrsach	small Celtic harp
cròmag	crook — walking stick
Cruachan	Peaks
Dearg	Red
Dòmhnall Beag	Wee Donald
'Dòmhnall Beag an t-Siùcair'	'Sweet Wee Donald'
dùn	fort, hill
'Eilean Fraoich'	'Heather Isle'
'Eilean mo ghaoil'	'My beloved Island'
Gàidhlig	(Scots) Gaelic
'Griogal Cridhe'	'Beloved Gregor' — 16th century lament
Guth na Bliadhna	*The Voice of the Year* (Gaelic periodical)
Hè mo leannan ho mo leannan	Hey my sweetheart ho my sweetheart
Se mo leannan am fear ùr	My sweetheart is the new man (traditional waulking song)
'Latha Inbhir Lòchaidh'	'The Battle (lit. day) of Inverlochy' (17th century Gaelic song composed in celebration of victory)

223

lochan	wee loch
machair	verdant sandy grass-land (no English equivalent)
meal do naidheachd	congratulations (lit. enjoy your news)
m'eudail	darling
'M'eudail m'eudail Mac 'ic Ailein'	'My love, my love is Clan Ranald'
Mòd	Gaelic music festival, similar to the Eisteddfod in Wales
'Moladh na Lanndaidh'	'In praise of Islay'
Muileach	person from Mull
O Dhia Dhia	Oh God, God
O Dhia 'gam chuideachadh	Oh God help me
O Dhia 'gam shàbhaladh	Oh God save me
O Dhia nan gràs	Oh God of grace
òran mor	(lit.) great song. Usually applied to the genre of song composed by the official or semi-official bards laureate of clans — usually laments or praise-poems for the chief, who was also traditionally the poet's patron
piob-mhòr	bagpipes
puirt a beul	mouth music — vocal dance music
sa mairch oan ra day	there's a march on today (Glaswegian 'English')
sgeulachd	story
sgian-dubh	dirk, dagger (lit. black knife)
sgùrr	diarrhoea in cattle
shin agad e	there you are
shin agad sin	there you have it
slàinte mhath	good health
sloinneadh	ancestry
Stob Coire nan Lochan	Pillar of Corries and Lochs
tarbh-uisge	water-bull — supernatural/mythical creature, believed to appear out of sea or loch, sometimes in human form, to entice maidens to their doom
'Tha smeòrach 's a' mhadainn chiùin'	'The mavis in the calm morning'
Thèid dualchas an aghaidh nan creag	(lit. heredity withstands the rocks)
'Thug mi gaol'	'I gave my love'
troich	dwarf